CLICK ON DEMOCRACY

CLICK ON
DEMOCRACY

The Internet's Power to Change Political Apathy into Civic Action

Steve Davis, Larry Elin, and Grant Reeher

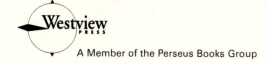

A Member of the Perseus Books Group

Copyright © 2002 by Westview Press, A Member of the Perseus Books Group
New Foreword and Preface to the Paperback Edition copyright © 2004 by Westview Press

Westview Press books are available at special discounts for bulk purchases in the United States by corporations, institutions, and other organizations. For more information, please contact the Special Markets Department at the Perseus Books Group, 11 Cambridge Center, Cambridge MA 02142, or call (617) 252-5298.

Published in the United States of America by Westview Press, 5500 Central Avenue, Boulder, Colorado 80301–2877, and in the United Kingdom by Westview Press, 12 Hid's Copse Road, Cumnor Hill, Oxford OX2 9JJ

Find us on the World Wide Web at www.westviewpress.com

Library of Congress Cataloging-in-Publication Data
Davis, Steve.
    Click on democracy : the Internet's power to change political apathy
into civic action / Steve Davis, Larry Elin, Grant Reeher.
        p.   cm.
    Includes bibliographical references and index.
    ISBN 0-8133-4183-3
    1. Political participation—United States—Computer network resources.
2. Internet in political campaigns—United States.   3. Presidents—United States—
Election—2000—Computer network resources.   4. Elections—United States—
Computer network resources.   I. Elin, Larry.   II. Reeher, Grant.   III. Title.
JK1764 .D385   2002
323'.042'02854678—dc21
                                                              2002008236

The paper used in this publication meets the requirements of the American National Standard for Permanence of Paper for Printed Library Materials Z39.48–1984.

First paperback printing, February 2004

10   9   8   7   6   5   4   3   2   1

This book is dedicated to Drew McGarr, Alan Kardoff, Mona Twocats, LuAnn Molloy, Dave Kaplan, and the other members of their online community. Though many others are not mentioned in this work, all are appreciated.

CONTENTS

ILLUSTRATIONS

Figures

FOREWORD TO THE PAPERBACK EDITION

Scott Heiferman, CEO and Co-Founder
William Finkel, Outreach Manager
Meetup, Inc.

CLICK ON DEMOCRACY FOLLOWS THE INTERNET'S ROLE IN THE 2000 election, from the early dreams that the Internet would have the same political impact that television did in 1960, to its ultimate disappointments as the campaign cycle climaxed. But the authors rightly recognize and argue that the Internet is a completely different medium, which aids political discourse in new ways. They describe a variety of examples of how this occurs, ranging across different kinds of political communities representing different points of view.

The Internet cannot be treated simply as another mass media outlet, driven by news releases and candidate statements. Instead, interactivity, engagement, and responsiveness are the elements that will define effective online campaigns. A candidate would be well encouraged to embrace the Internet for its many-to-many nature rather than to try to use the medium in the same manner as television or print. *Click on Democracy* effectively shows the differences between traditional media (as exemplified by mainstream news Web sites) and the new, effective forms of Internet-inspired communications. It is up to the candidates in 2004 and beyond to recognize these differences and embrace them.

Our organization, Meetup.com, is intimately involved in this new form of Internet-based political communication and activity. Meetup was launched in June 2002 as a way for people to find a group of neighbors with a shared interest. In part, our inspiration for the effort was Robert Putnam's *Bowling Alone*, a work that the authors of *Click on Democracy* also discuss at length. *Bowling Alone* outlines the decline of American community and the corresponding decrease in civic engagement. But Putnam is suspicious of the impact that the Internet is likely to have on rebuilding these communities, for two principal reasons: The Internet is more efficient at connecting strangers in far-flung locations who have things in common than it is at connecting neighbors who are different; and Internet communities are essentially one-dimensional forums, where all communication is written and societal cues are absent. We didn't see these aspects of Internet communities as inherent limitations; instead, we viewed them as an opportunity to create new and valuable forms of communities.

Meetup organizes local meetings for people with a common interest about anything, anywhere. We take the step of using the social interactions exhibited on the Internet and blending them with the real world. Following the model of civic organizations from earlier eras, Meetups occur on the same day of every month. We use modern technology to organize traditional face-to-face group meetings. The decentralized nature of the Internet helps people find their local niches and encourages word-of-mouth communication. Thus, a person in Detroit who is registered for the Republican Meetup can tell an online friend in Tallahassee about the Republican Meetup and that person can attend his or her own Meetup locally, as well.

Meetup was initially conceived without much explicit focus on politics. Using the Internet to spread the word about different events, we reached out to "weblogs," discussion forums, and chat-rooms to let people know about how to Meetup regarding political candidates. Fueled by grassroots political interest, the phenomenon quickly mushroomed. Our own story is entirely consistent with the theme of *Click on Democracy*, which posits that there is a latent yearning for civic engagement, which will percolate up from the bottom if provided with the right nourishment.

As we write this, there are over 150,000 people signed up for political Meetups, ranging from a candidate for treasurer in Kentucky, to an organization opposed to immigration, to, of course, Howard Dean, whose presidential campaign has been the source of much of the media attention we have lately received. But what all of our members have in common is a desire to be engaged in the political discourse in their country and their neighborhoods.

We don't know what the future holds for the Dean campaign, and we don't know what will happen with Meetup. But we do know that we are part of something important. This personal engagement of citizens with other citizens has been made possible through the Internet. The Internet allows politics to become local and personal again, and Meetup is at the forefront of that movement. *Click on Democracy* is at the forefront of works that recognize that potential.

PREFACE TO THE
PAPERBACK EDITION

IN THE TWELVE MONTHS SINCE THE ORIGINAL HARDCOVER EDI-
tion of our book first appeared, media and public attention being paid
to the political importance of the Internet has once again renewed,
rivaling the high expectations for the Internet that were generated in the
lead-up to election 2000, the event our book examines in detail. Most of
the new excitement has been driven by the use of the Internet in the
protests over the war in Iraq, and in Howard Dean's bid for the Democratic presidential nomination in 2004.

Just as in 2000, however, the primary interest in the Internet's political
potential remains focused on the Internet as an effective, efficient, flexible,
and low-cost substitute for the traditional activities of political organizations and media outlets: broadcasting, raising money, getting out a highly
controlled message. Howard Dean's use of the Internet to generate an
early lead in fund-raising, for example, has been the principal story line
for reports on the virtual aspects of his campaign. Similarly, the content
and style of the various candidates' Web pages, as a way to broadcast their
positions and present themselves, is another frequently covered topic.

In 2000, most of the great expectations for the Internet in these traditional political terms ultimately went unrealized. Overall, the Internet did
not generate a lot of money in comparison with traditional methods. It
failed to add a significant new dimension to how people learned about
political issues. And it did not yield big payoffs for politically oriented

business entrepreneurs. Although it may indeed be the case that 2004 will bring the first national election in which the Internet comes of age in these traditionally conceived political terms, it is also quite likely that the Internet's apparent political importance will fade as the field is narrowed and the campaigns and media outlets fall back on tried and true methods to reach their constituents and their customers. Once again, the pundits may conclude that the Internet is not yet ready to play a decisive role in American politics.

We see hopeful signs, however, that the Internet is increasingly being appreciated for its more subtle and, we believe, its more politically important role, as a facilitator of political community building and as a way to generate genuine citizen-to-citizen connections, which in turn create social capital and help to reenergize political activity and political interest. This is the story that we tell in our book about the Internet in the 2000 election.

We see this growing appreciation not only in the current media treatments of the Internet but also in the ways that some political organizations themselves are approaching the technology. It is gratifying to us that our book has been referenced in many of the stories that have explored this aspect of the Internet, from national and international publications like *USA Today* and *The Economist* to regional outlets like *The Hartford Courant* and Allentown's *The Morning Call*.

The Dean campaign and its use of Meetup.com is a prime example of the community-building potential of the Internet, as are the activities occurring through MoveOn.org. Dean's campaign has employed the Internet not only to connect itself with people interested in the campaign but also to connect these people with each other. The campaign has blended virtual and face-to-face communications and has ceded, for a presidential campaign, a remarkable amount of control to the grassroots participants. It has responded to the ideas and initiatives that percolate up from below, including his slogan, "People-Powered Howard," and the idea of Dean supporters in states many miles away from Iowa writing letters to potential supporters there.

Through the campaign, people who are new to political activities are doing things normally reserved for small numbers of political regulars. Last summer in Alexandria, Virginia, Helen Fall and her two daughters were writing letters to Iowa Democrats on behalf of Dean through their Meetup group, which Helen discovered while searching the Internet concerning the Iraq war. "I never participated in any kind of campaign before," she said to a *USA Today* reporter. In Bethlehem, Pennsylvania, Erin Washko told *The Morning Call* that she was inspired by the Meetups to participate for the first time in her life in political meetings, policy discussions, and fund-raising. Given the demands of two young children and a full-time job, the Internet's convenience made this possible.

The large turnouts at Dean's Meetups have taken their organizers by surprise, but it is no surprise to us that when people are provided genuine opportunities to become involved in something meaningful, and when those opportunities give them the chance to establish authentic interpersonal connections, they will take them. This is precisely the argument that we initially advanced over two years ago. Other candidates are now following Dean's lead, and it will be interesting to observe how effective they are in crafting additional ways to involve the public in their efforts.

For its part, Meetup.com, whose CEO has written the new foreword to this book, and which was formed out of concerns for the decline in community connections and social capital, is a prime example of the business potential of this phenomenon. Those who purchase its services, like the restaurants and pubs where the meetings are held, find that their participation is earning them a return on their bottom line. And Meetup.com itself appears to be on the verge of turning a profit.

The most important bottom line for democracy, however, is that in the 2004 elections, campaigns, media organizations, and businesses that are creative and that appreciate the community building and interpersonal connection potential of the Internet may discover that they can do well for themselves by doing good for the political process.

Syracuse, New York, September 17, 2003

PREFACE

IN NOVEMBER 1999, DEAN DAVID RUBIN OF THE S. I. NEWHOUSE School of Public Communications at Syracuse University sent an e-mail to the school's faculty, suggesting that the upcoming national election would be the first in which the Internet could play an important part. He invited any faculty members interested in researching the Internet's role to attend a meeting to discuss plans for an organized approach for the research, and possibly for writing a book. About twenty faculty members, some staff, and a couple of doctoral students showed up.

During that first meeting and several that followed, the group self-selected to ten members who stuck with it throughout the election and the writing process. We brainstormed what the impact of the Internet might be and what we should study. As students of the mass media, we expected to see the Internet play a major role in disseminating news and information. We saw the Internet as many others did—as a new way to distribute content. By Election Day we expected to see a more informed electorate and greater voter turnout. Our study thus focused on Web sites that already had been put up by the traditional media and by political candidates. The research team parsed out the areas of study: Someone would monitor traditional media sites, someone else nontraditional sites. Candidate sites, citizen sites, and parody sites were staked out. Two researchers decided to focus on Internet advertising. Two others proposed conducting online polling of Internet users, and another decided to interview them as a journalist.

By August 2000, however, we were demoralized. Media conglomerates were scaling down their Internet initiatives, and smaller online media companies were folding. Political party and candidate Web sites were often days behind the traditional media in posting news and information, and audits, polls, surveys, and our interviews revealed that few people were visiting political Web sites of any kind. It looked lifeless out there on the electronic frontier, and at a weekly meeting of the research team we considered calling our book "Election.dud."

At about this time we were joined by Grant Reeher, a professor of political science at the Maxwell School of Citizenship and Public Affairs at Syracuse University. He sat quietly during his first meeting with us, listening politely to our musings, asking a few questions, and jotting down notes. He seemed to take a special interest in our interviews with Internet users, some of whom had become quite attached to each other in an online community we had set up. Then he said, "You folks are sitting on a gold mine." We stared back at him. "You may have discovered 'social capital,'" he said, "and that is very exciting." Reeher pointed at the Internet users and said, "They are your story."

We turned our attention away from the political institutions on the Web, and began studying the dynamics of community building on the Internet by ordinary people. The more we looked, the clearer it became that Internet users—many of them new to the technology—were reconnecting with each other and forming virtual political communities online. The election was not a dud at all, but a catalyst for the formation of cybercommunities where new forms of social capital are being created. This became the story we tell in this book.

ACKNOWLEDGMENTS

A NUMBER OF PEOPLE MADE THIS BOOK POSSIBLE, PARTICULARLY Dean David Rubin of the S. I. Newhouse School of Public Communications, who got the project rolling.

Three undergraduate students made substantial contributions: Anthony Ronzio, who wrote the profile of Maria Mancini and was a great help in every stage from the beginning; Hae "Hedi" Hong; and Kimberlea Klein.

Emilie Davis worked many hours transcribing tapes of interviews and researching online resources. Kathy Sowards read early drafts of the manuscript and supplied the book's title. Martha Bonney, Bryan Greenberg, and P. H. Longstaff reviewed early versions and provided valuable criticism.

Our thanks go to many others as well: Thomas Hoban, Gabrielle Shapess, Jonathon Conan, Corinne Iasilli, Ann Kardos, Jessica Rozler, Danica Coto, Michael Lee, Christine Getzler, Chris Aliberto, Judy Johnson, Mike O'Mara, Ronald Kalinoski, Jeff Thomas, Arlayne Searle, Mylinda Smith, and Brett Heindl; Jen Newton, who created the charts and graphs; the wonderful members of the online community who helped us; all of those who took our surveys and polls; and all of those who agreed to interviews.

Advance Publications publicized our online surveys on its online newspapers, and GTE (now Verizon) contacted its Internet customers by e-mail for the same purpose. We thank them both.

Syracuse University and the Newhouse School provided funding and valuable resources that made our research and writing possible.

AUTHORS AND RESEARCH CONTRIBUTORS

Principal Authors

Steve Davis, former Washington/world and national news editor of *USA Today*, directed *USA Today*'s one-year coverage of the Persian Gulf War. He is currently an associate professor of newspaper at the S. I. Newhouse School of Public Communications at Syracuse University.

Larry Elin, filmmaker and interactive media producer, and author of *Designing and Developing Multimedia*, is currently an assistant professor of television, radio, film, and new media at the Newhouse School. He is also co-chair of the Media and American Democracy Institute at Syracuse University.

Grant Reeher, associate professor of political science at Syracuse University's Maxwell School of Citizenship and Public Affairs, is also a senior research associate at Maxwell's Center for Policy Research. He is author of *Narratives of Justice: Legislators' Beliefs about Distributive Fairness* and editor of *The Insider's Guide to Political Internships* and *Education for Citizenship*. He also sits on the board of directors of the nonprofit Social Capital Development Corporation.

Contributing Authors

Amy Falkner, award-winning former reporter, freelance journalist, and one of the "top 20 under 40" newspaper advertising executives, is currently an assistant professor of advertising at the Newhouse School. She authored Chapter 3, "Hype."

Barbara Croll Fought, Emmy Award–winning broadcast journalist, and coauthor of *News in a New Century*, is currently an associate professor of broadcast journalism at the Newhouse School. She is the author of Chapter 4, "Humility."

Contributing Researchers

Katy Benson, freelance feature writer, is currently in the masters program at the School of Information Studies at Syracuse University.

Chris Bolt is the news director of WAER-FM, in Syracuse, New York.

Hubert Brown, long-time public television producer and political reporter, is currently an associate professor of broadcast journalism at the Newhouse School.

Peter Moller is an expert on the Internet, dramatist, and coauthor of *Making Television Programs*. He is currently professor of television, radio, and film at the Newhouse School.

Liz Skewes, a former reporter for the *Tampa Tribune* and magazine editor, is currently on the faculty at the University of Colorado.

1

DON'T DO IT, DREW

IT WAS THURSDAY, AUGUST 24, WHEN DREW MCGARR, REAL estate agent, dropped the bomb on a tight circle of friends, political junkies all.

"If Al Gore wins, my wife and I have both pledged never to vote again. If Al Gore wins, we hang it up."

He said he meant it.

His friends were stunned. Indeed, they were alarmed to hear such a declaration from a sixty-year-old devotee of democracy who'd never missed a vote since he'd turned twenty-one. This was a man who loved voting, a man of such principle that he'd declared he questioned online balloting because he so believed in the process, in the public *act* of voting. "Over the years, my wife and I, we've always met and went to vote, and every time there's always that good feeling you have when you walk out of that school cafeteria, that lifted spirit," he'd once mused. He was proud that he'd brought up his three children—now thirty-six, thirty-seven, and thirty-eight—to feel the same way.

Yet in late summer 2000, he sounded depressed, punctuating his melancholy declaration by saying, "As I get older I seem to see the glass half empty."

His friends fired back. They tried to pump him up. One in particular, Alan Kardoff, voiced outrage. Alan could go on a bit, he could be hyperbolic, but he was genuinely passionate about politics. "Baloney. You're a

PHOTO 1.1   Drew McGarr

fighter," he told Drew. "You believe in America. The day you stop voting is right after you, like the rest of us, go to Eternal Rest. I feel the same way, almost on the other side. I never figured you for a coward."

Kardoff believed he spoke for his friends. "If you bail out, we have to all adjust and readjust. So do you. That is, unless your participation so far has been a charade. I know this is not true. Are you the only one who may feel a bit disenchanted?"

Dave Kaplan chimed in: "Alan is exactly correct on this! We need debate on issues. We need each other. Americans of all ideologies join together to form and maintain our imperfect government and society, but it is still the best of any in the world. Why should one part leave voluntarily, and cause unforeseen adjustments in all parts of the system?

"Hang in there," he urged Drew. "No matter how empty the top half of the glass is, the bottom half of the glass is always half full."

The conversation was percolating now; LuAnn Molloy threw her support to McGarr. "If Al Gore wins," she told the others, "I don't care anymore and renounce any interest in politics and will fit in with everyone else I know, too."

Now it was a debate in full flame. Mona Twocats weighed in. "No. No. A thousand times no. Even though I may disagree with your philosophy, it is imperative that we all continue to at least express our values at the

PHOTO 1.2   Alan Kardoff

PHOTO 1.3   Dave Kaplan

polls. I try to tell people that not voting is only voting by omission. There is no such thing as not being involved in politics. When you refuse to support your value system, you are voting against it."

And finally, Kardoff (a Gore man) wrapped it up, emoting in one of his signature stem-winders. He advised the group that, rather than giving up on politics, "I am fed up so much that my commitment to trying to help our nation elect the better candidates will be intensified.

PHOTO 1.4   Mona Twocats

PHOTO 1.5   LuAnn Molloy

"If Governor Bush and the secretary [Cheney] get in, I will write more e-mails during their term, if my CPU holds up and the economy doesn't fall apart. So, those who wish to leave have the right to do so. They have the right not to vote and join the other 53%-plus of eligible voters who are too busy to honor our patriots. There are a few people who will stay and fight, maintain their loyalty through action rather than hibernation and vote, vote, vote, regardless of what happens with the presidential elections. I think there are more than a few who will stay active citizens. When people are serious and get fed up, they don't crawl into caves. They stand up, stubborn, kick, stall, resist and fight for what is right. I am fed up. I am stubborn like a donkey, too."

Who are these Americans? And what neighborhood fence do they talk over? Drew McGarr is a real estate agent in Memphis, Tennessee. Alan Kardoff is a former business-school professor living in Melbourne, Florida. Dave Kaplan is a Des Moines, Washington, city councilman. A gay man, he came out not long ago. LuAnn Molloy is a mother of three teens in Minnesota who holds down two jobs. Mona Twocats, a Native American, is a Green party activist from Bakersfield, California.

How could such a disparate group come together, bond, and share such passion, empathy, and moral conviction?

On the Internet. All of them were part of an online community that they joined and nurtured during the 2000 election.[1] Kaplan says the Internet connected him to the world of gay Republicans and emboldened him to come out. He realized he was not alone through online conversations with others, many of them members of the Log Cabin Republicans, a national political organization of gays and lesbians. Thousands of miles separate these friends, but they might as well have been sitting around the same kitchen table as cranking out their passions on Compaqs and Dells from desktops in dens or on laptops propped on bedroom pillows.

What makes this group's conversation politically meaningful? What is the Internet contributing here to the vitality of America's political life? At the very least, the fact that the conversation is taking place is significant. And as we will soon describe in a much broader fashion, these kinds of conversations have declined in recent years, a fact that should worry us.

The Internet is the most efficient way for this diverse and scattered group to communicate at all.

And there is a deeper value. Political exchanges on the Internet are often dismissed as the chat-room babbling of the ill informed or the rude ramblings of people bent on venting. Peter Kollock and Marc Smith, editors of *Communities in Cyberspace*, describe online chat groups as either anarchistic or a dictatorship, depending on how moderated they are.[2] But as Drew McGarr and his friends illustrate, substantive discussions and real friendships can build and real passions spill. These people genuinely cared about each other. Over the Internet they built bridges to each other across chasms of politics, religion, economic status, ethnicity, age, gender, and sexual orientation. They accomplished this in ways not available to those without the Internet. The Internet helped to create a *community* or, as Paul Rogat Loeb puts it, "a virtual village."[3]

Loeb's vision looks back to Marshall McLuhan's hope, expressed in the early 1960s and never realized, that television would create a "global village." We think, however, that evidence emerged during the 2000 election to suggest that the Internet has promise to succeed where television did not. The McGarr story is playing out in hundreds, perhaps thousands, of similar online communities involving millions of people. During the 2000 election, as the national discourse turned toward politics, so too did many of these cybercommunities. While we wrote this book, the terrorist attacks on the World Trade Center and the Pentagon took place. We watched cybercommunities grow even closer, the discourse become more impassioned, and political action even more profound and meaningful.

This book describes the use of the Internet in American political life. It takes the 2000 election as its case study, but its arguments extend well beyond that event. It is based on extensive observation of Internet use, from the largest and most powerful institutions to the most average individuals. It comes to a hopeful conclusion. Our overall argument: The principal political institutions used the Internet as a new version of the older, one-to-many TV, radio, and print media and were in fact able to achieve some notable innovations in political communication. But they nevertheless failed to change political life in the dramatic ways many Internet and political observers had hoped to see. Instead, the greatest and most positive political impact was the way informal groups and individuals used the Internet to create and enhance *political communities.* In this way, the Internet helped to create an elusive and precious social good, often known in academic circles as "social capital."

The Decline of Social Capital

The community that Drew McGarr, Dave Kaplan, Mona Twocats, LuAnn Molloy, and Alan Kardoff formed in cyberspace exemplifies a degree of connection that has become increasingly rare in physical space. As social scientist Robert Putnam hammers home in his book *Bowling Alone,* Americans gradually have withdrawn from almost every form of civic engagement over the past forty years. Regardless of the barometer, "the last several decades have witnessed a serious deterioration of community involvement among Americans from all walks of life," he says.[4] By his calculations, we are 40 percent less likely to be involved in political or civic organizations of all kinds than we were in the mid-1960s. Membership has declined in organizations as wide-ranging as the PTA, labor unions, political parties, mainline Christian denominations, and even bowling leagues. Our own personal social connections have weakened, too. We are now less likely to visit friends, have dinner with our own families, or even have a drink in a bar with our coworkers.

All of these and many other indicators signal a serious loss of what Putnam and others call social capital: the "connections among individuals— social networks and the norms of reciprocity and trustworthiness that arise from them," which in turn enhance "the productivity of individuals and groups."[5] These connections also enhance our general happiness, our health, and the quality of our political life. The connections that generate social capital are fueled by relatively basic, but unfortunately diminishing, qualities: honesty, reciprocity, and trust. These qualities produce and are, in turn, reinforced by community.

As Putnam notes in his book, social scientists have long been concerned with social capital. Putnam's work draws theoretically on the works of economist Glenn Loury and sociologist James Coleman, in the 1970s and 1980s respectively, and before these on the writings of political reformer

L. J. Hanifan in the early 1900s. Social theorists and public intellectuals known as communitarians, such as Amitai Etzioni, have worried about social capital, though they may not refer to it as such. Sociologist Robert Bellah and his colleagues found a widespread sense of social disconnectedness in their classic *Habits of the Heart* but again, did not call it social capital.[6] Other social observers have noted it, as well. In a scathing indictment of the American political system, the journalist William Greider laments the decline of "connective tissue" in society.[7] And in a recent book on loyalty, the famed Clinton political strategist James Carville worries about "busted connectors."[8] As Putnam points out, Yogi Berra may have framed the problem best: "If you don't go to someone's funeral, they won't come to yours."

Although no one knows exactly what is causing the decline, it appears to have affected everyone, at every station in life. During the decades Putnam chronicles, we became a nation of suburbanites who spend about 25 percent more time in our cars than we did thirty years ago. Our roots are not simply shallow; they are hydroponic—veritably suspended in air. There are more two-income families, leaving many homes empty during the day and removing what had been a dependable supply of community volunteers. Our knowledge of and interest in current events, one of the most reliable indicators of civic engagement, is waning. We watch entertainment television more but the news less. Those who do watch the news are seeing less "hard" news—stories that deal with major events and issues affecting the community and country. Replacing it are tabloid forms of "infotainment" and critical journalism as news organizations battle for audience share with entertainment programming.[9]

The ideas of community, communication and democracy, and civics endure when put to the test of thoughtful discussion and scientific method and applied to the newest or to the oldest technology. That was apparent most recently in the work of Bill Kovach and Tom Rosenstiel, respected media critics who wrote *The Elements of Journalism: What Newspeople Should Know and the Public Should Expect*. Kovach and Rosenstiel produced their work based on the efforts of a group of twenty-five journalists, the Committee of Concerned Journalists, who did research, conducted surveys, and talked to dozens of citizens and news professionals at great length. The authors' conclusions and observations illuminate not just the media business but the evolving definitions of community and discourse, whether it is online or offline, mediated or unmediated, broadcast or video-streamed nationwide or traded among chatting neighbors. Kovach and Rosenstiel wrote:

> The news media help us define our communities, and help us create a common language and common knowledge rooted in reality. . . . This definition has held so consistent through history, and proven so deeply ingrained in the thinking of those who produce news through the ages, that it is in little doubt. It is difficult, in looking back, even to separate the concept of journalism from the concept of creating community and later democracy. . . . Even people who resist the label of journalist, who work on the Web, offer a similar goal. Omar Wasow, a self-described "garage entrepreneur" who founded a Web site called New York Online, told us at one forum that his aim, in part, was helping to create citizens who are "consumers, devourers and debunkers of media . . . an audience who have engaged with the product and can respond carefully."[10]

We read newspapers less. This decline is more pronounced among eighteen-to-twenty-four-year-olds (down 57 percent) than those over sixty (down 10 percent). What is true for television news is also true for newspapers—there is a preponderance of soft, human-interest news.[11] The news that is consumed is of little value. A generation of highly educated but less informed citizens looms as the entire population ages and the more informed die off.

Lost in the blizzard of disappointing survey results is the psychological toll inflicted on the individuals who collectively make up the statistics. We are a race of social beings who need healthy contact with each other but are spending less time even attempting to stay in touch. As individuals we seem to be inflicting on ourselves the most fearsome penalty we impose on our criminals: solitary confinement.

This combination—disconnection from each other and uninterestedness in community affairs—has taken a measurable toll on every form of civic engagement. Even forms of civic engagement that usually become

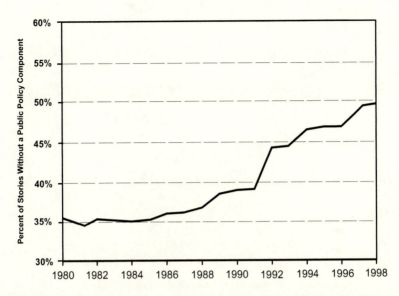

FIGURE 1.1 A Harvard study revealed a sharp increase in news without a public policy component. Source: Thomas E. Patterson, *Doing Well and Doing Good* (Cambridge, MA: Joan Shorenstein Center on the Press, Politics, and Public Policy, John F. Kennedy School of Government, Harvard University, December 2000), p. 3.

more evident during an important election year are suffering. According to Roper surveys taken between 1973 and 1994 we are 25 percent less likely to participate in any of the most common forms of political involvement, such as working for a political party, writing to an elected official, or signing a petition. Voting turnout in presidential elections has declined steadily to the point where in 1996, for the first time in the nation's recent history, fewer than half of all eligible voters went to the polls. In 2000, turnout was 51.2 percent, according to the Committee for the Study of the American Electorate—a slight increase perhaps attributable to the massive get-out-the-vote and registration efforts in battleground states, some of which took place over the Internet.

The decline in social capital is most acute among young adults. The most inactive generation of voters is between eighteen and twenty-four years old. In 1996 less than half the eligible voters in this age group registered and less than a third voted. These proportions rise steadily with age. Three-quarters of those over sixty-five are registered, and two-thirds

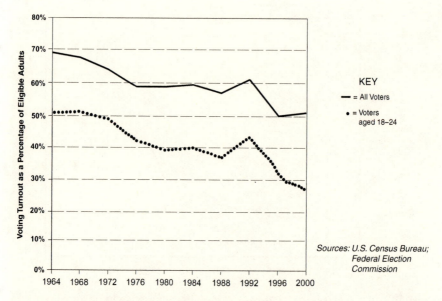

FIGURE 1.2   Voter turnout has decreased steadily over the last forty years, with youth voting showing the greatest decline.

voted. Each successive generation is better educated, more affluent, enjoys more leisure time, and is in almost every way more capable of participating in civic activities, yet younger Americans are withdrawing from the political process. Even the motor voter law, which made it possible to register to vote while getting a drivers license, and laws that made voting by mail the only method in Oregon and the preferred in Washington state, failed to significantly increase overall voter participation.[12]

The Internet and Civic Engagement

Can the Internet help reverse the decline in voting and other forms of civic engagement? Will the news media, political parties, special interest groups, and grassroots political organizations effectively use it to reach citizens? Can the Internet increase our consumption of and interest in the news and make us better, more informed, and more active citizens? Will the Internet engage the young to fashion new forms of civic engagement? Will they become more interested in politics?

Our study of the people who used the Internet during the 2000 election offers strong evidence that the Internet *is* having an impact, though not in the manner we expected. We found that the Internet provides citizens who are separated from each other by time and space a way to reconnect and become more concerned about each other and their society. Most of our evidence shows that they are doing this without the assistance of the media and political institutions.

The Flies around the Elephants

In the course of poll watching and survey taking during a national election, we often find it difficult to see anything that isn't very large and moving very slowly. We watch for and measure social, political, and economic movements occurring on a massive scale—huge herds of elephants crossing the plain. While watching the elephants, we fail to see millions of smaller, smarter, faster, more adaptable organisms, the very kind that better define the Internet and its users. When we looked more closely and noticed the flies buzzing around the elephants, we saw that ordinary people were successful where the institutions were not. Whereas the institutions regarded the Internet as simply a "tool" and largely mishandled it, everyday users adopted the Internet as an extension of themselves—what psychologists call a cognitive artifact—and used it to connect with others to form virtual political communities.[13] Unlike some technologies that preceded it, the Internet is part of what Bonnie A. Nardi and Vicki L. O'Day call an *information ecology*—"a system of people, practices, values and technologies in a local environment."[14] Contrary to the tool metaphor, which casts the Internet as an inanimate object that people must learn to use on *its* terms, the ecology metaphor embraces the Internet as something that evolves, changes, and adapts along with its users, often in unexpected ways.

The Critique of Virtual Communities

Scholars and social observers concerned about declines in community, connectedness, and social capital have tended to look askance at the Internet as a remedy. Some even see it as exacerbating the problem. The main reason is that the Internet does not establish *face-to-face* communication and connections, which they see as critical. In their view, genuine community requires that people jointly occupy a physical space where they share common experiences, needs, and desires and thus collectively develop identities, interests, and solutions to problems. It is the face-to-face discussions and shoulder-to-shoulder struggles for a common good that produce trust, honesty, and reciprocity, which are necessary for social capital. Although this vision of community is as old as recorded history, among modern scholars its image is rooted in the nineteenth-century work of the German sociologist Ferdinand Tönnies, whose concept of *gemeinschaft* still conjures up nostalgic memories of the tightly knit community.[15] The Internet, community-minded critics argue, cannot provide people with the means to establish communities that in any way substitute for this ideal. Admittedly, thinkers like Robert Putnam are keen to explore new ways of making genuine connections, but they focus on the physical, not the virtual.

In discussing the Internet's potential for regenerating social capital, Putnam observes that so far the social culture of the Internet is radically individualistic rather than communitarian and that the lower threshold offered by the Internet to expressing an opinion may in turn lower the quality of political discourse. He also argues that the Internet robs the participant of "social cues" and the depth and multiplicity of feedback necessary for "interpersonal collaboration and trust."[16] There was a famous cartoon in the *New Yorker* magazine in which a dog, seated at a computer, tells another dog, "On the Internet, no one knows you're a dog." This illustrates Putnam's point perfectly.

Thus the Internet makes it easier to misrepresent and lie. Putnam further posits that the Internet makes it easier for ever-narrower interests to come together, to the exclusion of others. Diversity in social interactions could further suffer with the Internet, as "local heterogeneity may give way to more focused virtual homogeneity."[17]

Putnam notes that historically, most of the cybercommunities on the Internet have been discussion groups composed of individuals with narrowly defined common interests. This "cyberbalkanization," in which the inhabitants of online communities self-select into self-interest groups, is anathema to the offline communities we actually live in.[18] In real-life communities, we have to deal with everybody we bump into, not just those with whom we are already in agreement. In addition, the Internet tends to be primarily a source for "passive, private entertainment," including the purchase of traditional retail goods, rather than a stimulant for active, real communication.[19] Finally, Putnam also notes the presence of the digital divide that separates computer access between the haves and have-nots.

For all these reasons Putnam doubts whether the Internet can be another telephone, versus another television; that is, something that can facilitate our interpersonal connectedness versus something that further isolates us and makes us less socially engaged.[20] Another way to frame the difference is that the Internet is creating virtual malls rather than virtual villages. Again, others have weighed in with similar concerns. James Carville, for example, flatly states, "email's not a real connection to me. It's words on a screen."[21] Can these supposed virtual communities hope to replenish the forms of social capital we are losing with something as apparently temporary and glib as a string of disconnected, sometimes invective-filled, and misspelled remarks by strangers?

According to Putnam and the other Internet skeptics, the self that exists on the Internet is a decidedly thin one. The anonymity, the lack of face-to-face or at least voice-to-voice communication, and the absence of physical proximity all limit the kind of community that can be generated virtually. We argue, however, that this kind of thinness of self also provides the opportunity for a kind of *thickness* of community that would not otherwise exist. Moreover, the terms *thin* and *thick* suggest a permanent condition, whereas what we have seen on the Internet is an *elastic self*. On the Internet, people are judged more on their behavior than on ascriptive characteristics. Boundaries of ideology, beliefs, and culture are not reinforced by appearance, voice tone, accent, and so on. Displays of arrogance and disrespect are more generally punished, without regard to the socioeconomic statuses of those involved. And people do connect. The Internet self can be both thick and thin—it is elastic.

Although the digital divide continues to keep some Americans at arm's length from the technology, the Internet nonetheless provides individuals with the ability to participate in and influence the political system in ways heretofore reserved only for those with either great resources or institutional affiliations with large, established organizations. Furthermore, the political communities initiated on the Internet often progress into face-to-face experiences and other real exchanges. Prior identities are unveiled, thus thickening the selves that originally existed only as user IDs. In these ways, the Internet communities can generate the kind of public spiritedness that their critics perceive to be inherently absent. In the remainder of this book we detail why we think that the future of the Internet in American political life may be considerably brighter, and its impact on social capital considerably more profound and positive, than do the skeptics we have just described.

During the latter half of our study, we found many instances in which enterprising Internet users employed its unique ability to create human networks. During Election 2000, some of these networks had specific purposes for short periods of time. They appeared, accomplished their stated goal, and evaporated. Others emerged and appear to be gaining momentum and growing; they are in it for the long haul. Either way, we began to see the use of the Internet for the creation of human networks as a hopeful and positive sign that it can have a positive net effect on civic engagement, social connections, and social capital. We found the Internet reached people who might otherwise never have become involved in the political process, and engaged them in activities that they never would have imagined possible with people they never would have met.

The Changing Face of Internet Users

During its earliest days, the Internet was populated by a homogeneous group of early adopters and technophiles mainly interested in the Internet itself. The chat-rooms, bulletin boards, and interest groups studied by social scientists during the dawn of the Internet were, perhaps not inappropriately, labeled as effete, self-absorbed, and exclusive. All those uninitiated in the ways of this select club were tabbed "newbies" and were often "flamed"—insulted for not knowing the correct etiquette. However, with the introduction of the World Wide Web, the Internet has exploded into

50 percent of American households in just the past few years. A *majority* of Americans now have access to the Internet at home or at work, the library, cybercafes, or other public locations. As more and more everyday people use the Internet, might they not use it for everyday things and behave in more socially acceptable, even normal ways? Is it possible that those aspects of their physical existence that make some forms of civic engagement difficult or impossible will become less relevant as people take their civic concerns and activities to cyberspace?

Alan Kardoff, a member of the online community that tried to "save" Drew McGarr, relies heavily on the Internet for a sense of connection to the larger society. "Personally, I'm a loner, I have no family," Kardoff said.

> Living alone, I developed a sense of community, some ties [on the Internet]. Some of the postings I didn't care to read, but it was virtually both sides. Doors opened to me that allowed me to have somewhat of a participatory life, a social life on the Internet that I wouldn't have otherwise. And I refute those who say it kept me more isolated. I got to meet people who I would have never had the opportunity to meet, and I got to feel a part of something. It's like when I answered Harris Polls, but this is more personal because I got to know the people.

Kardoff even made social connections through his use of eBay, the online auction house. Some social scientists contend that monetary transactions are, by their nature, antithetical to the notion of trust and reciprocity, and therefore community, but Kardoff's personal experiences indicate otherwise. "I've got a letter from someone in Idaho," he says.

> I've got a letter from someone in Omaha. A couple of people in Idaho who want me to come up to meet me. There's a professor of music up in Anchorage, University of Alaska, and I just enjoy the music he sells. So we've talked, and once I found out he's a conductor and a musician of all sorts, I started buying things from him just to see his name. There's a Holocaust survivor in New York, a doctor, and he took a liking to me. He's maybe in his mid-eighties. I purchased some things from him, and we started sharing. I owe him a personal letter. He adopted me and I adopted him.

Kardoff and his online connections are good examples of the positive side of cybercommunities, described by social commentator Howard Rheingold as "social aggregations that emerge from the Net when enough people carry on public discussions long enough, with sufficient human feeling, to form webs of personal relationships."[22] The difficulty of measuring "sufficient human feeling" notwithstanding, Kardoff derives important social pleasures online. Because the Internet is two-way and interactive, Kardoff gives back to the community by his active participation in it. He is to his online pals what they are to him—part of a reciprocal, honest, and trusting social network. As scholar Jan Fernback observed, "[Internet] users can assert victory in humanity's ancient struggle with nature by overcoming the constraints of geographical boundaries and form re-imagined social configurations."[23] The new generation of Internet users is quite different than that studied by cybercommunity critics as recently as two years ago.

The Internet that fosters the kind of attachment that Drew McGarr's circle experienced is just off and under the social scientist's and media scholar's number-crunching radar. This Internet brought thoughtful people together in ways that had gone unnoticed. The Internet we observed may be supplementing the village square and traditional forms of face-to-face connections with virtual communities and coast-to-coast connections that appear to be relevant and actually pertinent, meaningful, and valuable. Communities formed, activists organized, petitions circulated. People volunteered, contributed money, registered to vote, and some even voted online.

The Real Impact

So what is the impact of the Internet on society, as seen through the lens of the 2000 election? What clues were dropped during that year? What do they portend? These are the questions we explore in this book. The Internet's impact cannot be summed up in a sound bite. But it has changed everything it has touched and everyone who has touched it. The authors of this work tend to agree in principle and spirit with Doug Bailey, CEO of the Freedom Channel, organizer of Youth-e-Vote, and founder of the respected political newsletter *Hotline.* In an interview for this project, just a few weeks before the presidential vote, Bailey said:

> One view about the Internet and politics is that 2000 is supposed to be some kind of a gigantic breakthrough year, and because there's no candidate who has become the Internet candidate and has magically broken through, . . . the conclusion is that 2000 isn't a breakthrough year at all.
>
> The other school, of which I am a strong proponent, is that the notion that the Internet is not having a substantial impact on politics is just nuts. Of course it is. If you measure it by candidates who have invented themselves because of the Internet and have made a breakthrough, I can't name any, but that doesn't seem to me to be the point. The point is that more and more Americans are going to the Internet for their information—some to it exclusively for their information and some more to it as one of their sources for information, and every study that's done shows that that continues to rise.
>
> A major point that shouldn't be missed is that we are barely at the beginning of a gigantic transformation of how entertainment and information and communications happens in this country. . . . The capacity for sending and capacity for receiving become ubiquitous. That's a whole new world that is not only going to change our politics dramatically, it's going to change our culture and everything else. The world in which every one of us can become our own TV producers and pick what we want to see and when we want to see it, and what we don't want to see, that's just a whole new world, and that will change our world dramatically.

It is the way that the Internet behaved as a community builder, as a social-capital enhancer, that suggests the most promise for our nation's political life. This idea popped out at us as we puzzled over our data. Four more specific aspects about the way the Internet mattered merit a brief discussion, even at this early point. We will return to them in detail later, particularly in the latter half of the book.

First, the Internet was most effective when it was employed by those who saw themselves and others as active participants in an ongoing process rather than as passive receivers of information—recall the distinction we drew earlier between the telephone and television. This observation reinforces our broader argument concerning the Internet's potential value for social capital and helps to explain the "dud" yielded by the virtual versions of more traditional media and party activities and described in the next chapter.

Second, the communities that are produced through the Internet are of two kinds. The first are communities that would be recognizable to Robert Putnam and his colleagues, which begin on the Internet but are ultimately sustained and located offline. Indeed, Putnam argues this is precisely how the Internet might aid social capital accumulation (notwithstanding his virtual doubts, writ large, which we described earlier). But we found a second kind of community, vibrant and viable ones that began on the Internet and then flourished primarily on and through it. Both kinds are important.

Third, the digital divide persists. You will notice that our profiles in Chapters 6, 7, 8, and 9 are heavily populated by people who are well educated, well-off, or well connected, or all three. But there are also stories of completely "ordinary" people. We assert that the kinds of virtual interpersonal connections that we uncovered illustrate what can be accomplished within the entire population, given the appropriate public policies to enhance real access to the Internet. We will return to this in the final chapter.

Finally, by arguing that the Internet's positive impact was primarily interpersonal and community oriented, we do not mean to suggest that it was not *political*—quite the contrary. Part of the problem with civic engagement, especially among youth, is the assumption that *politics* can only mean narrow, partisan tactical battles and electioneering geared to the lowest common denominators of interest. Anything deemed political is thus tainted and to be avoided. But social connecting, talking, and doing is the very stuff of politics. Politics is the process by which we govern ourselves. It is the process of struggle, negotiation, and compromise. It is how we decide what we will do and who we will be. The story of Drew McGarr that opened this chapter illustrates this process as it occurred over the Internet. By enhancing those aspects of our lives, the Internet enhances politics, and by enhancing politics, it helps to reclaim the rightfully honorable place of politics in our lives.

The Story Ahead

The story of how we saw the Internet during the 2000 election chronologically parallels the actual events that led to the final Supreme Court decision that favored George W. Bush. In order to follow events that led not only to the selection of the president but also to our own gradual awakening to the true potential of the Internet to uplift civic engagement, we divide our book into four conceptual parts.

Chapter 3 traces the high expectations for the Internet from just before the first announcements of candidacy in late 1998 until the conventions in late summer. Many political eyes turned toward this media newcomer, and pundits wondered aloud if the Internet would have the same impact on this election as television had in 1960. Would there be a horrible cybergaff? A scoop that only the Internet could have pulled off? An Internet equivalent of Miss Lewinsky's "blue dress"? Would something be revealed on the Internet, and nowhere else, that would turn the election on its head? This is the story of the Internet's *hype*.

In those early days, a number of independent Web sites sprang up, some with venture capital funding, to cover the election. Media giants transferred staff and resources into their Internet "initiatives," as they called them. The networks bowed out of gavel-to-gavel TV coverage of the conventions, turning over some responsibility to their Web offspring. Some political parties and candidates welcomed Webmasters into their inner circle of strategists. People like Ben Green, Max Fose, and Lynn Reed became well-known among the campaign cognoscenti. Online voting was used for some nonbinding straw polls and for the Democratic primary in Arizona, only to be greeted with a lawsuit and an uncomplimentary task-force report urging states not to adopt the technology. A number of online get-out-the-vote efforts sprang up, determined to register millions of new voters. It was going to be a "wired" election.

Chapter 4 recalls the unsettling realization that the election did not orbit around the Internet. It is difficult to pinpoint the precise moment or inciting incident that led us to this conclusion. It came on gradually during the campaign, in part because of the trudging, lumbering sameness of the media coverage and party Web use. The Internet as used by the political and media establishment was not exciting, possibly because of the high expectations. Because the collapse of the entire dot-com universe occurred simultaneously, this was not surprising. Nobody, not even the world's great entertainers, could hold an audience on the Internet. Much of this story details how the media, the political parties, and the candidates failed to ignite citizenship. Far from scooping the traditional media, Internet media sites often trailed their older siblings in breaking the news. TV was still the more immediate way to get campaign news, and newspapers the more reliable. The candidates' sites were interactive billboards that combined negative advertising, stands on policy and issues, and instant opinion polls with e-commerce. Anyone who left an e-mail address with a candidate was inundated with e-mail from that moment on, often requesting a contribution. One lasting impression each candidate left on the Internet audience was of a guy pummeling his opponent with one hand and holding out a collection plate with the other. This is the story of the Internet's *humility*.

Chapters 5 through 9 tells the story of the *other* Internet. The story of Drew McGarr that began this chapter is one of the many hopeful signs we began to see as the Internet owned and operated by the citizen crystallized. Although we had been looking for indications that the Internet would influence the outcome of the 2000 election, and found few, we did discover that the Internet was providing citizens with new and better ways to be involved in the democratic process. Given the decline of social capital, our discovery is not a solution in search of a problem. The retreat of so many people from civic engagement over the last three or four decades will not be reversed solely by the Internet, but its increased use by citizens to begin, elevate, or improve their level of involvement is a reason to be encouraged. Over and over again we found Internet users who were reaching out to the greater society by using the Internet as an extension of themselves. This is the story of the Internet's *hope.*

We thus christened the collection of intrepid Internet users and their social circles *communities of hope.* We further subdivided the communities into those that were built around common *beliefs,* shared *identities,* civic *discourse,* and common *action.* Each of these types of communities closely parallels the communities that seem to be evaporating from civic life in the "real world." In these chapters are Republicans and Democrats, Greens and socialists. There are men and women of all ages and races, religious backgrounds, and economic classes. They come from the Deep South, the Northwest, the inner city, and the suburbs. Some are pro-choice, others pro-life. Some support gun control and others gun ownership. They are environmentalists. They want the government to leave business alone. They want to outlaw capital punishment. They want swift and sure criminal prosecutions.

Those profiled in these chapters of hope for civic engagement used the Internet to communicate, inform, proselytize, organize, promote, and petition and as a soapbox for self-expression. They gathered others around them and developed bonds that may last as long and as steadfastly as non-virtual friendship. These individuals represent others who may be shaping the Internet into a tool for reenergizing democracy.

Granted, the distinctions between these four kinds of communities are to some degree artificial. This is inevitable, as members of any community share something in common concerning all four qualities. In addition, identity and beliefs usually lead to political action, action that in turn strengthens identity and beliefs; furthermore, an identity often supplies the roots of more specific beliefs, and in turn these beliefs can strengthen and develop senses of identity. And of course all of this depends on discourse. The communities we describe will thus overlap in type. Nonetheless, we believe that in organizing and naming them as we have, we have accurately captured the core aspect that unites each community.

We conclude the book with our ideas about the future of the Internet's role in American politics.

Our Methods

Andrew Calcutt observes in his book *White Noise: An A–Z of the Contradictions in Cyberculture* that those who study the Internet usually "begin with the technology, and then move on to examine its application in society."[24] This is backwards. The Internet is a reflection of the society that uses it, not the other way around. "We live in a social system that for two hundred years has brought larger and larger numbers of people together in the act of making our world, while at the same time pulling them apart and alienating them from each other and from themselves," Calcutt argues. "Moreover, this is a social system that relies on innovation, but finds itself ill-at-ease with new developments." We are uncomfortable, he suggests, with the very technology we may come to depend on to glue our social system back together. Taking this to heart, our study focused on people, not systems, and on individuals, not institutions. The flies became our focus, not the elephants.

The observations and conclusions in this book are built on two years of study of online election content of all kinds but with a special and concerted emphasis on those who created the content. This involved approximately two hundred interviews. The authors talked at length with professionals and citizens representing the full range of Internet sites and users: major media, Webzines, and nonpartisan sites; citizens who used the Web and those who merely cruised it; and firms that tracked every move and every mouse click. As part of the project, we recruited one hundred everyday users from across the country for interviews; about one-third of them voluntarily joined a message group and talked online from midsummer right through, and past, the final Supreme Court decision that ended the election.

We probed news stories, attended conferences, and conducted an extensive literature search. We obtained the results of available surveys and polls. More than six hundred college freshmen answered our online survey that probed the interconnection of the Internet and politics, and three dozen of them sat down for in-depth conversations. Comments from these students—future voters and new-style news and information consumers—are scattered throughout the book.

2

ELECTION.DUD

*In the same way Gutenberg's Bible hastened the end of The
Church's stranglehold on fifteenth-century Europe, in the same
way Thomas Paine rallied troops to fight King George, in the
same way Upton Sinclair cleaned up the meatpackers with a
single stroke, the Internet is liberating the Great Unwashed.
... The Internet supersedes every mode of communication ever
invented. Except a simple handshake and hello on the street.*

Matt Drudge,
The Drudge Manifesto

FOR ALL THAT THE WEB IS, CHARLES ELLISON WAS STRUCK BY
what he *could not* find there: a site that spoke to blacks who were middle
class, educated, upwardly mobile, and sophisticated about politics and
policy. Certainly, there were sites that targeted African-Americans, but
they were mostly general interest, often with a heavy sports and entertainment slant. Ellison, who was working in Washington, D.C., as a producer
at C-SPAN, began to discuss a magazine venture with friend Roderick
Conrad, and they quickly realized a Web site could be accomplished much
more quickly and at much less expense. "We had dreams, we had visions
for a huge, interactive, international community," Ellison said.

PHOTO 2.1   Charles Ellison

The then twenty-seven-year-old Ellison and Conrad began to brainstorm just a few blocks from the Capitol, sometimes working at one of the
Xando coffeehouses that would inspire the black-and-yellow color
scheme of the site they planned and quickly brought online in June 1999.
Their choice of "politicallyblack.com" for a name sounded like a giddy,
perfect fit. It was the beginning of a classic fifteen-month tale, what Ellison described as riding a fifteen-foot Maui wave at its height, but at its
nadir, the classic dot-com demise: wipeout.

The independent site quickly drew media attention—from salon.com,
Black Enterprise magazine, Fox TV, C-SPAN, and many more—and eventually attracted a private suitor as well, in the form of Netivation, a publicly traded company on the NASDAQ stock exchange. Conrad and Ellison—a father with two young daughters who was paying for the bills out
of his personal savings and from his C-SPAN check—sold the business to
Netivation in October 1999 but continued to run it with editorial independence. Ellison and Conrad hadn't been making money, which was an
understandable and pressing mandate from owners who envisioned a
whole suite of sites (politicallylatino.com and more). But the business
model failed. The content drew 5 million hits a month at its peak and as
many as 1,000 e-mails a day, but not nearly enough advertising dollars. By
September 2000 the operation was shuttered. The bottom line: No one

was going to pay for content in the Web world, and advertisers had figured out the truth about banner ads. No one read them, no one clicked through.

Ellison's story does not fit the classic grassroots model: Its aim was to merge activism, information, and political news with a profit, and it was not built on the backs of volunteers. But it is informative nonetheless for the niche it fit, for the dream its founders held, and for the promise, perhaps, for an S. B. Woo– or Joe Bogosian–style success story in 2004 or beyond (see the profiles of these entrepreneurs in later chapters).

"We were growing at a time when people were still sort of experimenting with the Internet and examining how it could be used for public discourse and how it could contribute to the common good and trying to find that balance between using the Internet for civic engagement and profiting from it," said Ellison, whose mother is African-American and whose father is Scotch-Irish. "We were having fun with it, and we were also using it as a public service to our community, but at the end of the day, the bottom line was, 'If you want to keep this site going, it has to generate some kind of profit.'"

Ninety percent of African-Americans voted for Al Gore, but Ellison did not approach his audience that way. He toiled to present a balanced read and to provide a forum for all kinds of voices. He said he heard criticism from some people in the black political establishment, who felt he should have sought their blessing before he launched the site. Some people were surprised to read his bio, which noted that he'd worked for a time for Republican Newt Gingrich, the former Speaker of the House.

If you can't do it through a newly created or independent site, then I've advocated for many longstanding black interest groups or organizations such as the Urban League or NAACP to do such a thing. What's hindering this is persuading these very old organizations, who have an old guard of political figures in their corridors who have not yet recognized the power of the Internet, to galvanize a community. The kings and queens of the black political establishment are from the era of forty years ago of physical, live, in-person grassroots mobilization. But this Internet, they're still trying to figure it out; it's still something that they haven't yet come to accept fully. It is something that confuses and confounds them. The Internet is something that I believe right now is kind of scaring the black political establishment. And not just the black political establishment, either. I think it's just the political establishment in general. It terrifies them. It's going to have to come from a new generation of pioneers and forward thinkers.

In retrospect, the high expectations for the Internet in the 2000 election made sense. More Americans were online, and more people used it to be engaged in the political process than in 1996. By December 2000, according to a study by the Pew Research Center for the People and the Press, 56 percent of all Americans were online, and 18 percent regularly went to the Internet for news and information.[1] Page view and site visit reports showed that a considerable number of Americans went online to study candidates, issues, and news. For example, Voter.com, a voter education Web site, reported 600,000 unique visitors during the party conventions in August 2000.[2] Web White & Blue 2000, a voter education project supported by the Markle Foundation, reported that its Web site received 7,518,608 page views from June 28 through November 8, 2000.[3]

To accommodate these Internet surfers, more than 3,200 Web sites devoted to some aspect of the 2000 election appeared by mid-May 2000, each waiting for virtual foot traffic.[4] The Web sites were updated daily, sometimes more than once, and information was archived in vast virtual vaults. Literally millions of pages of political information were created, metatagged, hyperlinked, and posted on the Internet. This took place during the most exhilarating and unbridled growth ever of new-media startups and initial public offerings, and it seemed as though cultural critic Neil Postman was absolutely accurate when he asserted, "The Technopolist stands firm in believing that what the world needs is yet more information."[5] True believers in the Internet's power were adamant in their conviction that more and deeper information would reenergize democracy.

Some Web sites were put up by the traditional news media, such as *The New York Times* and other newspapers, as well as ABC, CNN, and other television entities. Web sites such as Pseudopolitics.com and Salon.com, which did not have a traditional media lineage, joined them. Political parties and candidates and hundreds of average citizens put up Web sites.

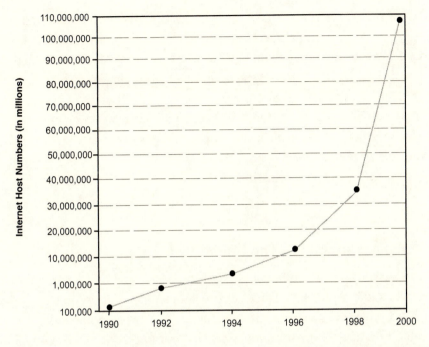

Source: Metrix.net (http://www.mids.org)

FIGURE 2.1   Penetration and use of the Internet have grown steadily during the past ten years, and this fueled great expectations for its use in Election 2000.

Nonpartisan get-out-the-vote organizations created Web sites to increase voter knowledge and voter registrations. One feature of these sites was online registration—potential voters could register to vote by filling out and submitting their applications entirely online. There were sites devoted specifically to the pre-voting-age youth and one, Youthevote.com, conducted an online mock election one week before the real one involving more than a million high school students. Even commercial sites joined in. Lane Bryant, the women's wear retailer, promoted an online registration effort over its Web site using its spokesperson, pop star Queen Latifah. (Today, many of these sites are archived—frozen in time for historical purposes—at http://archive.alexa.com/collections/e2k.html.)

The primary players in the online drama were the political parties, the candidates, the media, and the electorate. They were joined by a smattering of public interest groups, watchdog groups, get-out-the-vote campaigns, pollsters, and academics who watched the whole thing unfold. Each learned something about how to effectively use the Internet in a national election. Ben Green, Webmaster for Al Gore, cited the importance of having adequate "back room" technology. "We were able to handle far more site visitors than the Bush site because of our server configuration. That's the only way to explain why we had twice as many page views than they did after every debate," he declared.[6]

Despite some encouraging indications, there were four problems with the wired election.

Problem Number 1—The Online Media

The increase in the number of political Web sites and the size of the potential audience for the content were eye-opening and hopeful signs to most observers and many entrepreneurs. The television networks and cable news channels, for example, decided not to provide gavel-to-gavel coverage of the Republican and Democratic party conventions and instead dispatched their Internet subsidiaries to shoulder much of that responsibility. At the time, it appeared to the networks that they could continue to air their highly rated comedy and drama shows during the convention weeks and Webcast the convention to online political junkies. The convention Web coverage looked surprisingly like a televised event, with streaming video pushed down the distribution pipe at the Web audience.

At the Republican convention in Philadelphia, a huge tent was erected just outside the convention center and dubbed "Internet Alley." Web-site work areas were located one after the other under the big top, and reporters seated shoulder-to-shoulder posted their stories on laptops connected to servers. Webmasters rearranged graphics, inserted new links, dropped in new jpeg photos fresh from the convention floor, and refreshed the Web sites constantly. The competing Web sites rushed to be just a little faster, a little better, and a little slicker than the others. But in the mad dash to find, write, edit, and post news, almost nobody thought of the back channel—the fact that the Internet is a two-way communications system, not simply a distribution system with a voracious appetite for content.

The traditional media viewed the Internet as another distribution system and were motivated by the same quest for ratings that drives their print and broadcast business model. The media tried to market their content and brand their Internet presence by cross-promoting their Internet campaign coverage on television, radio, and in newspapers. Even the Public Broadcasting System continuously urged viewers of its *NewsHour with Jim Lehrer* to visit PBS.org for additional information. Some media coverage of the election on the Internet seemed halfhearted and uneven. Several papers used the same reporters to write and post stories for their Web site as for their print newspaper, creating an Internet product composed of "shovelware." The term is used derisively by new-media aficionados to describe interactive media content that is initially created for another medium and simply ported over to a Web site.

But if the news media had hoped to launch their Internet initiatives into the limelight by luring voters during the election and then holding on to that audience afterwards, they failed. In January 2001, NBC, CNN, *The New York Times,* and several other media giants announced massive layoffs and a general downsizing of their Internet groups. Even some of the companies that measured Internet usage went offline. Gone by June 2001 were PC Data and Media Metrix, companies that collected, processed, and sold Internet usage data to dot-coms, Wall Street analysts, and advertisers.

The news media did not reenergize news consumption by creating new outlets on the Internet. Those who visited Internet news sites tended to be the people who watched television news, read newspapers, and were generally informed about political news already. Although the Internet population swelled to more than half the country during the 2000 election, true believers in the Internet's power to create an informed electorate were disappointed to find that the most frequented sites featured the day's weather and that one of the most popular search topics was "Pam Anderson," the buxom former star of TV's *Baywatch.*[7]

Furthermore, the Internet news audience is small compared with the traditional media—TV, radio, and newspapers—and is not growing at a rate that will offset the steady decline of news consumption. For example, Americans are watching less TV news. As recently as 1994, three-quarters of Americans told Pew pollsters they had watched some kind of news on

TV the day before. Now, slightly more than half say so. TV has lost one in every three news viewers; the networks, in particular, have been staggered by the steep decline in their audience share. Cable news has remained flat. Pew's numbers show that two-thirds of us claim to read a newspaper regularly, though less than half responded "yes" when asked if they'd read one the day before.

Problem Number 2—The Cybercandidates

The major political parties and individual candidates weighed in early in the 2000 election and used the Internet in every conceivable way, though it did not replace yard signs and door-to-door canvassing, $200-a-plate dinners, baby kissing, TV advertising, stump speeches, or anything else that works dependably. Arizona senator John McCain raised a few million dollars online and hosted the first "cyber cocktail party/fundraiser." Some massive e-mail lists were built, and millions of e-mail messages were sent by campaigns, citizens, and candidates. Al Gore supporters built their own Web pages—five-minute cookie-cutter creations—and became instant-message friends. Gore himself sat "At the Table" for occasional Webcast chats with college voters, live from his Web site.

The Bush camp seemed to win the debate-night battle, burying the Gore forces with e-mails refuting and disputing in real time almost everything the vice president said. John McCain brought us "impulse giving" by inspired supporters who wrote electronic checks before thinking twice, but it didn't get him the nomination. Steve Forbes and Elizabeth Dole announced their candidacies online but faded fast. Bill Bradley, the Democrat who understood the Internet's potential as well as McCain did, was defeated early and often. George W. Bush bought the first TV ad ever to promote his URL, but to him the Internet seemed only about money. Soon after the election he e-mailed his partisans, "Please give up to $5,000 to my Recount Committee. All givers will be posted on my Web site."

Political parties, candidates, and other partisan groups created Web sites to publish election material, raise funds, organize, register voters, and make contact with the media. The political party operatives developed a top-down hierarchy, usually placing the Internet initiative somewhere under the communications director. From that vantage point, Web sites were used largely to distribute information and take in contributions. The political parties assembled massive e-mail lists that enabled them to broadcast pleas, directives, and "personal" messages to thousands of supporters and fence-sitters. Ben Green, Gore's Webmaster, employed every technological trick he could to outdo the Bush site. "We had live Webcasts every day," he said. "We even did one from a moving school bus in Iowa."[8] He was particularly proud of the instant-messaging feature that he installed on the Gore site, making it possible for Gore supporters to identify each other the moment they came online.

Despite the bells and whistles on their Web sites, it is possible that Gore and Bush made just as much political hay with the Internet when it was the central theme of a speech, rather than the technology for disseminating the message. Bush hammered Gore over and over about Gore's comment that he had "taken the initiative in creating the Internet." Gore made the "digital divide" an early primary campaign issue in stump speeches at historically black colleges, such as Morgan State University, where he promised universal Internet access.[9]

Candidates and their parties used the Internet in three distinct ways. First, they provided a public face for their cause with Web sites that set forth their agenda and presented their issues, published the text of speeches, countered the opposition's claims, and generally updated site visitors with breaking news and stories. The graphic design was carefully chosen to reflect the image they hoped to project. Second, they used the Web sites to make more intimate contact with campaign workers, volunteers, and contributors. This particular use required more interactivity and two-way communication, as well as back-room technology to process e-mail and online contributions and create a database of party loyalists. The third use of the Internet was to distribute e-mailed broadsides to political reporters. Although e-mailed messages did not replace phone calls and faxes, candidates used e-mail far more regularly to reach reporters with late-breaking news or announcements than in 1996, owing in part to the proliferation of reporters toting Internet-enabled laptops.

Political Web sites attracted mainly party devotees and did little to promote a national discourse, although the Democrats did boast that their convention Web site counted a quarter-million unique visitors a day.[10] However, nonaligned voters seemed to ignore sites put up by the presidential candidates. Part of this avoidance may be attributable to the growing popular distrust of the executive branch as reported by the National Opinion Research Center. Its report showed a steady decline in the public's trust and confidence in the president from 1972 to 1998.[11]

Problem Number 3—The Applications

During the campaign, we watched anxiously for what computer software people call the "killer app," the hugely successful application that would capture everyone's imagination. It never happened. We considered the possibility that the Internet could bring to the democratic process something unique and special. Perhaps this technology could address one of the perennial problems with elections—voter turnout. Online voting became a hot topic during the primaries, when the Arizona Democratic party used it, and the idea was revisited when the vote in Florida exposed the fragile and dilapidated state of our current voting system. The response to online voting was a host of technical, legal, and social objections, most of which quashed any prospect of turning toward the technology any time soon.

A California task force assigned to study the possibility of online voting in that state issued a scathing indictment, based largely on the technical shortcomings that it thought would introduce fraud and privacy problems. The Voting Integrity Project, a Virginia-based voting-fraud watchdog group, sued the Arizona Democratic party over its use of online voting, claiming it violated the Voting Rights Act, which outlaws making voting more difficult for one group than for another. The Voting Integrity Project claimed that online voting violated the spirit of the law by giving Internet users an unfair advantage. The Pentagon explored online voting by allowing military personnel stationed overseas to vote over the Internet in the presidential election, but only eighty-four voters took advantage of the $6.2 million experiment. At a cost of $74,000 per voter, it is a figure that makes Steve Forbes's pursuit of individual voters seem stingy.

Michael Cornfield, George Washington University professor and cofounder of *Campaign Web Review*, a biweekly electronic newsletter, points out that the technology itself is not a replacement for the social contract, of which voting is only a small part. He writes:

> Suppose I asserted that we could strengthen the institution of marriage by allowing people to be wed on the Internet. You'd laugh at the idea, wouldn't you? The flaw lies not with the concept of online weddings; it's that the medium in which the ritual of marriage is performed has little to do with all that must precede and follow for a marriage to be right, for it to last.
>
> The same goes for the institution of democracy. Yet we are hearing similarly harebrained claims on behalf of the magical properties of the Internet. Higher turnout! Broader participation! Fairer elections! Healthier democracy![12]

Problem Number 4—The Digital Divide

The most serious problem inherent in the political use of the Internet is the digital divide—a class system based on computer ownership, Internet access, and computer literacy that corresponds with wealth and divides the country roughly in half. Studies have shown conclusively that affluent and educated whites dominate the online population in disproportion to the general population. They generally enjoy high-quality, home-based Internet connections. Minorities and the poor do not. According to a U.S. Commerce Department report titled "Falling Through the Net," released in 1999 and filled with data current through 1998, most people who enjoy Internet access are typically white or Asian-American, well-educated, affluent, and urban. Those without access are African-American or Latino, poor, and rural. The study, bolstered by others conducted by firms such as Forrester Research and Jupiter Communications, casts a pall on the euphoria surrounding the emergence of the Internet and the hype that dominated the early months of the campaigns.

The Commerce Department study looked at where people accessed the Internet—at home, at work, or elsewhere. People who access the Internet at home have private, personal access any time, day or night. Those who depend on the computer at work or in public places have time and contention obstacles. Blacks and Latinos have less access anywhere—home, work, or public places—than whites do at home. Not only do whites enjoy

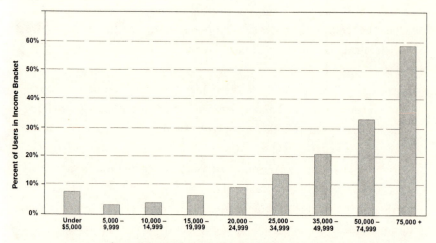

Source: National Telecommunications and Information Administration, Department of Commerce

FIGURE 2.2　The digital divide frustrated those who thought the Internet would bring democracy to the masses. Too many low-income Americans do not have access.

access to the Internet in greater numbers, but the quality of their access is demonstrably better.

Jerry Morrison, co-founder of Strategic Consulting Group, uses the Internet as well as direct mail and other means to recruit campaign volunteers under contract with various Democratic party candidates. He is skeptical about the Internet as a tool for reaching minorities. "In the three years we have been in business, we have not recruited a single minority on the Internet. Not one," he said.

If the Internet could be used for political purposes, it might just reach and benefit only those with access and further alienate the rest. This divide raises serious doubts about the Internet's contribution to existing political instruments and institutions, such as the news media and political parties, and its potential for creating new democratic tools, such as online voting. Deborah Phillips, founder of the watchdog group the Voting Integrity Project, is a vocal critic of online voting. She compares the Internet to a turnstile where "whites and affluent people can rush through to the train, but blacks and other minorities [who do not have Internet access] have to go through slowly, one at a time."

Internet connectivity is regarded as more than simply another advantage of wealth and education. It is not just a trapping of advantage, like a luxury car or an in-ground pool, but a tool that adds to the user's wealth and education. It is not just a symbol of class disparity but a device that increases the size and scope of the gap. Anyone with Internet access can easily imagine how true this is. The Internet is a source of information, knowledge, communication, and commerce for those with access to it, and its fruits are gradually becoming perceptibly more important for typical users' healthy personal financial diets. For example, it is easy to follow minute-by-minute market trends and trade stocks online.

In April 2000 lawyer Rafael Velasquez founded the National Voter Registration initiative, which targets minorities of all kinds, particularly young, first-time voters. His group, based in Los Angeles, focused not on any particular ethnic minority but rather on low-income households and on what Velasquez calls "social minorities." "We are inclusive of everybody."

"My opinion's changed [about the Internet]. In the beginning, I thought that access to information in itself can only be positive and so I encouraged, for example, Internet voting. I was very supportive of that. And now my stand is not that firm anymore. I have seen that none, virtually none of the low-income families or households that I want to encourage to participate in democracy, really know anything about the Internet. I think it would probably widen the gap." Velasquez said he overheard two people talking at a barbecue, discussing getting on the Internet. One said he couldn't afford a computer to get access. Hearing this kind of anecdotal evidence has Velasquez second-guessing the access and online issues. "I don't know if it's hurting them," he says, "but it does exclude them."

If the Internet remains elusive for the poor, argue its critics, its effect will be antidemocratic. Power to communicate, persuade, conduct commerce, and otherwise become enriched in the information economy will further accrue to the educated and affluent, strengthening a class system based on technical literacy and reinforcing traditional hierarchies.

By the time of the Democratic convention, as we watched coverage by Internet news sites dwindle and dot-com workers use the occasion to hunt for their next job, we concluded that, if the impact of the Internet could be measured on the Richter scale, it would barely register. The news media and the political candidates failed to skillfully employ the Internet and ignite the election. Voters continued to rely on other media for their information and news. The technology was deemed too flimsy and makeshift to replace paper ballots. Many considered the Internet too elite and undemocratic because of the digital divide. We even considered calling this book "Election.dud," a reflection of what we then thought was the impact of the Internet on the election's outcome.

3

HYPE

WHEN YOUR DAD IS THE MAYOR OF MIDLAND, TEXAS, AND you're born on Father's Day weekend, you get your picture in the paper. You're the fourth of four children, and your dad figures that's four more votes for the Republican party someday. Your dad gets appointed as a delegate to six Republican National Conventions. You attend four, running messages and working as a page. Your next-door neighbor just happens to be the minority leader of the Republicans in the Texas House of Representatives, and he hires you as a legislative aide. You intern at the Texas governor's office and eventually join his reelection campaign. There you meet your future wife. The governor decides to run for president; you sign on to run the Web operation while your bride-to-be works in the press office. You schedule your wedding on December 9, a month and two days from the day you hope your candidate wins the presidency of the United States.

That's Cliff Angelo's life, started in spectacular political style when he and his dad, Ernest Angelo Jr., appeared together on the front page of the *Midland Reporter-Telegram* in west Texas. Twenty-seven years later, father and son stood outside the state capitol in Austin, Texas, on November 7, 2000, in the cold and drizzle, waiting for a presidential acceptance speech from then governor George W. Bush that would not come.

"One of the saddest times I've ever had in politics was standing in the rain in Austin waiting for the governor," said Ernest Angelo Jr., who was mayor of Midland from 1972 to 1980 and a delegate to the Republican

PHOTO 3.1   Cliff Angelo with father, Ernest Angelo Jr.

National Convention from 1976 to 1996. "Cliff and [his wife] Jill and all
the young people on the campaign were euphoric, of course, and they
weren't thinking anything bad, but I've been around long enough. I got to
thinking, 'This thing is too close and there is something terribly wrong.'
And of course, they finally said what it was.

"I felt for them more than any time I ever have for anybody. To have
their political innocence destroyed in one evening is kind of tough. But it
all worked out."[1] It worked out to the liking of both the political novice,
Cliff, finishing his first presidential campaign at the helm of the
www.georgewbush.com Web site, and the political veteran, Ernest, a man
involved in politics for more than forty years who couldn't send an e-mail
if his life depended on it.

Dad is a "political nut" who has had the same crewcut since 1953. He
got paid $75 a month to be the Midland mayor, and nothing for all his
other political work. And he didn't mind one bit. He's slightly embar-
rassed his wife or his secretary has to send and receive his e-mail, but
Ernest sees the potential in the Web:

Communications with like-minded people is the big thing on the Internet. I
was in a political meeting and the speaker was involved with a nonprofit organization that works the legislature on issues. One of the things they are see-

ing is that they are able to communicate with a big constituency through the Internet that they can't reach through the commonly understood media. So much of the media is antagonistic to the philosophy that we're supporting— not just unfriendly but antagonistic. [The Internet's] got a lot of potential.

His son was excited about the potential of the Web, too, as were others who had great expectations the Internet might "democratize" the United States beginning with Election 2000. Political veterans and neophytes alike speculated that the Internet would change the way candidates campaigned and raised money, that citizens would devour election news, and that many Americans would be inspired to volunteer for campaigns. People would find political information everywhere online, and without the intermediaries that concerned Ernest, Cliff, and others.

"It gave John Q. Public the tools to go out and really be politically motivated," Cliff said. "They could log on both [candidate] sites and choose what they believe in. We gave them the tools to go out to their friends and the rest of the public and have their say on voting for the president."[2]

Cliff did not envision he would be an architect in the building of a presidential campaign. "My dad was involved in politics; I never thought I'd be involved in it," said Cliff, who moved on to be senior advisor for privacy to Commerce Secretary Donald Evans. Cliff's dad never expected his son to leave the University of Texas—three credits from graduation—to help the governor of Texas become president of the United States.

After working in the governor's state office in 1996, Cliff moved over in March 1997 to Bush's gubernatorial reelection campaign team to run the computer network, manage the e-mail systems, and handle Internet security. In November 1998 Bush was reelected, and by April of the following year he was contemplating a presidential run. His www.bush98.com was moved to www.georgewbush.com, and it was retooled by Cliff and his team of vendors and volunteers in just five days after the exploratory announcement. And Cliff, the baby of Ernest and wife Betty Lou's children, needed to explain to his technology-challenged dad why he had to forsake school to run the governor's computer operations for the presidential campaign.

Ernest was very pleased about the opportunity presented to his son, even if the father couldn't offer much advice. The expertise Ernest gathered running phone banks as Texas chairman of Reagan for President in 1980 and as deputy chairman and campaign manager for the 1980 Texas Reagan-Bush campaign seemed of little use in the new digital era. "The old telephone banks, they're never going to work again," said Ernest, even though in 1980 he helped organize more than 20,000 volunteers that way. "These days, people won't spend the kind of time that that effort required." Now the Internet allows everyone to seek and receive information on their own timetable. "And you don't have to get them up from their dinner table or away from the NFL game or whatever to do it, to communicate."

The new technology was embraced by the son, who as an eleven-year-old page at the 1984 convention watched in wonder as a fax machine "the size of an average desk" spit out a barely readable printout. Even in 1998, the Bush team was using a fax distribution list for the press. In Cliff's reign, fax machines disappeared. "But now the e-mails they send out, I cannot even tell you how many e-mails," Cliff said. "And the press wanted it, as often as you could send it out."

The press validated Cliff's sense that candidate Web sites were not just a novelty. Hype about the Web's role in the presidential campaign started to build after Bush announced in April 1999 that he was exploring a run. And what was a Web team of one—Cliff—originally hired as the information technology manager on a Bush campaign of just seven people total, quickly ramped up to nine working the Web on a campaign staff of nearly two hundred in Austin by the summer of 1999.

"I remember the press starting to talk about it and CNN covering the fact that we had Web sites," Cliff said. "At the press briefing for the exploratory [announcement], we had computers set up there with the system on it, and the press wrote about it. They knew that it was going to be something important."

But just how important? The media and political pundits heaped all kinds of expectations on the Web. This was supposed to be the year of the "Internet election." The most common pronouncement: The Net in 2000 would have as much or more impact than TV in 1960. These great expectations for the Web could be grouped into four major areas.

First, as addressed by the Angelos, there were great social and civic expectations for the Web. It would expand the number of people participating and volunteering for their candidate. It would make the political process more inclusive and legitimate. The Web would raise the quality and quantity of political information and make it easily accessible. There would be a wider variety of viewpoints. People would be more involved news consumers. Voters would be smarter as a result. Younger people, especially, would be more engaged because this was their medium.

Second, the Internet would prove to be the ultimate communications tool. E-mail, not telephones, would empower the parties to rally supporters and talk directly with voters. There was a nod, but just a nod, to how the Internet could empower individuals, though it was envisioned that this would take place through the most basic interactive tools, possibly initiated, as Cliff described, through the candidate sites.

Third, the Internet had great potential for revenue. The candidates would raise millions online. Budgets for TV campaign ads would be downsized a bit and some ad dollars shifted to startup political portals and traditional media news sites, where voters would flock for information.

Finally, the new technology offered by the Web would begin to make other media seem mundane. Rotating, 360-degree Web cameras would transform convention coverage. Interactive banner ads using animated video and sound would intrigue potential voters. E-journalists would pounce on a "blue dress" moment, using the Internet's speed to display the story faster and in more detail than their offline brethren.

This chapter revisits these four themes to reset the stage for what often turned out to be unrealistic and hyped Internet expectations. The Internet helped the media tell the story of the election; indeed, for the tail end of 1999 and the first eight months of the 2000 campaign, the Internet often *was* the story. The hype set an impossible standard. In contrast, there was no hype at all about how the grassroots might use the Internet, what eventually would be the most exciting element—and most overlooked—of all.

Great Expectations for Social and Civic Change

Charles Bowen has been online since 1981 and has written or cowritten nearly two dozen books on computer communications and technology.

More than a year before the election, he imagined that the Web would provide an abundance of online campaign news and political information. He anticipated the Internet's coming-out party in his weekly Internet column for *Editor & Publisher* magazine. "Now comes Campaign 2000, and by all sorts of measures—even if it's simply the sheer number of political-oriented Web sites—this looks like the election year that the Internet comes of age in the political arena."[3]

The role that the media play in American democracy is unquestioned. Exhaustively studied television replays of the Kennedy-Nixon debates show that imagery is often more powerful than substance for determining ascendancy. According to radio listeners, Nixon won the debate. Television images and widespread newspaper photos of Edmund Muskie weeping in New Hampshire undermined his bid for president in 1972. The investigative reporters who dug up the Pentagon Papers, uncovered the Watergate scandal, and revealed Tom Eagleton's and Gary Hart's secrets remind us that the truth can topple dishonest governments and ruin candidates. Now surely this new medium—the Internet—would magnify a candidate's greatness or expose a glaring weakness faster and better than broadcast or print. W. Russell Neuman, a professor at the Annenberg School for Communication at the University of Pennsylvania, proposed that, if the Internet made a difference in the 2000 presidential race, it would be in how a candidate failed, not in how he succeeded. "What we are going to see in this campaign is that the candidates are going to make some mistakes," Neuman said in an interview with *The Washington Post.* "Somebody is going to have the equivalent of the bad make-up job on Richard Nixon in 1960, and it might make a difference."[4]

More important, the Web was projected to inspire the masses. Story after story in online and offline media painted the picture that Web activity would result in a renewed interest in politics from an apathetic electorate, less than half of whom (48.9 percent) voted in 1996.[5] The commonly espoused theory: A better-informed electorate would be more likely to participate in the democratic process.

And it seemed to be working. Everyday citizens put up thousands of Web pages supporting Gore or Bush or their own cause or candidate. Some were prompted by templates available at the candidate sites, others just did it on their own. "It's kind of democracy at work," said political consultant and former Republican National Committee Deputy Chairman Eddie Mahe, commenting on the sites in *The New York Times* in May 2000. The *Times* reported that, at the time, there were already almost 7,000 of what it called "home-grown" Web sites, with either the Gore or Bush name in them. "Historically," Mahe said, "those same things have been in every campaign. The difference is they used to be said in a bar or at the corner coffee shop. But now, on the Internet, everybody has a megaphone."[6]

The Gore Web team encouraged supporters to shout the Democrats' message. With a few clicks, online visitors to the Gore site could build a page that linked to position papers on issues they found important and then e-mail that page. Issue-oriented groups such as "Educators for Gore" or "Firefighters for Gore" could create a customized campaign page built around their causes, then send that version to like-minded friends. "We basically opened up our publishing system to the general public," said Ben Green, director of Internet operations for Gore.[7] "We used our site to rally our supporters and get our message out aggressively." [8]

Steve Forbes also believed that concerned citizens would rally to his message online. He declared his candidacy for president before any others, and he did it on the Internet. The Conservative News Service quoted Forbes as calling his effort "the first full-scale campaign on the Internet."[9] He said he utilized the technology of the Web because he believed it would involve more people at a grassroots level. Rick Segal is managing director of Hensley Segal Rentschler, the Cincinnati, Ohio, communications firm that created the Forbes site. Segal said online campaigning would spur people to download material that identified them as Forbes supporters, and it would help activists get their hands on the yard signs, bumper stickers, and other campaign paraphernalia that are fixtures in American politics. And instead of calling up the campaign office, they could volunteer right on the Web site. "I think this is really going to represent the rebirth of grassroots conservative political action," Segal said.[10]

Political consultants were intrigued by the Web's potential power. Former Bill Clinton strategist Dick Morris started vote.com, a site including news briefings, links to articles about the election and politics, and a feature to measure public opinion—a question of the day. These ranged from news-related issues and entertainment questions to political topics such as "Should John McCain run as an Independent?" and "Do you believe Al Gore has been honest in his past fundraising activities?" Vote totals were forwarded to appropriate political figures, including members of Congress and the president. Morris in his book *vote.com* argued that the Web was supplanting traditional media as the driving force in political life. Soon, he predicted, money would be less important in politics because the free Web would replace paid TV ads, and the ability to talk back to political figures via e-mail would encourage direct dialogue. He said he firmly believed people would feel more a part of the process, and that sense of connection would lead them to the polls:

> The key goal of our site is to create a way for the Internet to encourage direct democracy. We need a way that people can express their opinions even when a pollster doesn't happen to call. It can make government a completely interactive process in which people are involved on an ongoing basis in all the decisions. [The Internet] can transform our system into a national, local, and even global town meeting. [11]

News and political Web sites tried to recreate the town meeting concept online. Web White & Blue 2000 hosted a daily online issues-oriented exchange among the presidential campaigns. The unedited "Rolling Cyber Debate" was carried simultaneously on the seventeen Web White & Blue charter sites—high-traffic sites that together reached 85 percent of America's Internet audience.[12] Those sites included the news media and other major portals, such as ABCNews.com, America Online, Yahoo!, CNN.com's allpolitics.com, Excite, MSNBC.com, and MTV.com's ChooseorLose.com. Web White & Blue 2000's front page provided links to political stories at these top outlets. The online debate was designed to supplement the televised presidential debates by providing the candidates a forum to offer longer answers. Each of the high-traffic Web sites linked to www.webwhiteblue.org, bringing a potential audience of about 70 million Americans. Doug Bailey, former Republican political consultant, worked with former Clinton spokesperson Mike McCurry to help bring the various Internet outlets together for the nonpartisan project, which was initiated by the Markle Foundation in October 1998.

At the time, AOL CEO Steve Case had a favorable outlook for the Web-politics combination offered through Web White & Blue. "We predict that the presidential election in 2000 could turn based on what happens on the Net," he said in a 1998 www.cnet.com interview. "People feel disconnected from the political process, voting is at an all-time low, people feel like they don't understand what is happening. We feel the Net can be a tool to address that and to put more information at the fingertips of the people."[13]

Bailey cofounded two other political information Web sites—Freedom-Channel.com and Youth-e-Vote 2000—that were intended to take advantage of Web technology and to foster political involvement. Youth-e-Vote 2000 hosted the first-ever national online student vote. FreedomChannel.com, a nonpartisan, nonprofit Web site, used streaming video to give voters direct access to candidates' statements. The site provided every presidential, senatorial, congressional, and gubernatorial candidate with "Net time" of up to ninety seconds per topic on a drop-down menu of issues ranging from world trade policy, to race relations, to education, to Medicare. Approximately 2,000 video clips were available to voters. "When television was invented," Bailey said in an interview with the magazine *Fast Company,* "nobody thought much about how it was going to change politics, or if we could use it to improve the process. So we're asking ourselves those questions, trying to figure out how to use the new technology to reach people, because the medium has the power to change politics."[14]

Certainly part of the Web's charge was to act like a magnet, attracting a younger, Net-savvy crowd to politics, particularly eighteen-to-twenty-four-year-olds—those presumed most likely to use the Internet but the least likely to vote. Only 32.4 percent of this age group voted in 1996. The figure wasn't much better for twenty-five-to-twenty-nine-year-olds; only 40.2 percent of that group voted.[15] Both age groups register and vote in numbers considerably lower than the population as a whole. The thinking was that the Web might be their only source of political knowledge and might be the impetus to get them to register and then to vote. A Pew Internet and American Life study measured Internet usage in two periods in 2000—May–June and November–December. The study found 61 percent of voting-age citizens under the age of thirty had Internet access in the first time period; that increased to 75 percent in the second half of the year. Meanwhile, just 12 percent of those ages sixty-five and over had access in the first time frame; that number rose only slightly to 15 percent in the late stage of the survey.[16] Couple that with an April 2000 study by the Round Table Group, which showed the Internet quickly displacing traditional media such as television and newspapers as the prime source of important information for America's youngest adults.[17] The study showed that 67 percent of Americans aged eighteen to twenty-four lived in households that used the Internet to gather information, compared to a nationwide average of just 46 percent who used the Internet for that purpose.

Among those young adult Internet users, 59 percent said that their household received more "useful information" from the Internet than from the newspapers, and 53 percent said that they received more "useful information" from the Internet than from television. Eighty-four percent of eighteen-to-twenty-four-year-old Internet users said that their household was more likely to use the Internet to retrieve useful information than go to the public library. When they needed to answer a specific question, 68 percent of households were more likely to consult the Internet than turn to a newspaper, and 67 percent were more likely to consult the Internet than rely on television.

None of this was news to those involved in making the Web user-friendly for young voters. Kim Alexander, president of the California Voter Foundation, which was issuing its seventh online voter guide for the 2000 election, estimated 1.5 million Californians would seek political information on the Web before the November vote. Alexander predicted many of them would be younger voters. "They aren't watching TV news, they aren't reading newspapers," Alexander said in an interview with the *California Journal*. "Those mediums don't cry out to them. They expect to find what they want on the Internet, and our role is to make that information available."[18]

Of course, that role implied two things: (1) Young voters would consider political information "useful" and look for it in the first place, and (2) they could find what they were looking for.

Bill Castner, then eighteen, said he had used the Web for political purposes. He was checking his e-mail several times a day and getting his news links from his AOL browser. The electrical engineering major at Syracuse University surfed Star Trek sites and kept up with Trekkie newsletters. Both his parents are Republicans; his favorite high school teacher back in Victor, New York, was the Republican chair of Ontario County. He described himself as pro-life, and he opposed affirmative action. An Eagle Scout, he e-mailed his member of Congress to support the Boy Scouts' opposition to gay scoutmasters. Castner was staying in touch with his troop through a Web page he set up and still acting as an assistant scoutmaster. "The Internet has helped because I have sent a couple of e-mails to representatives about legislation to repeal the federal Boy Scout charter," said Castner, who e-mailed U.S. Representative Tom Reynolds of New York to protest the potential repeal. "The Internet definitely makes that easier. You don't have to look around for addresses or stamps or envelopes. The news story I read had a link to contact your representatives."[19]

The under-thirty segment wasn't the only group e-mailing government leaders. A May 2000 survey for the political and government services portal E The People (www.e-thepeople.com) found one in eight American households had sent e-mail to a government official, while twice that had visited a government Web site; 12 percent had visited a candidate site. Also according to the survey, 26 percent of American households said they were more inclined to back a candidate who communicated with them via e-mail.[20]

Everything seemed to be in place: Nearly 60 percent of U.S. households had Internet access and the potential voters—including the coveted new young voters—were tuned in. The candidates, the media, and political portals were launching their sites, which would serve as the foundation for new and personal involvement in the political process. Internet watchers anticipated an election that they believed would be determined in cyberspace.

Great Expectations for Communication

In 1996 political Web sites had lots of details but they were, for the most part, incredibly boring. Low bandwidth, slow servers, and underpowered personal computers limited how engaging and interesting the political Web sites could be. Few candidates considered the Web important enough to devote funds for all-out development anyway. Campaign Web sites were largely a higher-tech extension of traditional campaign brochures, loaded with pictures and policy statements and having limited interactive capability. It was intriguing to project that in 2000 the candidates would utilize the Web's power to connect with the public and create their own private media organization on the Internet, bypassing the mainstream press. Wrestler-turned-politician Jesse Ventura won the Minnesota governor's office in 1998 by using the Internet effectively. His Webmaster, Phil Madsen, started www.jesseventura.org in February 1998 with about $200 and little Web experience. The campaign, which had only two paid staff members, relied on its Web volunteers to enter 5,000 names gathered at the Minnesota State Fair into a database. Within days, these 5,000 volunteers were sent bumper stickers and a fund-raising letter. All Web site visitors were encouraged to sign up on "Jesse Net" and to receive occasional e-mails about the campaign. It was the grassroots volunteers who drove Ventura's statewide get-out-the-vote Drive to Victory Tour two weeks before Election Day. The seventy-two-hour tour was organized, executed, and updated online. Ventura's site rallied help:

> If you are located near the tour route, help take pictures and upload graphics, video or audio to this site. The idea is for a group of people in your town to have their picture taken with Jesse. Then, by the time they get home, they can see that picture on this web site. The Ventura campaign does not have this capability right now, but with volunteer help from Jesse's Internet friends who have these skills, we can make it happen.[21]

They did make it happen. Crowds of five hundred or more gathered at small-town rallies all along the route. And on Election Day, Ventura eked out a victory over the two major-party candidates, collecting 37 percent of the vote. The *Minneapolis Star Tribune* postelection analysis story stated that Ventura "accomplished several extraordinary feats" in winning the election: "Among other things, he was possibly the decisive reason for the surprisingly large statewide turnout, drawing new voters to the polls, nearly all of whom voted for him. Among the youngest voters casting ballots—those under age 30—Ventura won hands down, getting nearly half those votes (46 percent)."[22]

Many came to believe Ventura won because of the Internet, even though Madsen wasn't so sure. "The Internet is not about technology; it's about relationships," Madsen said in his "Notes Regarding Jesse Ventura's Internet Use in His 1998 Campaign for Minnesota Governor," posted at the jesseventura.org Web site. "While it's true that we could not have won the election without the Internet, we did not win the election because of the Internet. We won because our candidates, campaign staff and volunteers engaged the voters in a number of meaningful ways."[23]

The buzz about Ventura's online efforts grew louder as 2000 approached. With the list of Ventura's successes in mind—recruiting new voters, especially a large number of younger voters—the 2000 candidates set out to duplicate the relationship building of Ventura's effort. They also added the latest in Web technology to their sites, offering multimedia replays of ads and speeches and plenty of ways for supporters to sign up for e-mails and donate money. Site visitors could read up on the candidate's family, search out positions on issues they cared about, follow the candidate's schedule on the campaign trail, scan a host of positive press clippings, or sign up to volunteer. If they were members of a key voting bloc—female, Hispanic, veteran—they could find a page specifically designed for them.

But the press releases, video playthings, and $32-a-case "George W. Bush Drinking Water" that could be ordered online at the GOP site were not the point. Building relationships meant collecting the e-mail addresses of supporters, contributors, and volunteers. At a January 2000 meeting of Republican party leaders, party chair Jim Nicholson outlined several new strategies, one of which promoted the use of the Web to spread the party's message without "going through the filter of the news media."

"We have recognized over the last 120 days that it's a New World, where you go digital or die," Nicholson said in an interview with *The New York Times*.[24] He also announced that he hoped to enlist 100,000 "e-mail activists" by the start of the Philadelphia convention in August. Nicholson defined an e-mail activist as a Republican who would forward the party's message to at least ten friends. The campaigns and the party organizations counted on the

American people's willingness to turn over their e-mail addresses. The math: If someone sends an e-mail to ten people, and each recipient sends it to ten more, by the ninth transmission it will reach 1 billion people.

Certainly there is an element of preaching to the choir with e-mail. Yet the campaigns hoped to take advantage of a technique Web advertisers had coined "viral marketing." The theory: Receiving a message from a trusted source—the friend who forwards you the e-mail—makes you more likely to open the e-mail and the message more believable. That made the campaigns determined to collect as many names as possible. Bill Bradley used the organizational ability of the Web to drum up a crowd on short notice, according to ZDNet News:

> The campaign stacked an important Democratic Party event with Bradley supporters by using e-mail alerts. Tyler Chafee, a field organizer for the campaign, received word late on a Thursday night that two days later, the Democratic National Committee would be holding a forum. Not only would Bradley be allowed to speak, but the public would also be invited to attend.
>
> There was little time to activate a phone tree to leave messages for supporters, especially when the schedule for the forum kept changing. So he went to the campaign's database. It listed about 700 supporters who lived near Washington, D.C., whose names and e-mail addresses had been collected during Bradley's appearances and through the campaign Web site. Chafee launched an e-mail about the event around midnight that Thursday, and by 8:30 the next morning, 100 people had replied that they would attend. As the details changed, Chafee sent steady updates to the group by e-mail.
>
> In the end, Bradley was greeted at the event by as many as 300 supporters. "He was shocked to find hundreds of people standing at the curb to welcome him with their own homemade signs," Chafee says. Gore's supporters were surprised as well.
>
> "They didn't think those kinds of numbers could be produced without some sort of major effort that took weeks," Chafee says.
>
> Chafee, who has worked as a field organizer in several campaigns, says the experience changed his thinking about the ability of a campaign to hold rallies. Like many political advisers, he had found that the time and resources involved in organizing rallies was rarely worth the trouble in the end.

"Crowd-building is always this trade-off in politics," he says. "But if you can create a rally-like atmosphere with less than an hour's work, it changes the way you can do politics."[25]

In addition to organizing the faithful, part of the goal in collecting e-mail addresses was to convert the undecideds. According to a Media Metrix survey conducted before the conventions, registered Republicans comprised 36.8 percent of the online population aged eighteen and over, whereas Democrats represented 27.9 percent; 35.2 percent of online adults were either not affiliated with one of the two major parties (11.7 percent) or not registered (23.5 percent), making for a potentially large number of swing voters.[26]

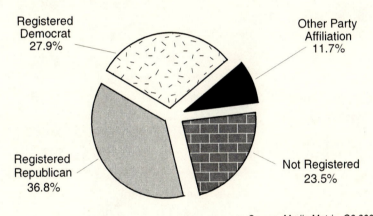

Registered
Democrat
27.9%

Other Party
Affiliation
11.7%

Registered
Republican
36.8%

Not Registered
23.5%

Source: Media Metrix, Q2 2000

FIGURE 3.1   More Republicans than Democrats were online during the 2000 election.

The fact that there was a higher percentage of registered Republicans online is perhaps one indicator of the digital divide, or as Media Metrix called it, a "Dollar Divide." Through August 2000, households making $25,000 or less were the fastest growing segment on the Web but still represented the smallest segment overall.[27] Republicans are traditionally from higher-income households, the same ones that were early Internet adopters.

The survey conducted before the conventions reported that 75.6 percent of online users indicated they planned to vote in the 2000 election.

The percentage was even better—96.1 percent—for those fifty and over, the most politically inclined demographic group on the Web.

By the Republican convention, the GOP, independent of the Bush campaign, had a database of 250,000 names. Further, 150,000 of the most

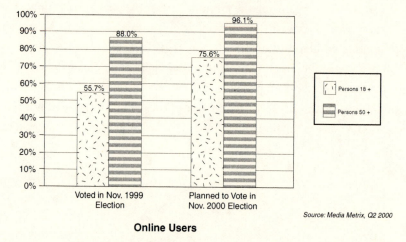

FIGURE 3.2   Online users planned to vote, apparently in greater numbers than those not online.

faithful received daily updates from the convention. If the party lacked an e-mail address for a donor, someone called and tracked it down. The goal: double the number of "activists" to half a million before Election Day. At the same time, the Gore campaign said it had collected 150,000 names. Every new e-mail registrant was thanked and then asked to volunteer. The Gore campaign unveiled a revamped www.algore.com site in a live Webcast to kick off the Democratic National Convention. The new site emphasized e-mail, InstantMessageNet, which allowed Gore supporters to chat with each other in real time, and links to various state- and issue-oriented groups. The idea was to connect Web surfers and turn them into campaign volunteers.[28] "E-mail is the primary means of organizing," said Green, director of Internet operations for Gore. "It sets a low threshold for people buying into the campaign. The logical progression is then to volunteer and then donate money."[29]

The Internet was supposed to serve as the ultimate communications tool—people to the party and party to the people, give-and-take. This connection between individuals and between individuals and organizations would show off the Web's interactivity, its great advantage over other media. And it would dovetail quite nicely with campaigns' reliance on youthful volunteers—those in their twenties who are typically unattached and unencumbered by family obligations and enthused about throwing themselves into a political cause. Taking a page from Ventura's playbook, the campaigns would capitalize on the young's penchant for being online. The Web was their domain. They had computers and knew how to use them, sometimes to the exclusion of the other media.

"I don't go out and buy newspapers unless I'm bored. I can't remember the last time I bought The New York Times.*"* (Christina Hinchey, Syracuse University student)

"The last time I watched the evening news on television was over Christmas vacation. Before that? Oh boy . . . " (Joe Burns, fellow SU student)

These were not the voices of two disconnected, disaffected, disinterested college students. Hinchey was elected president of the College Democrats and Burns to the same office of the College Republicans on this upscale campus in central New York, where tuition alone ran $21,500 a year. They were getting their news online and donated money online. They networked, talked, and organized online, and they volunteered online. They worked to get out the vote online.

Burns in particular ascended to a lofty status for a twenty-year-old during Election 2000. He was the number-3-ranked "e-precinct volunteer" for the presidential campaign of Republican challenger Steve Forbes. Burns was the lead anecdote in a front-page *Wall Street Journal* story about Forbes's online strategy. It was the kind of story that fueled optimism that the Internet would alter the political landscape in every way imaginable. The *Journal* article introduced Burns, who sounded like the volunteer of the future—hardly more than a teen, but with a veteran political operative's reach and influence:

> From a red-brick fraternity house overlooking the snowy campus of Syracuse University, Steve Forbes supporter Joe Burns knocks on the virtual doors of voters 1,000 miles away in Iowa.
>
> It's hard to tell if anybody's home.

The 20-year-old junior hunches over a laptop in his third-floor room and bats out electronic e-mail pleas to 10 Iowans he has never met and perhaps never will. But this afternoon, five days before Monday's big Iowa caucuses, he hopes to rally them to the cause of Mr. Forbes' long-shot bid for the presidential nomination.

Three missives bounce back because the e-mail addresses were wrong. One message reached a state Forbes organizer who doesn't need any goading. But Mr. Burns isn't discouraged. "Four years ago, I wouldn't have been able to do anything to help Steve Forbes in Iowa," says the history and political-science major. "I think the Internet is the future of political campaigns."[30]

Burns is the perfect political prototype, the classic young grassroots volunteer who provides so much of the energy for the 24/7 campaigns. Despite his youth, he helped organize and coordinate the county legislature campaigns of a half-dozen Onondaga County Republicans in 1999. Working nationally for Forbes, Burns signed up 125 e-volunteers for his man before Forbes's early exit after Delaware. Burns helped Forbes with his get-out-the-vote (GOTV) drive in Iowa and, later, New Hampshire. Working on a Compaq laptop, Burns popped canned iced teas from his mini-frig and e-mailed strangers, encouraging them to ignore the cold and the snow. To his surprise and relief, he didn't receive a single cross reply from his e-mail targets; indeed, several voters replied that they did intend to support Forbes.

Burns remembered the Forbes camp sending him three lists of ten to twelve names each in Iowa. "I believe they had me send the first list a follow-up e-mail," he recalls. "At first I thought there was a possibility of ticking people off. With two [e-mails] I was a little more nervous. But as much as it seems people will be ticked off, [e-mail] really seems to work. When I was nervous, I shouldn't have been."[31]

Christina Hinchey, the other SU student, remembers scrapping with her brothers over television fare: CNN, her choice, or cartoons? In 2000 she was ordering exactly what she wanted from the online magazine *Slate* and *The New York Times;* they dumped political stories into her e-mail in-box, where she read them when she wanted and when she could, feeding her ninety-minute-a-day online political habit.

Hinchey, a Hillary Clinton backer, used her credit card to charge a $200 donation to the first lady's U.S. Senate campaign—"It hurt," Hinchey says—and Hinchey also volunteered for her online. "I clicked on 'volunteer,' and they called me."[32] (In a testament to old-time check writing, Burns recalled that after Forbes dropped out, he went online to give to Bush but gave up when the server locked up. He never went back; the urge had passed.) The Clinton campaign played it smart, by keeping it personal. Whenever Hillary's camp had a job to farm out, Hinchey heard by phone. "At least five days a week, there'd be a [phone message]. There must be fifteen different people who called me." She was tasked to tape-record Bush and New York City Mayor Rudolph Giuliani at separate Syracuse campaign stops and also to pick up copies of paperwork for ads that were running on local TV stations.

Hinchey, who campaigned for state representative Jim Magnarelli (who bested Burns's candidate), impressed the Gore campaign by writing her own e-mail message rather than sending out one of the campaign templates. Her message to fellow campus Democrats stressed that the next president might name as many as four justices to the U.S. Supreme Court, something Hinchey noted was critical for many pro-choice college students.

"We are trying to be innovative," she said. "It's hard. What is it that college students care about and what would make them care?" The campaigns cared about the growing number of college students online, because they reflected a great source of volunteers. By the end of 1999, Internet research firm eMarketer said 87 percent of college students were online, representing by far the most active single group on the Internet.[33]

The campaigns believed the Web would be a great fund-raising tool. But they would need to look elsewhere for donations.

Great Expectations for Revenue

The Web offered great potential as a tool of commerce, and as the NAS-DAQ sped toward the unheard-of 5,000 mark, the hope was that politics online would attract users and, therefore, advertisers would follow. Ad sales managers across the country discussed plans to sell banner ads and sponsorship packages for traditional media Web sites, upstart e-zines, and political portals. Web sites devoted to political coverage, such as voter.com and politics.com, would compete in cyberspace with the likes of CNN and *The Washington Post,* news behemoths that planned to dedicate whole sections of their Web sites to politics. The expectation: Politics on the Web would generate high traffic numbers that mainstream advertisers and dueling candidates would value. Political consultants came forward, hoping their talent at fund-raising would translate well on the Web. Some of the consultants were new at politics but masters of Web commerce. Others were old political hands who created an Internet application for their customers. From eContributor.com to eCommercial.com, dozens of companies declared themselves open for e-commerce.

Phil Noble, president of PoliticsOnline, told *The Detroit News* in November 1999 that the Internet was poised to collect political donations and more. "The Internet will do for politics what the machine gun did for Bonnie and Clyde. We've only stuck our smallest of small toes into the water of cyberpolitics. The Internet will revolutionize politics as we know it."[34]

The Web has proved particularly useful to underdog candidates, those who have nothing to lose and everything to gain. The buzz in 2000: The Web would make a race of what was originally considered to be shoo-in nominations for Gore and Bush. "The underdogs are forced into situations where they need to maximize their financial resources, which the Internet can help with," said Lynn Reed, Webmaster for Bill Bradley, whose campaign collected more online by early January 2000 than the frontrunner, Gore—$1.3 million to $800,000. "And they need every trick in the book to try and get some traction. So they're more likely to experiment and try new things. The candidate who is ahead of the game and is going to win comfortably by traditional methods doesn't have to experiment in the same way."[35]

John McCain wore the underdog mantle when his startling nineteen-point victory over Bush in New Hampshire started another round of media frenzy about the power of the Internet to bring about change. McCain capitalized on the New Hampshire win because he'd prepared to take advantage of it by putting his Internet operation in place. McCain's close friend and deputy campaign manager, Wes Gullett, laid it all out in a memo at the start of the campaign after he talked with Governor Ventura's people. "[Wes] went to McCain and said, 'You can do this. You're the same sort of candidate, and you're going to ignite the same sort of feeling in this independent vote,'" said Max Fose, McCain's Webmaster. "And John McCain said, 'Well, do whatever you need to do. Let's try new things. If we fail, we fail. We don't have anything to lose.' We never thought we'd have a chance, and so it was great to have that freedom."[36]

Tom Hockaday, who ran the online fund-raising arm of the McCain campaign, said McCain raised 25 percent of his money online. Hockaday called it "the splash of cold water" that made everyone realize the Internet could be a force.[37] Hockaday recalled that on primary day in New Hampshire, "McCain was out of money. He had a couple hundred thousand dollars, but you can't put the [campaign] people on the plane [for South Carolina] with that."

The pop-up window proclaiming victory went up on McCain's Web site just after 7:00 that night, and the money started pouring in. When Fose checked an hour later, $20,000 had come in online. It didn't let up. By 7:30 the morning after, more than $162,000 had rolled in via the Web. According to a *Newsweek* report, down in South Carolina aboard McCain's "Straight Talk Express," McCain staffers shouted the latest numbers to a horde of reporters on board the bus. Before long, McCain's Internet momentum was feeding on itself. Media reports about the surge generated more clicks on the Web site.[38] Donations came in at an average of four per second; contributions piled up at the rate of $19,000 an hour. Volunteers signed up quickly, as well—at the rate of almost three a minute. McCain mentioned www.mccain2000.com everywhere he went, and the money kept on coming, totaling about $500,000 in twenty-four hours, and more than $800,000 in forty-eight hours. More than $2 million was raised in just a week. There was concern that computer servers would crash, Hockaday said. He recalled that it was more than a week before a "lull"—four minutes between donations—occurred, sometime between 2:00 and 3:00 A.M. It took nearly ten days for the flood of money to stem. Another bright spot, according to McCain handlers: 40 percent of the donations came from first-time political givers, and 34 percent of the contributors were younger than forty. The average contribution: $119, compared to the average of $30 taken in through direct mail. McCain was still in the race financially as well as politically.

Fose said that while the first $500,000 poured in online, a phone campaign netted only $67,000. In fact, he added, he could not have bought enough phone lines to take in a half-million dollars. "So without the Internet, we would have raised $67,000," he said.

The key to success, Fose said, was simple. McCain asked people to go to his Web site. He didn't just mention he had a Web site or hope displaying a podium banner would do the trick. In every TV interview, in every speech, he said: "I need you to go to my Web site."

"In past years, when candidates like Gary Hart and Pat Buchanan won in New Hampshire, they got a bounce from media coverage, but they weren't able to take advantage of it," Fose said. "They couldn't get their volunteers organized and the contributions in the door before the next primary. Now we can do it overnight—and it's practically free."[39] It wasn't exactly free—there are costs associated with running a Web site, and McCain's was estimated to run about $300,000—but it certainly was fast. Everything was faster, and that includes crediting accounts. Online credit card contributions allowed fund-raisers to accelerate the transaction process from about twenty days to twenty seconds online. Money was instant cash; it went directly into campaign accounts, bypassing the usual check-clearing ritual. The Federal Election Commission (FEC) enhanced the Internet's impact when it ruled Web donations could be eligible for matching funds as long as the candidates complied with campaign finance law.

The Web also made campaign contributions so much less intimidating, especially for younger, Internet-savvy voters. Hesitancy to give evaporated among those trained in the ways of Amazon.com and travelocity.com. The Mellman Group, a survey firm for veteran direct-mail consultant Cravers, Mathews, Smith and Co., had identified this group in September 1999. The Mellman survey pointed to a growing and largely untapped reservoir of "socially engaged Internet users" who could be targeted by campaigns online. The rapid development of the Web had created a universe of potential online activists and donors that was larger than the pool of people being reached by direct mail and decidedly younger. The traditional direct-mail universe was approximately 6 percent of the U.S. adult population, or about 12 million people, two-thirds of whom were age sixty or older. According to the report, the number of Americans with Internet access who reported giving time or money to social causes represented 25 percent of the adult population, or approximately 50 million people. Not everyone who had Web access was willing to be politically active online in 1999. Still, 16 percent of wired Americans said they were willing to send an e-mail to an elected official, and 8 percent said they would donate to a charity or to public interest groups over the Web. In addition, the study said the Web population tended to be more politically interested and active.[40]

Michael Hamilton of Hoboken, New Jersey, a twenty-eight-year-old New York University student who donated $250 to John McCain, was typical of the new breed of e-donor. "I felt very strong about McCain, but without the Internet I don't know if I would have given him money," Hamilton said in a *New Orleans Times-Picayune* story. "I just wouldn't have known how to do it otherwise."[41]

John "Trey" Richardson, president of the Washington-based e-Contributor, a nonpartisan political fund-raising site, estimated that in 1998 not more than 2 percent of donations were made online. He predicted the figure for the 2000 campaign cycle would go as high as 20 percent.[42] And Internet fund-raising is more cost-effective than either direct mail or telemarketing. Direct mail typically costs 50 cents per dollar raised, and telemarketing can run as high as 70 cents per dollar. Richardson pegged the Internet cost at about 10 cents for every dollar made. E-Contributor makes money by taking 3 percent of what its clients raise.

Other political consultants and Internet marketers hoped to guide candidates toward the light—away from the familiar twenty-seven-inch TV in the living room and toward the glow cast by a fifteen-inch Web screen. Their specialty: online advertising. This would be a sea change. Political commercials were the third-largest TV advertising category in 1998, trailing only automotive and retail ads, according to a study by investment firm Bear Stearns Cos. In fact, television overwhelmingly dominated political advertising that year, sweeping up 83.5 percent of political advertising expenditures.[43] The Internet did not show up in the statistics. It didn't in 1996 either, when the Web was in its infancy. TV has been taking the majority of advertising dollars from politicians for years. Political advertising was first measured as a category in 1970, at $12 million. That number ballooned to $400 million in 1996 and to nearly $500 million in 1998, according to Competitive Media Reporting (CMR)/Mediawatch.[44] Unlike other categories, political advertising is cyclical. In the odd years, local and state elections produce lower spending. The even years, presidential and congressional years, see significant spending. Recently, advertising about ballot issues, in addition to candidate advertising, has driven up the total.

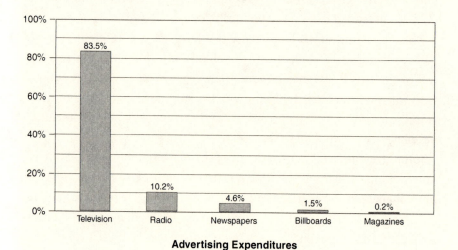

Advertising Expenditures

FIGURE 3.3   So few dollars were spent for political advertising on the Internet in 1998. Source: Dan Morgan, "The TV Bazaar," *The Washington Post,* May 2, 2000, A1.

Online ad salespeople were undeterred. Although rare, there had been a few examples of Internet political advertising success going into the 2000 campaign. In 1998 gubernatorial candidate Peter Vallone bought banner ads in his unsuccessful attempt to unseat New York governor George Pataki. According to a 1998 E-Voter study, Vallone's online banner ads did influence voter awareness and attitudes. The ads, which ran on www.nytimes.com, focused on several key election issues and sought to change voter opinions of both candidates. The study's findings suggested that Vallone's banner ads helped create a fourteen-point negative swing in Pataki's overall favorability rating.[45]

Examples such as these were used by Internet consultants to persuade candidates that spending advertising dollars on an untested medium such as the Web made sense. They also pointed out the rising costs of television advertising and the commissions paid to the campaign consultants who placed the TV ads. Those people could pocket commission checks based on a percentage of the overall TV ad time purchased. Online advocates theorized that those days were over. "The traditional media adviser . . . the guy who buys a ton of ads for a campaign and makes serious money off TV—that guy's nervous," said Jay MacAniff, spokesperson for Aristotle Publishing, a high-tech political consulting firm. "Your print shops who do the mailers, the pamphlets, the door hangers, the fund-raising letters—those guys are real nervous. They have entered into the category of 'old school' overnight."[46]

Phil Noble, president of PoliticsOnline, did not think online advertisements and campaigning would be the difference between defeat and victory in 2000, but he did believe it would have an impact. "We are just seeing the first wave of what will become in time the dominant advertising medium," he said in an interview with ZDNet News in February 1999.[47]

Political Web insiders touted the Web's ability to target and measure response. Alan Gould, president of Gould Communications Group, said in the same ZDNet interview that AOL was one of the market leaders for online advertisers because it could break down its 15 million U.S. users (at that time) demographically and geographically. Gould was in talks with two candidates running in the primaries. "One fact is highly persuasive with both campaigns," he said. "If you target correctly on the Net, you are more likely to reach registered voters" than through traditional advertising avenues.[48] AOL wasn't the only one trying to generate ad revenue from politicians. Yahoo! and other major portals, as well as the top media news sites, prepared Web sales pitches. 24/7 Media, a major online ad network, opened an office in Washington, D.C., in 1999 to be closer to political decisionmakers.

Web users had become more accustomed to online advertising. Yearly expenditures for Web advertisers doubled, from $1.9 billion in 1998 to $3.6 billion in 1999, according to estimates by eMarketer, a leading Internet business statistics firm.[49] Banner ads were popping up in all sorts of places—including e-mails. Rebecca Gorny, a Democrat who lives in Los Angeles, said she was sent an e-mail video ad for a candidate and thought it was pretty innovative. "I don't think they're intrusive because a person can choose to play it or not," she said, adding she thought such devices might encourage people to look for more information about the topic and maybe get more involved in politics. She described the Internet as being the best way for underdogs and third-party candidates to get their message in front of what advertisers love most—a captive audience. "You can channel surf on TV and get away from it," she said. "On the Internet, the information is there in ad banners and in e-mails in your in-box. TV can't deliver it to you. The Internet can."[50]

At least one company took full advantage of its computing power to target online ads with pinpoint accuracy, something impossible with print and broadcast media. For the last twenty years, Aristotle Publishing has maintained up-to-date voter lists and sold them to campaigns for use in various kinds of voter targeting, from direct mail to door-to-door canvassing. With a new Internet application, Aristotle used its voter registration records (it had almost 150 million registered voters on file) and its own computer model to help campaigns target Web ads. The voter information was cross-referenced with data collected by portals, Web sites, and Internet service providers. Aristotle said it could target clusters of voters of special interest to candidates—say, married women in their thirties who were registered as Democrats in swing states, such as Pennsylvania. "This is like combining the best of direct mail with the best of TV," Aristotle president Dean Phillips said in a 1999 ZDNet News interview.[51]

The campaigns responded. On December 21, 1999, the Bush campaign announced it was launching an online advertising effort with the help of Aristotle. The interactive banner invited the curious to calculate how much the Bush tax plan would save them. The scrolling text read: "How much will the BUSH TAX CUT save YOU? Find out right in this banner." The banner ran on 1,500 sites in Iowa and New Hampshire. "Thus far," Bush e-campaign manager Greg Sedberry said in a February 2000 interview, "the reports have been very positive on click-throughs [when respondents click on a banner ad] and time spent calculating." He called the Internet "the fastest-growing medium in politics."[52]

This particular campaign identified voters registered as Republicans or independents who were likely to vote in the Iowa caucuses or New Hampshire

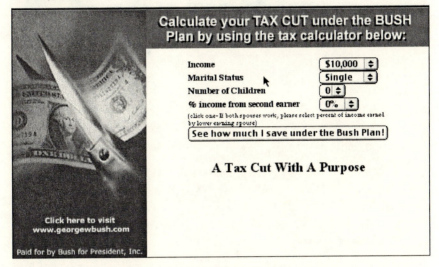

How much will the BUSH TAX CUT save YOU?

Calculate your TAX CUT under the BUSH Plan by using the tax calculator below:

Income	$10,000 ⬍
Marital Status	Single ⬍
Number of Children	0 ⬍
% income from second earner	0% ⬍

(click one- If both spouses work, please select percent of income earned by lower earning spouse)

See how much I save under the Bush Plan!

A Tax Cut With A Purpose

Click here to visit
www.georgewbush.com

Paid for by Bush for President, Inc.

FIGURE 3.4   A tax cut ad run by the Bush campaign included an interactive device for calculating your cut.

primary. In that way, the process added a more targeted layer than just geography or a basic age and gender demographic, such as adults ages eighteen to forty-nine, a typical demographic audience that TV salespeople pitch to.

McCain used the Aristotle technology to help him round up volunteers for a petition drive to put him on the Virginia primary ballot. His campaign was able to send banner ads exclusively to Virginia registered voters from December 9 to December 16, 1999. Just $1,500 bought McCain about 10,000 impressions of five different banner ads appearing on hundreds of Web sites, said Fose, McCain's Internet manager. "We were literally a week away from not being on the ballot in Virginia," Fose said. "The crisis alarm was sounded—try anything. So we went and bought some banner ads from Aristotle."[53]

The ads earned 198 click-throughs. That's a 2 percent response rate, which is much higher than the industry average click-through rate of 0.3 percent. It ultimately gained McCain ninety-seven volunteers to help collect signatures to get on the state ballot. Respondents to the ads could click

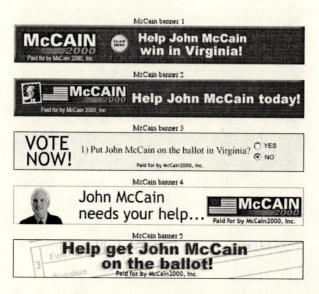

FIGURE 3.5 McCain banner ads ran in Virginia to help him get on the ballot in that state's primary.

through to a page where they would fill out a request, and the McCain camp would call and explain how to find and sign a petition. Or the campaign would drive one out to the volunteer's home. "You just have to be a registered voter in Virginia's open primary, so the message was 'You're a registered voter. Sign a petition and get John McCain on the ballot,'" said Fose. "It was very effective. It probably helped us get a couple thousand signatures." McCain spokesperson Molly Ives felt at the time that the Web really made the effort succeed. "We filed over 20,000 signatures in Virginia today, and clearly this can be credited in part to our outreach efforts on the Web."[54]

Finally, while political consultants and media conglomerates developed Web sites and e-commerce experts zeroed in on likely fund-raising and advertising targets, everyday people played the Internet version of prospecting for gold. Cybersquatters bought domain names, speculating that the candidates would want them and would be willing to pay. Once spurned by the Bush campaign, one such site, www.gwbush.com, became so popular that it started charging money for banner ads and merchandise. Pete Lucas of Bridgewater, New Jersey, held at least five combinations of Gore-Lieberman addresses and several combinations of Bush-Cheney.

He said in an August 2000 interview that he might use several "R-rated" addresses related to "George W. Bush" as leverage to get the Bush campaign to pay. "I fully expect some five-digit sales down the line (maybe not here) but with my other domains," Lucas said. "It's very tough with politicians, as many feel they have the God-given right to domains and are constantly worried about bad publicity."[55]

This concern led the Bush team to buy up scores of domain names in July 2000, just before the candidate was about to announce his vice presidential running mate, as well as domains for potential spoof sites. Many of the logical combinations of *Bush/McCain* and *Bush/Dole* had long been snapped up by cybersquatters, some waiting almost two and a half years to see if their combination won. Internet domain name registrar Network Solutions released a list of fifty domains purchased by Bush campaign manager Karl Rove that included any *.com, .net,* or *.org* combo of "texasgovernor.com" and "governorbush.org" or domains associated with potential running mates such as "bushwhitman.net" and "bushpataki.net." Most of the spoof names included some version of "bushblows.com," "bushsucks.org," or "georgebushbites.net."

"We had initially purchased a bunch of domain names that included georgewbush.com, and then in 1999 we decided to purchase about seventy more names," explained Cliff Angelo. "A lot of them were the 'anti' variety. . . . Obviously, you can't buy every iteration of someone's name, and it gets to be very, very expensive. We bought all of those to protect his name because, for instance, aolsucks and billgatessucks are huge sites, very, very well trafficked. We knew we didn't want that to happen."

The fish that got away? www.bush-cheney.net. Young researchers at the Democratic National Committee (DNC) in Washington snapped up the rights to that domain name on July 22, 2000. Ten minutes after Bush announced his running mate on July 25, the site was up with a catalog of Cheney's conservative House votes and dealings in the oil industry.[56]

Great Expectations for the New Technology

The site put up by the DNC highlights the difference Web technology can make in a campaign. Responding to Bush's vice presidential choice in such detail would have taken much longer than ten minutes in 1996—at least a press cycle in the media, with the journalists in control of the story, and much longer if responding by negative television ads.

The candidates were anxious to show how tech savvy they were. Al Gore told Yahoo!'s *Internet Life* magazine that he was willing to consider installing a Webcam in the Oval Office. "Maybe so," the vice president said about the possibility of a probing Internet eye, if the public views were "episodic."[57] Gore's team took advantage of Web technology to make an initial big splash, using the latest gee-whiz technology to launch its effort. The first online ads it bought announced a Webcast to kick off the campaign in June 1999. These weren't static banner ads but fifteen-second ads using Real Player technology that included Flash animation and music. Real Player is part of RealNetworks, Inc. Real Player software locates and allows the user to play audio (live music, radio broadcasts) and video (news broadcasts and music videos) over the Internet. The Webcast was advertised only on the Real.com Network; ads were embedded in the preset stations in Real Player. The "cool" factor was very high, and so was the response, according to Ben Green, Gore's director of Internet operations. "I think [the ad] was able to achieve a click-through rate of 6 percent," said Green, noting all the regular banner and button impressions they bought received less than a 1 percent click-through. "The Flash stuff people really liked, and it's neat. You click on it and the Real Player opens up a browser and takes you to the Gore site. We got great results out of that."

Gore's team had other gadgets, including a Web "roadcam" that filmed clips of the vice president every day and a Webcam stationed at Gore's headquarters that offered a twenty-four-hour view of the activity there. Green felt this would be a big incentive to make daily visits to the site. That sentiment was shared by a number of Web sites searching for a high-tech hook that would draw Web users back time and again. Sometimes the goal was just to lure visitors to the site with innovations like the candidate matching program, which walked users through a series of questions on education, abortion, health-care reform, taxes, and defense spending and then matched them with the candidate who most closely resembled their beliefs. These devices were quite popular at the political sites or those targeting certain ethnic groups or voting populations.

The news and political portals geared up for election coverage, and in particular the conventions, to showcase the "gee whiz" aspects of the Web. Rotating Webcams, hatcams—any part-of-the-body cams—would allow users an unparalleled opportunity to peek into every crevice of the conventions.

Searching out Web technology "firsts" was one approach that online news directors used to prove to their corporate managers and to the world that their Internet news organizations were legitimate and important. Carin Dessauer, election director at CNN Interactive, helped secure the first online news interview with a sitting U.S. president—Bill Clinton—on February 14, 2000. "That was a very dramatic moment for the importance of the Internet and the ability to reach out globally utilizing numerous media," said Dessauer. The interview was later shared with the sister cable TV and radio networks.[58] The first online interview with candidate Bush, according to Dessauer, came with a twist on the normal reporter-interviewee format: the promise that the electorate would actually be involved. "It's one of those 'Why-not?' [things]. [I]t hasn't been done before," she said. "What can we do that is new and different? What can we do that showcases the online medium and also combines the strengths of the CNN newsgroup and also really enables a person being interviewed to take questions from real people?"

The Web afforded online news organizations other distinct technological advantages: speed and unlimited availability. Tim Noah of slate.com had worked for two of the three major news weeklies and the *Wall Street Journal* before filing the "Chatterbox" column for *Slate.* The site is known for what Noah describes as a "unique blending of fact and opinion."[59] *Slate's* goal: to be an agenda setter in the campaign. Noah was quite tickled that the Web afforded him the opportunity to zip by the competition. "With certain kinds of items, items that actually have some news that the newspaper might follow on, I am pleased to exploit the technology that allows me to go to press immediately and therefore scoop the newspapers," Noah said. "It's one perverse advantage to there being so few Internet magazines that do journalism in anything like the traditional way. If you have a scoop, it's really easy to scoop everybody. Nobody can move as quickly as you can."

ABC News dedicated online journalists to each of the two main presidential candidates and another group to political stories in general. Ann Compton was pulled off the broadcast White House beat and put on the Web site. She created a five-minute daily Webcast called *On Background*. "The convergence of that kind of intensive coverage and the Internet works so well," Compton told the *Washingtonian* magazine. "These off-air reporters come up with so much good inside information that's perishable, and this way we can put it on 24 hours a day."[60]

The Web world pulled out all the stops for the Republican convention. Upstart Web operation pseudopolitics.com scored a first when both major political parties granted it a skybox, enabling it to compete—literally and figuratively—in the rarified air normally reserved for the broadcast networks. Much of the preconvention discussion and debate centered on the Big Three's decision to significantly scale back television coverage and cable television and the Internet's willingness to make up the difference. ABC and CBS planned to broadcast only five hours of the convention and NBC about half that much. In 1976 each network aired about fifty hours of convention coverage.[61] Web site operators, meanwhile, talked about going around the clock. Instant polls and 360-degree Webcams would fill the void left by Dan Rather, Peter Jennings, and Tom Brokaw.

Pseudopolitics.com and America Online spent at least $20,000 for the right to occupy those skyboxes. Pseudopolitics, hoping to reap an advertising blitz from its prime position, called attention to itself with an illuminated "on the Net" sign, instead of "on the air." And much to the delight of its staff, the Pseudo logo rested neatly in the CNN shot when the cable channel trained its camera toward the convention hall stage. For AOL, the big box was a marked difference from 1996, when it was initially denied press credentials, then finally was sent up to the nosebleed seats with the college press. In 1996 several companies—including CNN, CompuServe, Prodigy, and MSNBC.com—offered limited convention coverage. In 2000 virtually every media company offered major Web coverage. However, Pseudo and its online brethren weren't interested in following the lead of their broadcast competitors.

"We don't plan on covering this like network television. Otherwise, why should we be here?" said Sam Hollender, executive producer and managing editor of pseudopolitics.com, in May 2000. "This is going to be something very different from them. We're going to dive headfirst to make sure this experience is as special and state-of-the-art as it can be."[62]

TV was state-of-the-art in 1948, the year widely recognized as the launching pad for television thanks to live network coverage that year of the conventions. Only 162,181 television sets had been sold in 1947, but that number tripled in 1948. Yet as far as technology goes, the convention broadcasts weren't an impressive effort, nor were the actual viewing numbers large. The conventions were watched by 10 million people in a nation of more than 125 million, and the coverage was rudimentary.[63] Both conventions were in Philadelphia, at the time the third largest city in the United States, simply because the broadcast range was only fifty miles and TV execs wanted to reach as many people as possible in that radius. "Only on the East Coast could you be sure there were programs and reception, and then only in the major cities did AT&T's coaxial cable provide a fuzzy picture on those massive living-room consoles with their tiny, seven-inch screens," wrote Zachary Karabell in his book *The Last Campaign*. At the time, he added, skeptics assured each other that TV would never replace radio.

Web sites weren't anticipating the same kind of problems with their technology in 2000; they were expecting this would be their breakout year. If the coverage could be new and different, that was all the more impetus to try it. Potential broadband limitations did not stem the excitement and anticipation—even though only 16 percent of U.S. households were estimated to have broadband access in 2000.[64] And where better to kick off this Internet news revolution than the same city that hosted those 1948 conventions? The First Union Center rolled out 6,600 miles of fiber-optic cable—enough to stretch from Philadelphia to Tokyo—to accommodate the newcomers. The new Web whiz kids took their place among the estimated 15,000 media throng. Their Philly address for July 31–August 3, otherwise known as Media Pavilion No. 4, was quickly christened "Internet Alley." The high-tech bells and whistles they packed were a far cry from the 1996 Republican convention in San Diego, where the closest thing to Internet Alley was a Radio Row of conservative talk show hosts. This time some fifty-five Internet news outlets set up shop in the Alley, and even more were scheduled to make the trek to Los Angeles for the Democratic convention August 14–17, where they would be housed along "Internet Avenue."[65]

Bold predictions were made: More than fifty years after that historic television signal was beamed, the year 2000 would sound the death knell for televised political coverage. "This may be the last television convention and the first Internet convention," Doug Bailey, president of FreedomChannel.com, said in a *Columbus Dispatch* interview just as the Republicans were getting set to open the convention.[66]

The newcomers would need to overcome something that didn't factor into the 1948 coverage. Conventions used to feature high drama and suspense about who would be the nominee. In more recent elections, with the advent of the primaries, the party's nominee became known well ahead of time. In addition, party leaders long ago scrubbed most of the conflict from the convention. It got so bland, in 1996 Ted Koppel stomped home from San Diego in midconvention, declaring there was nothing newsworthy going on. The only question ABC execs were wrestling with this time around was whether Colin Powell's speech could be fit into the halftime of *Monday Night Football*'s preseason affair between the San Francisco 49ers and the New England Patriots.

So thousands of new-media journalists converged on Philly in search of a new angle and a new audience—searching for that defining moment in the evolution of news on the Internet. With approximately 150 million Americans online—fifteen times the number in 1996—the stage was set for the Web to make its mark. To get away from the potentially dull proceedings, politics-only sites such as grassroots.com, speakout.com, and politics.com prepared to set themselves apart by taking the convention directly to the people. The plan was to let Web users from around the country share their gripes online about a candidate's speech, register their opinions in polls, and even interrupt an online video interview if they thought a politician had pontificated too long. According to *The Industry Standard*, speakout.com, in a partnership with MSNBC, was set to debut its patent-pending "Ntercept." [67] Ntercept was an online political mood meter that enabled surfers, for example, to rank a speech on a scale of 0 to 100 by moving a bar up and down the meter with their mouse. Speakout said it could handle up to 8,000 participants at a time and compile results of polls within minutes, producing a "national EKG" of what people thought.[68] "In the past, we were all couch potatoes sitting back basically having to absorb the [television] convention coverage as dogma," said Joshua King, Speakout's vice president of national affairs. "It shouldn't be left to the pundits to analyze and give feedback to how these politicians are speaking."[69]

The general emphasis was to engage the Web users, making them feel like delegates. Political and news Web sites would offer streaming video coverage and live audio feeds of nightly sessions. Visitors to sites could download archived speeches, chat online with others, and interview delegates and journalists. They could complete instant polls, play online games, take political quizzes, and access loads of data on the candidates and the party. AOL featured a twenty-four-hour Webcam, a "pre-game" streamed Web show, chats and delegate diaries, and for those with high-speed connections, live feeds of convention speeches.

"The Internet is changing politics irrevocably and it's changing journalism irrevocably," former Watergate reporter Carl Bernstein, executive editor of voter.com, told *The New York Times*. "This will be an intersection where you will see both."[70] In addition to covering the convention with a team of forty people (larger than most newspaper contingents) voter.com issued delegates "smart cards" that could be used to gain access to kiosks tipping them to the best late-night parties.

At a party for the news media throng on the night before the Philadelphia convention officially started, many on the dot-com crews were easy to spot—funky glasses and a whiff of irreverence. And they were abuzz with the message of their industry: to give viewers the sort of experience they could never get with television or print. At Insightmag.com, *The Baltimore Sun* described what might be called robo-reporters who were sent out onto the convention floor. With a keypad on one wrist, an Internet screen on the other, a minicomputer at their waists, and a camera strapped over one ear, six reporters would conduct interviews at parties and on the convention floor and simultaneously feed the Web. "Whatever a reporter sees, you'll see—I want to demystify this process," said Paul Rodriguez, editor of *Insight* magazine. "We're going to show you how the sausage is made."[71]

Pseudopolitics offered Web users the opportunity to become virtual camera operators with its live, 360-degree streaming video from a choice of several camera angles, ranging from views of the Texas and Wyoming delegations to the schmoozing in the skybox itself. Along with the images, the Web outfits delivered software that let the user rotate the picture or zoom in and out. In addition, Pseudo hosted live coverage from noon to midnight on the days of the convention and partnered with *Salon*, *George* magazine, and *The New York Observer* for a nightly Webcast. The Pseudo programming had no beginning and no end, no prepackaged sound bites, no hair-sprayed host. The "EJs" rambled on while also conducting online chats. The EJ monitored the chat-room, whose members received a live audio feed from the skybox discussion and could send in questions or snide comments or give guests a Roman-style thumbs up or thumbs down. The EJ often, and gleefully, interrupted on-air guests with the comments.

"My job is to be obnoxious," said one EJ, identified as Jaxx, in a *Boston Globe* story that described the Pseudo atmosphere as a blend of *Wayne's World* and *Animal House* in a place the size of Elizabeth Taylor's bathroom. "If people in the chat rooms don't believe what they are hearing, I'll let the online people know about it."[72]

All the excitement in the chat-rooms bubbled over in the Pseudo skybox, which was *the* place to be for this convention. Scheduled guests such as Rick Lazio, Arianna Huffington, Jimmy Breslin, and Al Sharpton gave way to impromptu visitors who just wanted to check out what all the buzz was about.[73] The box got more crowded as nights wore on, attracting everyone from curious journalists who wanted a beer to politicians making sure they didn't miss out on history. Pseudopolitics marketing coordinator Tammy Braman noted that while the Big Three's skyboxes were somewhat quiet, the Pseudo box was treated to a full house.[74] She said Pseudo was demonstrating a new way to cover politics and reach out to the eighteen-to-twenty-four-year-old voter. The reaction the site was getting was something never seen before, according to Braman, and the results were just part of what was to come. Braman, young and energetic just like the visitors Pseudo hoped to attract to its site, gushed about the Web's seemingly limitless potential and the moth-to-a-flame effect the technology would have on Web users: "The Internet is going to take over the earth," she said. "The technology just isn't play anymore."

4

HUMILITY

JUSTIN FRIEDLAND REMEMBERS EXACTLY WHERE HE WAS WHEN he got the phone call. He was sitting in the lavish skybox in the Staples Center in Los Angeles, then about 80 percent complete, directing thirty staffers who would produce pseudopolitics.com's twenty-four-hour coverage of the upcoming Democratic convention. Pseudopolitics.com, a Web site startup covering the 2000 elections, hired Friedland because of his expertise covering conventions as a TV producer. On the other end of the phone line was his long-time friend David Bohrman, CEO of pseudopolitics.com.

Bohrman was blunt. He was scrambling to keep the company viable, but venture capital wasn't materializing. Coverage would be cut way back. "All the people who were supposed to leave from New York the next day weren't coming," Friedland recounted. "That left us with a skeleton crew." Such scale-backs weren't new for the TV producer. He had been asked before to cover a story and then, a few days later, told to produce something else but for nothing. "I just pulled out my file and said, 'Okay, here's what has been done, here's what hasn't been done. Let's stop what hasn't been done so we don't have to pay for it.'"

Friedland was disappointed that the Los Angeles coverage would be far different from Philadelphia, site of the Republican convention just a week earlier. There, onlookers had fawned over pseudopolitics.com and its state-of-the-art technology and impressive presence. Pseudopolitics had

PHOTO 4.1　Justin Friedland

unveiled 360-degree Webcams that enabled Internet visitors to view the convention at any time. Pseudo was blessed with an energetic staff of new-media wunderkinder who rushed about purposefully and gathered, wrote, and posted stories continuously. This, many people thought, was the future of news coverage—live, real time, nonstop, media-rich publishing.

In fact, in Philadelphia Pseudo and its coverage became the number-two story to the nomination of George W. Bush himself, as nearly every media outlet covered this intrepid online newcomer. The Pseudo skybox was often packed with reporters from other news media. Staff from ABC-News.com drifted across the hall to marvel at pseudopolitics.com.

But Friedland, now in Los Angeles, was told the site wasn't sustainable. During the lull between conventions, his boss, Bohrman, frantically raced to leverage the attention and raise more capital, but investors were not buying the "field of dreams" business model, a euphemism for "supply an attraction, and demand will result." The site did not attract sufficient hits, advertisers were not pleased, and investors became cautious. The demise of pseudopolitics.com closely parallels the dot-com implosion that occurred during 2000 and into 2001. There was no demand for political news on the scale provided by Pseudo, and the high cost of supplying it simply drove the company into the ground.

After all the lauding, bragging, and hype about the Internet and its political impact, detailed in the previous chapter, the reality was sobering. Although there were many examples of the media and the political parties using the Internet purposefully and successfully, the actual impact fell so far short of the unreasonable expectations that the Internet itself seemed to fail. The business model could not support many media initiatives, and like Pseudopolitics, they ceased operations or cut back. Although they offered a wealth of information, they attracted few but political junkies, and advertisers shied away. There was, of course, the problem that the election was going to end in November, and then what?

Political party and candidate sites failed to fully utilize the Internet's power to motivate and communicate. Those sites failed to lure voters to learn more about the candidates, to donate, or to volunteer in the numbers hoped for. In an example of missed opportunity, political party and candidate Web sites failed, for the most part, to enable citizens to engage in real dialogue with the candidates, perhaps the single most significant distinction the Internet could offer.

Pseudopolitics.com is the poster child for many Internet companies that evaporated in the free-falling dot-com industry. In August in Los Angeles, pseudopolitics.com's 360-degree cameras disappeared, replaced by a convoluted process of videotaping live events and then shipping the tapes to New York for digitizing and uploading to the Web site. A Federal Express courier replaced live streaming pictures. The on-site staff shrank from thirty to seven. Gone as well was the wall-to-wall action and excitement that filled the Pseudo skybox in Philadelphia. The Los Angeles scene appeared calm, even boring. One night, staffers from *George* magazine sat and watched the speeches, drank white wine or Evian, and quietly discussed which of the evening's parties to attend. Friedland searched frantically for guests, who previously had waited anxiously for their turn in front of his camera in Philadelphia. A Pseudo executive crouched under his desk trying to fix the Internet connection when it stalled halfway through President Clinton's speech, cutting contact with live chatters and Pseudo headquarters in New York. And Pete Austin, Pseudo's lone camera operator, shot everything he could for packaging to New York but missed one of the biggest events of the week: the protests during the Rage Against the Machine concert.

The Internet Bubble Bursts

Pseudopolitics.com wasn't the only cyberflop of the Democratic convention. Compared with the glitter and glamor of the Republican convention, Internet Avenue in Los Angeles resembled an abandoned strip mall. Staff worked the booths for the first day or so, but the buzz about the Internet had quieted. Workers at the Lexis-Nexis booth had a hard time giving away convention buttons and booklets that listed top Web sites. Reporters from the traditional media showed more interest in model Christie Brinkley and the World Wrestling Federation's "The Rock" than in Internet Avenue. Many Web reporters and other dot-com employees handed out business cards in search of a new job.

Pseudopolitics.com managed to operate for forty-five days after the Democratic convention ended, but then Bohrman was forced to pull the plug. All 175 employees were fired and joined thousands of others whose dot-com careers paused. Friedland returned to his Westchester County, New York, farm, more concerned about the welfare of his old friend David Bohrman than Pseudo's demise. "I'm really sorry Pseudo couldn't find the funding," Friedland said. He expressed admiration for Bohrman's talent for recruiting smart people and generating a real excitement for covering politics. "I believe that what we were doing at Pseudo was four years too early. It was the right idea, we were just too far ahead of ourselves."[1]

Most of the political portals, both the profit-making and public-interest, found themselves struggling to survive in cyberspace.[2] Consider the following three snapshots:

By summer, ad revenues at the nonprofit grassroots.com didn't match expectations. Despite bringing in two big-name former White House staffers to lend credibility (Clinton spokesperson Mike McCurry and George Bush chief of staff John Sununu), the site didn't attract enough audience to keep the computers humming. By Election Day it had morphed into a site to sell software to political organizations.[3]

One of the most promising enterprises, voter.com, held on through Election Day but disappeared three months later. With more than $15 million in venture capital, the planners had hoped to transform politics by engaging candidates and citizens in meaningful dialogue. The splashy site offered a news service, voter guide, and sample ballot. A twenty-six-year-old from the investment industry ran it, along with political heavyweights such as Craig Smith, the former political director of the Clinton White House; Randy Tate, formerly of the Christian Coalition; and Carl Bernstein, one of the journalists who broke the Watergate story. Although they reported 3 million site visits in November, they couldn't maintain steady traffic. When they lost out on a deal for an additional $40 million, voter.com closed its doors.[4]

Politics.com stumbled too, despite the lofty ideals of founder Howard Baer. He envisioned his site as a powerful aid to democracy by giving citizens quality information, an easy-access campaign contribution database, and forums to post both opinions and questions. As the election came to a close, the site was sold, never realizing its potential. Baer summed it up in an interview with the *San Francisco Chronicle*: "The American public is just not that interested. Not enough people kept coming to the site to make money."[5]

Internet sites suffered the same audience fragmentation that befuddles the television networks: not enough viewers to go around. While site visits bubbled up around Election Day, the traffic pattern didn't reach the volume needed to sustain the sites month after month. Another factor in the downfall: The political sites just couldn't compete with the content-rich news sites of established media companies.[6]

There was value in the depth of information on political portals such as voter.com, but the public didn't respond. One study showed that only 9 percent of those who said they used the Internet for political information visited a nonpartisan Web site.[7] Although 35 percent of all Americans reported they used the Internet to get information about politics, campaigns, or issues in the news, only 14 percent said the Internet was important in providing them with information that helped them decide how to vote.[8] Combined with the general slide of the dot-com industry, the political portals couldn't begin to reach their lofty goals of reinvigorating democracy.

Online Political Advertising

One of the expectations that media sites had, and in fact depended on for their survival, was that the campaigns would shift advertising expenditures to the Internet. For reasons we explore in this section, the campaigns did not oblige, and their unwillingness to advertise on the Internet contributed to the media Web sites' demise.

Peter Chang registered for MSNBC.com and slate.com as a twenty-eight-year-old Philadelphia resident. A Gore supporter, he surfed the Web weekly throughout the 2000 campaign, but he never saw a political ad. Anita Suarez, forty-seven, of San Diego, registered to vote through latinovote.com and visited news sites. She too never saw a political ad. Neither did Bobby Norman of Mobile, Alabama, a Bush supporter who read about the election at nra.org, the National Rifle Association's site.

Chang, Suarez, and Norman were all fictitious people, cyberghosts invented by us to collect data on online political advertising. In an experiment, fourteen imaginary people were registered for Yahoo! and Hotmail e-mail accounts. Each had addresses and zip codes in swing states. They covered all age brackets, and some had ethnic surnames. These voters signed up for e-mail newsletters and surfed on sites that reflected the profiles created for them—gay, senior citizen, suburban mother, NRA member, environmentalist. Some signed up for e-mail from a political party or candidate. Others were intentionally left to appear undecided. They got lots of e-mail, most not worth discussing. While many of the in-boxes of the males in our ghost community received the e-mail "DO YOU LIKE HOT WOMEN?" and various other come-ons, none received a political online ad.

Even though the technology exists to target ads at specific Internet users, few of them saw any political advertising from the parties or campaigns or even from political portals or news organizations promoting political coverage. AdRelevance, an Internet-audience measurement firm, said the total banner-ad effort of three political parties (Democrats, Republicans, and Libertarians) combined for a little more than 29 million impressions that cost about $860,000. Compare that to the more than $163 million the Brennan Center for Justice estimates that the parties and candidates spent on TV ads.

Ben Green, the director of Internet operations at Gore headquarters, described the Internet ad dollars as "a thimble in the ocean."[9] And it was a bit of a surprise, according to Marc Ryan, director of media research at AdRelevance. "With all the noise that was made about the Internet over the last year and a half, going into the elections we thought 'Betcha we'll see a lot of ads here,'" Ryan said. "And the reality is we didn't see a heckuva lot, which is really surprising because here's an opportunity to reach markets that you can't reach through TV—an opportunity to target individuals, to target different genders, to target different age groups, to provide custom-tailored messages to specific individuals."

The campaigns balked at that opportunity. The Bush campaign tried to repurpose the "Uncle Sam Wants You!" slogan dating from World War I and placed "We Want You . . . to Click into the Party" banner ads. The Republican National Committee (RNC) paid for these ads along with another, "The Future President Wants to See You." The goal: to gather some 100,000 e-mail addresses. The RNC got 1 million responses, far exceeding its expectations.[10] The Republicans were more aggressive Internet users than their Democratic rivals during the 2000 election. According to AdRelevance, the GOP ran more than 19 million impressions, compared to the 8 million that the Democrats ran from July through November 2000.[11] The bulk of the GOP ads ran during the conventions and the debates; a few ran in the days leading up to the election. The tactic was to ask users to join the party, sometimes using incentives such as a chance to win a Palm Pilot or a trip to Washington, D.C. The ads linked to gop.org or e-champions2000.com, a Web site affiliated with the GOP.

The primary goal? Get names, according to Larry Purpuro, RNC deputy chief of staff. It wasn't an exact science. "We did it everywhere," said Purpuro about the ad placement and site promotion, which included media buys ranging from Yahoo!, MSNBC.com, and the *Drudge Report* to FreeLotto, *Maxim*, and Zeeks.com. "It was just throw everything against the wall and see what sticks. We tested a dozen different advertising forums. They weren't exclusively advertising; some were newsletters." The RNC ran about twenty different banner ads on approximately thirty-five sites, according to AdRelevance, which used rate card costs to estimate that the GOP spent $662,511 on the ads.[12]

The Democratic National Committee (DNC), by comparison, ran a single banner ad on Yahoo! the week of the Democratic convention, according to AdRelevance. It estimated the DNC buy at $161,474. The ad was static—just an announcement that the convention was taking place at the Staples Center in Los Angeles, August 14–17.

The Gore campaign said it ran online ads that were never seen in the Media Metrix sample. Green, the Gore campaign Webmaster, told the authors about two online ads that were tested in swing states and a final big blowout of $100,000 worth of ads that the DNC ran in a three-day burst near the campaign's end. The latter was a get-out-the-vote (GOTV) effort on Yahoo! and AOL that ran in ten swing states, including Florida, according to Green.[13] And it was large—nearly 5 million impressions.

The two test ads ran statewide in Pennsylvania and in the Columbus, Ohio, area targeting women ages twenty-one to thirty-five on Yahoo!, Green said. The ads ran during the Republican National Convention concerning a red-hot topic: abortion. Green said the more provocative the ad, the better it performed. "We tried two approaches: We tried what I call the shock approach, where it was black-and-white and flashing text saying, 'The Republicans want to take away your right to choose,'" he said. "And the other approach was sort of a softer approach, without such a radical font, without such a radical color contrast. It didn't work as well."

Green maintains the Democrats' issue-based approach was a better idea than the GOP data-collection approach. "We were speaking to the issues that were important in the election and not some sort of bland thing that's like, 'Oh, you can win a Palm Pilot if you give us your e-mail address,'" Green said. "It was a real difference in the approaches. They were trying to collect information from political junkies to pad their e-mail lists and make their e-mail list bigger. We were more aimed at swing voters, people whom we were trying to persuade one way or the other. People that we knew were with us and we wanted to motivate them to come out and vote."

Purpuro defended the Republicans' e-mail database effort. "The one thing we did do right was that we focused on the fundamentals and the idea of building an e-mail database that is critical to any organization," said Purpuro, who estimated the party spent about $1 million to promote the domain name. "At the end of the day, that's going to be your most effective means of reaching people and the most efficient way. . . . The Web sites that have a large community of like-minded individuals and have their e-mail addresses are going to be the ones that are most viable."

Not all the campaigns felt good about their online advertising efforts. Lynn Reed, Bradley's Internet manager, tried to reach voters by targeting Juno users in New Hampshire, Iowa, and California and Hotmail subscribers in Iowa. She didn't anticipate the difficulties. "A lot of these people that sell banner advertising claim that they can target, and perhaps for corporate standards they can," Reed said. "But for political standards, where we need to find likely voters or likely Democrats, how do you possibly target well enough to make it worth the expenditure?" Reed said the campaign spent $25,000 on the ads, which featured the headline "Tired of politics as usual?" It then flipped to another message with a picture of Bradley and a link to his Web site: "I am. See what I'm going to do about it."[14] Reed said only fifteen people clicked on the ad, at an average cost of $1,666 per person.

Some software vendors do have technology to target likely voters. Aristotle Publishing, mentioned in Chapter 3, can identify fund-raising or volunteer prospects. Aristotle's database includes twenty-five demographic, geographic, and psychographic characteristics cross-referenced with the names of 150 million registered voters. It includes a person's age, sex, telephone number, party affiliation, and estimated income and whether he or she rents or owns a home, has children, and has an ethnic surname. It also provides the make and model of voters' cars, whether they are campaign donors, their employer and occupation, and how often they vote. A dollar sign pops up next to the name of a voter identified as a "Fat Cat," a wealthy donor.[15] The data are compiled using information from state motor vehicle departments, the Postal Service, and the Census Bureau, among others. It can be used for direct mail or telephone soliciting or polling or to target Web users. Although the service is extraordinarily useful for political messaging, the party that chooses to use it may have a bit of damage control on the privacy issue.

"The ability to monitor the cost-effectiveness of [online] advertising is a big plus, but it's also a minus," explained John Phillips, chief executive officer of Aristotle Publishing.[16] "There's an adage that 50 percent of the money in politics is wasted; the question is which 50 percent. Is it the emery boards the money is wasted on, the TV spots, online ads, bill-boards, what else—the balloons? But it's clear there is a lot of waste there. The difference is that online, the performance is measured on a cost-per-click or a cost-per-e-mail acquisition, whereas in these other areas, vast sums are expended and there is no accounting for 'Did these balloons lead us to pick up another volunteer that we can raise money from?'"

Max Fose of the McCain campaign decided banner ads weren't worth the investment. The upstart campaign saw mixed results from its four on-line advertising efforts. The effort to get McCain on the Virginia ballot worked, but messages about campaign finance reform that ran in San Diego and ads stating McCain's position against the Internet tax didn't perform well. The McCain camp was averaging a $1 contribution to the campaign per unique visitor, and when it applied that "income" against how many people were clicking through the banners to get to the McCain site, the ads were not worthwhile.

"We looked at what banner ads cost and did the math, and they were, say, a 2 percent click-through rate," Fose said. "A 2 percent click-through rate wouldn't even pay for the ad. Now if it would have just paid for itself, we would have done it because we'd have gotten more people signed up to the campaign. Unless there was a specific goal, like petitions, it didn't pay to do it, because the math just didn't work out."[17]

Green doesn't think that click-through is the be-all, end-all to measure the success of an online effort. The last-minute DNC buy finished with what Green termed typical click-through rates (0.3 percent). Green pointed out that the Gore campaign eked out wins in New Mexico, Wis-consin, and Iowa and suggested that the get-out-the-vote banner cam-paign contributed to those victories. "We won by 500 to 1,000 votes and you can't help but think, maybe it was the banner impressions we ran," Green said. "I tried to sell it to everybody—'Don't look to click-through as the measure of success for this. "Did we win the state?" is going to be the measure of success, and then I can tell you afterwards how many ads were shown in that state.' If you show 100,000 ads in Florida and you end up winning or coming up short by 537 votes or whatever, it's not that much of a stretch to say, well, if we hadn't run those ads, maybe we would have had a couple hundred fewer votes and the outcome would have been different."

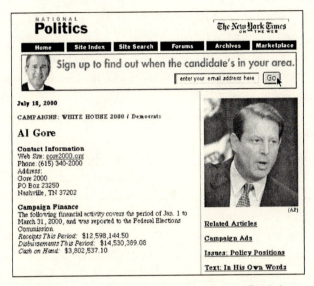

FIGURE 4.1 In an ironic happenstance, a Bush banner ad appeared over a story about Al Gore, on *NY-Times.com*

Ryan, director of media research at AdRelevance, speculated that, because it was a close race, the campaigns were loath to advertise on the Internet. "Do we really want to experiment with the Web, something that hasn't been proven yet, at least in an election period, when it's a head-to-head battle on TV and every dollar spent on TV is probably well spent?"

Campaign Sites Failed to Attract an Audience

Lisa Boerner is the prototypical Web user and campaign worker—young adult, well-educated, politically astute, and trained in communications. Her job in advertising takes her online eight hours a day. Boerner's earliest memories of activism come from the day her mother insisted that the then ten-year-old accompany her to work because the president, Ronald Reagan, was going to speak there. Her mother discussed candidates at home, and on every election day she took Boerner with her into the voting booth. "I knew at a very young age who the senators were and what their role was," remembered Boerner. "By the time I reached high school, I worked with the Clinton-Gore campaign, the first one."

She continued her activity at college in Michigan, working for local candidates and joining the annual Labor Day march, where candidates trek across the Mackinac Bridge. During the 2000 election, Boerner spent about two hours per week online reading political news. In typical surfer fashion, she would see a headline at gotonet.com, the portal Web site where she worked, and link to a Seattle Web site to get the full story. She clicked over to local news sites to see how they covered the campaign as the candidates traveled the country through the summer and fall. A former advertising manager at Amazon.com, Boerner understands good communication and has a keen eye for good Web design. None of the campaigns' Web sites impressed her.

She clicked over to the Bush site (georgewbush.com) in early 2000 because she heard it touted as one of the best. Boerner was looking for information about Bush's position on capital punishment, since a controversy was brewing in Texas about a pending execution. Boerner was disappointed that she couldn't find anything on it, nor did much else interest her. "It seemed like there was a lot of duplicated content," Boerner said. "It was not that deep, and it didn't give me enough of what I was looking for in terms of information about the candidate." She liked the Gore site (algore2000.com) for its section on issues but became turned off by all its requests for money. She found it far too promotional and biased for her liking.

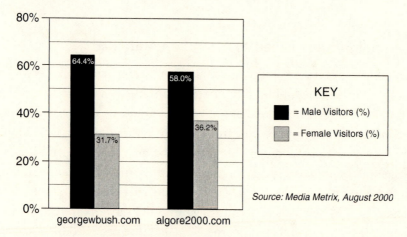

FIGURE 4.2 Candidate site visitors by gender

The net conclusion from a number of polls is that partisan Web sites attracted a small percentage of the total online population, and that group tended to be party loyalists. A Harris Poll in February 2000 showed that only 16 percent of people online visited at least one candidate site.[18] Furthermore, the Pew Research Center for the People and the Press found that only one-third of online users who went to candidate sites found them useful.[19] When Harris asked people to rate the campaign sites in early 2000, 16 percent rated them "excellent," and 74 percent labeled them "pretty good," but the only site that spurred discussion by at least half of those who went there was that of Republican candidate Alan Keyes.[20] Candidate sites did not attract undecided voters. Researchers at Media Metrix found traffic at the Gore and Bush Web sites appeared to be highly partisan, with only 8 percent of the total who visited either site also visiting the competition's.[21]

Thirteen viable candidates had launched Web sites by the summer of 1999, from Libertarian Larry Hines's simple photo and text to fellow Libertarian Harry Browne's colorful billboard of links to the party's supporting sites.[22] Most of the earliest sites resembled online campaign brochures. An early study in 1999 by two scholars ranked the Web sites of George W. Bush and Bob Smith (U.S. senator from New Hampshire) as the worst. Lamar Alexander's and Al Gore's ranked as the best.[23] A Harris Poll in February gave Steve Forbes's and Alan Keyes's sites a grade of "excellent."[24] Nearly all the candidates redesigned their pages throughout the campaign. By Election Day, the Bush and Gore sites had flashy graphics, interactive activities, and streaming audio and video. Both featured position papers, speeches, media releases, chat areas, youth sections, a Spanish version, links to state parties, and links to contribute or volunteer. Interestingly, the most popular aspects of their sites were the issues sections and biographies.[25]

The Bush campaign spent more than $1 million on its Web site, georgewbush.com, and claimed it was the first to put up a searchable donor database where visitors could find out who had given and how much. However, few used it.[26] The site also featured live streaming videos crafted to look as though they were broadcast from a conventional TV news set. The Republican National Committee spent even more, an estimated $5.9 million, for a site that featured Bush and included many other GOP candidates.[27] At algore2000.com the staff boasted that its Web site was first to stream video and that they produced a record sixty-five live Webcasts. Both campaigns filled their Web sites with features to appear more cutting edge and knowledgeable about technology. However, few Net users could see these features without broadband.

Lessons Learned

These pioneering Web sites became petri dishes for future online campaigns. During 2000, consultants and campaign staff puzzled over how to use the Internet effectively. Coming out of the election, there are key lessons the campaigns could share.

Open the Back Channel

The campaigns tended to view the Web as a mediated, "one-to-many" broadcast technology. Their message was carefully worded by a team of editors and electronically published for consumption by the masses. The campaigns largely disregarded the Internet's unique feature as a two-way medium: They could get information not only to voters but also from them. The Gore people did install instant messaging, enabling site visitors to communicate with each other. The candidate himself was still shrouded.

This is perhaps the most difficult paradigm shift for future campaigns—the notion of opening lines of direct access to the candidate with an unseen, unpredictable, online electorate. However, the Internet is first and foremost a communications technology; e-mail and instant messaging have become indispensable parts of the typical Internet user's daily routine, and as we will show in later chapters, the Internet is quickly becoming an integral component of community building. Candidates who avoid communication with online communities and continue to broadcast at them will do so at their own peril.

Make the Web Part of the Strategy

Despite John McCain's success with the Internet, the Bush and Gore campaigns never put the Internet front and center in their plans. They didn't invest enough time, money, or effort in their Web sites, didn't promote them aggressively, and didn't include Web experts in their top strategy sessions.

Tuesday, July 25, 2000: An important day in the Bush campaign. George W. Bush would announce his vice presidential candidate. The country watched to see if the pundits' prediction that Bush would select Dick Cheney was correct. But those who visited the Bush campaign Web site didn't know it was Cheney until several hours after TV carried the event live. Even then, georgewbush.com posted only a small notation that Cheney was the man, followed sometime later by a thumbnail mug shot and ever-so-brief biography.

Cliff Angelo, e-campaign manager for Bush, admitted his team was behind the curve. Although it had designed the Web site for easy updating with the vice presidential candidate's name, the Web staff didn't learn it was Cheney until the official announcement to the general public. The notice it finally posted came from the campaign communications office sometime after that. To add insult to injury, the Bush site was hacked twice.[28]

None of the campaigns spent much money promoting their Web sites, either online or in other media. Only the Republicans attempted to lure young voters by placing banner ads on youth-oriented Internet sites. And rarely did a campaign post its Web address within the view of the television cameras covering the candidate.

Political consultant Wes Gullett, who worked as the deputy campaign manager on the McCain campaign, said 2000 wasn't a watershed year because people running the e-campaigns weren't in key management positions. "Where we've had success we've been in the inner circle," Gullett said. "Where we haven't had success we've been working with the Web guy who is seventh tier down, in a small office around the corner." Neither Ben Green, the director of Internet operations in the Gore campaign, nor Bush Webmaster Cliff Angelo, regularly sat in on the top strategy meetings. Angelo told the authors he wished his team had more of a buy-in from the entire organization.[29] But support for a new, untested medium requires a cultural shift in a bureaucracy in which factions compete for attention. "They simply didn't devote the necessary resources," the RNC's

Purpuro said. "I think John McCain proved that the Web has potential. But the reality is that our folks, with[in] a short period of time, went back to the traditional means of running the trains on time."

Stay in Touch with Supporters

Besides running the same old trains, the campaigns did, to their credit, lay some new tracks. They were very successful using the Internet to establish and maintain contact with party loyalists. E-mail became a digital surrogate for the phone bank and door-to-door canvassing, and it was by far the closest the campaigns came to using the Internet effectively.

Gore volunteer Ed Rudd provides an insight into how the e-mail multiplier technique worked. A political professional, Rudd had worked with the campaigns of Gary Hart, Ernest Hollings, and Michael Dukakis, among others. Less active now and calling himself a "liberal Libertarian," Rudd practices law in Gadsden, Alabama. During the primaries, he joined the e-mail lists of several presidential candidates, including Bradley, Buchanan, Gore, and McCain. He liked what he saw in Gore, so one June day he responded to a Gore e-mail that asked him to spread the message of the day—that Gore is a friend of the environment. Rudd went to the Gore Web site and read the message posted there. Comfortable with it, he decided to pass it along. So he clicked over to AOL and searched for people in his former home state of Colorado who described themselves as environmentalists in their AOL profile. In about twenty minutes, he'd compiled a list of twenty-one people and forwarded the list to Gore headquarters along with a personal note of support. The campaign then forwarded his endorsement to the Colorado AOL users, with any replies directed back to the campaign rather than to Rudd.

The marketing industry calls this "viral marketing"—a series of forwarded or replicated e-mails spreading across the Internet faster than a virus. It proved to be a successful recruiting technique for many of the campaigns.

Rudd believes his online efforts did more than encourage loyalists. He said he brought in undecided voters and Libertarians. His repeated communications to the editor of the newspaper in a nearby town resulted in an invitation from its online editor to discuss the election after the second presidential debate. During that forum Rudd mentioned that he ran an e-mail discussion group and several people joined it. "So that was bringing in more people to be active participants in the campaign, at least through receiving the e-mail," he said.

Eventually his contact lists burgeoned to 1,000 individuals. As an e-precinct leader for Gore, Rudd got sample mailings a couple times a week. He was impressed that the e-mails targeted the recipient's vocation and interests. Even he and his mother received different messages, on different days. His messages related more to professional and legal issues. His mother, an educator, got e-mails about education and women's issues. She received excerpts from *The New York Times*'s endorsement of Gore. He got a link to the entire editorial.

Rudd preferred to customize his e-mails rather than simply forward the Gore mailings to the e-precinct chairs. Sometimes he'd pick something from the "Jews for Gore" or "Environmentalists for Gore" messages he received, cut and paste something from the Internet, and send it out. "I like what I do better than what they send me," he said.

His mailings went out several times a week, telling of Gore activities, pointing people to a certain online article, or attaching an example of a sample letter to the media. Rudd said he tried to go beyond just discussing the campaign, and to encourage action. He sent out a list of all the media outlets in the state, urging his e-mail community to write them a letter. He sent so much e-mail that eventually AOL, his Internet service provider, set him up as a legal commercial account.

Sometimes the notes would start a dialogue. For one mailing to 1,000 people only five people wrote him back, but Rudd saw that as encouraging. He spent about two hours a day reading information on the Internet and writing messages. Rudd called this online activity "more laid back" than the old days, when he left home to work on presidential campaigns. But he said it made him feel involved. In fact he thinks he might even have more influence for the amount of effort he puts in than in the old days of shoe-leather campaigning. The fact that Rudd's sense of political efficacy seems higher through online activity than through his past off-line activity is worthy of note.

Thousands of others sent or forwarded e-mails for other candidates. Some developed their own newsletters; others merely forwarded the stock letter from the campaign. The idea paid dividends. The Bush camp called its effort the "e-Train," a series of succinct e-mails designed to energize the grassroots and collect more e-mail addresses.[30] Four days after sending out the first e-Train missive in September 1999, the Bush campaign netted nearly 19,000 new e-mail addresses.[31]

Even before the primaries, e-mail proved a useful technique for the campaigns. More than 5,000 volunteers signed up the first day the Elizabeth Dole Web site came online, and two-thirds of all volunteers for that campaign came through the Web site. Most had never been involved in politics before, particularly women who felt disengaged from the political process.[32] "I think it was a great campaign, involving people who were otherwise disaffiliated," noted consultant Kathryn Coombs, who worked for Dole. She added that the Web reaches people other media don't. Coombs believes the multiplier effect from viral marketing can be sixfold. She once sent out an e-mail to 5,000 people, and 30,000 people visited an "e-mail your state legislator" site the following day.

By the campaign's end the Democratic National Committee and the Gore campaign said they gathered more than 800,000 unique e-mail addresses.[33] The Republicans said they surpassed them, topping 935,000 on Election Day.[34] It is ironic that something with the insidious-sounding name viral marketing actually helped the campaigns personalize an online experience and, in a small way, enhance the connections that people felt with one another and the candidates.

Organize the Volunteers Online

Prior to the New Hampshire primary, the Bill Bradley campaign e-mailed five hundred people, notifying them of a meeting in New Hampshire. Two hundred fifty showed up. Lynn Reed, Internet manager for Bradley, said such an event would never have happened if it wasn't for e-mail, because the campaign couldn't afford a phone bank and the mail would have taken too long. Part of the Bush campaign's strategy was to use e-mail for organizing on a local scale. A Bush intern spent hours setting up a yahoo.com account for every county in the country. The campaign found it an efficient messaging network, far better than the phone tree. With e-mail, everyone got the messages simultaneously. "In terms of organizing large numbers of people there's not a more cost-effective way to do it," said Ben Green, who designed a similar campaign for Gore. Ed Rudd said he received an e-mail thank-you from the Gore team every time he did something for them. He said that, with such an easy way to communicate, campaigns of the future must exploit the technology or fear losing not only a volunteer but a vote.

McCain's campaign invited e-mail to come in from supporters but was overwhelmed with the volume. His Internet manager, Max Fose, called the Internet "the new paradigm . . . the ultimate grassroots organization tool." By the end of McCain's campaign, Fose said McCain received e-mail from upwards of 5,000 people a day. Once someone e-mailed the campaign, its e-mail autoresponder sent a prewritten reply that included the campaign Web address, thus driving potential volunteers back to the campaign's Web site to get involved. Many people were put off by cookie-cutter responses from the campaigns, however, particularly when those responses merely herded them to an electronically published document. Such shortcuts only undermine the value of the Internet for one-to-one dialogue.

McCain also combined e-mail with phone banks. The McCain staff sent a volunteer the names of ten registered voters. The volunteer called each potential voter and then e-mailed back the results, including any new e-mail addresses of McCain supporters and undecided voters. Within twenty-four hours in New Hampshire, 1,200 people agreed to make additional contacts, 9,000 by the end of the state campaign. The callers, Fose said, ranged from a lawyer to a Denny's dishwasher. After making ten phone calls, "they are committed," Fose said.

Build a Community

Such commitment can become a community. The campaigns fostered message sending and shared Web space by like-minded people and helped to connect them with each other. It drove many of them to political action both online and in physical space. Users of the Gore Web site posted more than one million messages on its Town Hall section, the most active part of Gore's Web site. People used Gore's instant messaging (IM) feature, where supporters could chat. Gore Webmaster Ben Green called the results "phenomenal," noting that 30,000 people were using IM by election day.[35]

Specialty Web pages also served a community-building function. A firefighters' labor union created a "Firefighters for Gore" community in the "Voter Outreach" section of algore2000.com. Visitors there could use another ready-made feature to send e-mail to ten friends and invite them to visit the newly created online community site. The campaign hoped to connect the Gore faithful, as well as the uncommitted, with something that affected their daily lives. Groups constructed more than 40,000 such sites through the Gore Web site.[36]

The campaigns began, with these small steps, to foster discourse and community building. These efforts suggest that the larger institutions are not incapable of using the Internet to generate social capital, a thought we will return to in our final chapter. However, they must go beyond connecting supporters with each other and use the Internet to connect supporters with the leaders.

Promote Empowerment

E-mail, instant messaging, viral marketing, and personalized group Web pages empowered users. Campaign consultant Max Fose said people tired of being preached to on the campaign Web sites or through other one-way communication from the campaigns. Here they could become actively involved, invoking the older notion of a political party that recruits and organizes people to do things. "The only thing we ever get asked to do as Republicans is give them money," said Fose. "We're never asked for our advice. We're never asked how to help. We're never asked to provide assistance for creating a group of like-minded people or any of that stuff. We're just asked to give money so they can pay the professionals to do it in some scientific way."

When people did share their opinions with the campaigns via e-mail they were brutally frank, and far more candid, the consultants said, than during phone solicitations or campaign events. "You get more of an indication how the campaign is or isn't touching people's lives," consultant Kathryn Coombs said, noting that some people poured their hearts out online at the Dole Web site. "They're also more willing to tell you to go fly a kite, so you get some good honest feedback that you wouldn't otherwise be getting."[37]

The Value of Online Information

It's 10:00 P.M., and as you walk down a suburban street of quaint, older homes in Fayetteville, New York, you probably conclude that everyone is asleep at the cream-colored Georgian-style home on the block. But Daniel Chakin is still awake. As he clicks out the lights and his wife snuggles down to sleep next to him, Chakin reaches for his Palm VII. He scrolls through news from csmonitor.com, nytimes.com, and salon.com. The news from the Internet, downloaded to his hand-held Pilot, literally puts Chakin's hands on political news 24/7.

PHOTO 4.2 Dan Chakin

Staying in touch came easily to Chakin, forty-five, who has been at the forefront of computer technology for twenty years. Formerly a computer salesperson, Chakin runs his own Internet-based business that sells accounting software for Palm devices. He stays online all day, using the Internet as his primary source for political information. Still, his favorite time of the day to reflect on the news is the late evening. It sure beats his old method: using an irritating bright book lamp to read magazines full of days-old news. "Now, if you ask me a question—Bush-isms, statistics, primary results—I have them all right here," Chakin said, holding up his Palm VII.[38]

Because of information on the Internet, Chakin said he knew more—and knew more quickly about issues in Campaign 2000—than ever before. And that, he said, is good for democracy. "A better-informed and educated voter is one who will be involved," Chakin said. "And if you're involved, you're more likely to vote and take an active role in the political process." Chakin took such a role. He first worked in politics as a teen in the 1972 George McGovern campaign and then majored in political science and psychology in college. Later he volunteered on local campaigns and also worked for the Bill Bradley Senate campaign in the late 1970s, an experience that fostered deep loyalty. There was no question whom he'd support in 2000—Bill Bradley. Chakin published a political newsletter that he e-mailed regularly to nearly 1,800 people from his personal Internet e-mail address list. Like Ed Rudd, he became a digital publisher, but his operation ran separately from Bradley's campaign.

"I would read all that I could possibly read, from news columns to columnists, distill what I thought was of value, and send it off to my Bill Bradley list," Chakin explained. His sources ranged from news sites such as CNN.com and MSNBC.com, to the biting humor of columnist Molly Ivins, to political sites such as democracywatch.com. Some days he checked information at presidential history sites to augment his e-mail message. Chakin said he tried to be bipartisan, knowing his e-mail list included both conservative Republicans and liberal Democrats. "In every e-mail I sent I said, 'Here is my purpose for sending this: If you don't want to be on this, don't hesitate to say thank you but no thank you,'" Chakin said. "And many people did that—not a lot—but enough for me to know that not everyone wanted to hear about politics. But people with very different points of view than mine really appreciated it."

Chakin's publishing venture would have been much more difficult, if not impossible, before 2000. Chakin and others interested in political news could tap into a vast amount and variety of information. The Internet was made for political junkies willing to drill down ten levels to get detailed information or original documents.

As noted earlier, the political portals and campaign Web sites didn't attract a large following, but the news and other informational sites did. The Democracy Online Project at George Washington University reported that 35 percent of Americans used the Internet to get information about politics, campaigns, or issues in the news. That's up from 25 percent just two years prior.[39] The Pew Internet and the American Life Project found the audience grew during the campaign.[40] The zenith was achieved on Election Day, and traffic continued to be strong through the recount controversy. Political news pages showed as much as a 366 percent increase in traffic on Election Day over the previous day.[41] Twelve percent of Americans went online for political news on Election Day, and even more (18 percent) checked out news the next day, according to the Pew Research Center. That was four times the normal traffic for news. And it remained steady for a week.[42]

News consumption trends and habits indicated the new medium took a bite out of the old: TV news viewership and newspaper readership.[43] The most popular news sources for campaign information: MSNBC.com and CNN.com.[44] People went to news from national or local news outlets most frequently, according to Pew, followed by news from commercial online services, such as AOL.[45] Why was Web political news and information sought out during 1999–2000 more than ever before? Surely the increase mirrors the swell of people online. But at least three other factors stand out: timeliness, depth in content, and breadth of viewpoints.

Timeliness

Dan Chakin liked the instant information at his fingertips. He often compared and contrasted sources. For political junkies and for those inside the news business the news gathering changed dramatically from 1996 to 2000 due to the Internet. Picture this example from convention night at nytimes.com: National Editor Eric Owles was arguing with writer Julian Barnes about changing his story. Owles's boss in New York just phoned to complain that Barnes's story needed updating by adding the latest quote from John McCain's speech to the top. A *New York Times* print reporter doing duty at nytimes.com, Barnes disagreed with Owles. "I was trying to make it artful; if you put the quote up top, it just doesn't make sense," Barnes said.

Owles knew that Web reporting doesn't allow time to develop the artful story—this was breaking news. It had to go—now.[46] If nytimes.com didn't have it, people like Chakin went elsewhere. The new twenty-four-hour cycle for election news increased the pace for all reporters.[47] "There's a sense of urgency here that *The New York Times* has never seen before," said Owles. No longer is the best stuff saved for the morning paper. If something was happening, said Owles, it went on the Web.[48] News professionals interviewed for this book believed that their election coverage helped cement online news as part of the media landscape.[49]

Depth

Readers of online news found a variety of political information: news, opinion, timelines, cartoons, video, and links to more of the same.[50] One news editor called the Internet the "killer app" because of its capacity to offer volume and context in ways the other media can't. The Internet merged the video of TV, the photos and graphics of magazines, the political commentary of talk radio, and the details of newspapers. In addition, it offered a feature no other media could—a search function.

Web users searching the Center for Responsive Politics found detailed information about campaign contributions on its site, opensecrets.org. Donations were categorized according to a variety of measures, including state/region, industry, and profession. Although such information had always been available to journalists and campaigns, the site made it available to everyone.

Other examples of political content on the Internet included:

- voting results, down to the county level, when polls closed on primary days
- maps showing where to vote by neighborhood
- easy online registration, with 25,000 people doing so at voter.com alone

- a first-ever mini-documentary on political convention history, "Ballots to Bits," streamed at washingtonpost.com
- court documents from *Bush v. Gore*, the postelection judicial fight
- moderated chats, such as one at ABCNews.com with Sam Donaldson interviewing comedian and commentator Al Franken
- entertaining features such as animated cartoons of bobbing Bush and Gore heads on stick bodies at CNN.com; a dunk-the-candidate game at foxnews.com; and the Scuttle Button, a puzzle made from old campaign buttons, at washingtonpost.com
- streamed political Webcasts such as MSNBC's *Politics Only*, a five-day-a-week mini-newscast, and a daily show, *Political Points*, a partnership between ABCNews.com and *The New York Times*[51]

The amount of digital information, along with the variety of sources, was cause for some concern about accuracy and truth. Take, for example, drudgereport.com. Site founder Matt Drudge made a name for himself by digging up—and e-publishing—behind-the-scenes Washington information. But some conjecture published as fact proved to be false:

> Texas Governor George W. Bush is on the verge of selecting his running mate for the race to take the White House. Now, the DRUDGE REPORT, which was first to report that Sen. Dole had chosen Jack Kemp in '96 [beating CNN's Bob Novak by forty-eight hours], can reveal: Oklahoma Governor Frank Keating is Bush's current choice for the slot! While other names continue to swirl around Bush, Keating has emerged as not only the front-runner, but he is now considered by campaign insiders to be the de facto nominee.[52]

But a study by a consortium of academics and journalists found the Internet to be largely dependable. "Contrary to the idea that the Internet is full of opinionated argument or unsubstantiated innuendo, campaign sourcing on the Internet was strong. More than one-in-five (21 percent) of all lead stories had more than seven sources. And overall, more than half had at least five sources."[53]

Breadth

The Web offered a variety of viewpoints from established news organizations, alternative news sources, and public-interest groups. Chakin, the political junkie who reads news in bed at night, said one of the best features of Internet news is the unfiltered access. "There's a difference in that which is fed to you by radio and TV and actually reading and making your own interpretation, slowing down to read, or going to a hyperlink to get more," Chakin said.

Chakin's desire mirrored that of many citizens during Election 2000. For the first time, the Pew Center found that a majority of voters (53 percent) thought news organizations exerted too much influence on the outcome of the presidential election.[54] The new information providers on the Internet offered a complement and competition to the mainline media. A public-interest site, webwhiteandblue.com, enlisted seventeen top-traffic Web sites to carry its icon and link so users at yahoo.com or aol.com could easily reach it. The site listed the platforms and points of view of many presidential candidates at times when the most popular news sites tended to report mostly on the front-runners.[55] While these alternative sites didn't attract a large audience, they did provide a breadth of viewpoints not always seen in traditional media.

The hope that the Internet would engender a wealth of original stories didn't materialize. Too many of the established regional and national news organizations simply put their newspaper or broadcasts on the Internet, with minimal additional content. An Election Night study by the well-respected journalism organization the Poynter Institute found too little reporting about ordinary people and too few stories that were interesting. These evaluators expressed disappointment that even the alternative new outlets, such as *Salon* and *Slate*, didn't create much original content. "*Salon* posted a colorful and compelling story about Hillary Clinton, which was terrific, but stories like that were rare," the report noted.[56]

However, the Internet did give readers more opportunity than they'd had in previous elections to share their opinions. E-mail empowered them by putting them in immediate touch with writers. Timothy Noah, writer of the "Chatterbox" column at slate.com, said he appreciated when his writing sparked a dialogue. Occasionally it made more accurate journalism. Noah recounted to the authors how his readers quickly corrected his interpretation of Florida election law in an article lambasting Florida secretary of state Katherine Harris. Thus came his mea culpa: "Correction, 11/28: The plague of misunderstandings and misinformation besetting Indecision 2000 finally caught up with Chatterbox: I completely botched this one."

"It's sort of that perfect accountability you have on the Web. Even if the reader had no idea what the statute said, they could read it themselves," Noah said. "I ended up saying, 'wow, I really blew this.'"[57]

The Cart before the Horse

Eric Owles, of nytimes.com, says nobody in the profession really believed the hype that the Internet would impact the 2000 election the way television did in 1960. "But what has happened has not been revolutionary in terms of the people who watched, but rather in what you're able to do and the level of interaction you can get with candidates," Owles said. Indeed, the most stunning successes of the Internet, particularly by the media and political institutions, were those instances when the media stopped mediating and the political parties stopped spinning. When the institutions stopped using the Internet only as a means to control and distribute messages and used it also to enable two-way communications, connections occurred. Many of these connections led to what its participants described over and over as a sense of community. Connectivity is the genesis of community, and community is the foundation of civic engagement. It is at that point that there is interest among us in each other, and news and information is sought after. The early expectations that the Internet would energize democracy because of the amount and quality of information was, perhaps, putting the cart before the horse.

The campaigns made noble attempts at community building and organizing but still didn't risk pushing the medium to its full potential. The amount of information available tantalized the political faithful—those already engaged—and only occasionally intrigued the average voter. The institutions showed a pulse and the first stirrings toward building community. But to completely comprehend and appreciate the Internet's contribution one must look elsewhere, outside of and underneath the large institutions.

5

HOPE

JOSEPH A. MORRIS, A CHICAGO ATTORNEY AND FORMER
president of the United Republican Fund of Illinois, says he's basically a
low-tech guy. He uses e-mail, of course, and the computer is an important
tool for both his occupation and his other activities, but he's not part of the
cyberculture. He doesn't know a megabyte from a Google search. But for
ten days in November 2000, he was both Internet cult hero to the Republican recount killers and notorious spam-meister to the editors of nearly
every major newspaper in the country. It all started when Morris exercised
his right and, he thought, civic duty to write a letter to the editor and to
public officials, which he copied to thirty friends with a recommendation
to do the same. His message went out by e-mail on November 9.[1]

Morris was miffed that Al Gore had not conceded the election to Bush
and was instead demanding that votes be recounted. Morris's message to
his friends suggested that they write to their editors and public officials,
making it clear that Gore should relent. Morris said people "must bom-
bard the news media and our public officials. If it becomes widely reported—and it will—that there is a groundswell demanding that Gore
back down and not embarrass the country, he will have to relent."[2] Morris
included a list of newspaper editors and government officials, complete
with phone numbers and e-mail addresses. The editors of the *Chicago Tribune*, *Chicago Sun-Times*, *New York Post*, and *The Boston Globe*, among
others, were targeted.[3]

PHOTO 5.1   Joseph A. Morris

To Morris's surprise, his e-mail took on a life of its own as it circulated among Republican address books. Within days, his basic message, morphed slightly by the hands of thousands of friends of friends of friends, started clogging the in-boxes of major newspapers from coast to coast. Republicans everywhere rallied around the idea that a virtual grassroots uprising, vented on the media, would yield some press. The weight of public opinion would have to make an impression. Perhaps an editorial demanding that Gore back down or at least an article describing the size and scope of the scorn for Gore's recount bid would result. Some papers, such as *The Philadelphia Inquirer,* had to install blocks on their e-mail systems because they could not handle the 4,000 e-mail messages that came through. Editors at *USA Today, The Washington Post,* and the *Los Angeles Times* reported getting thousands of similar e-mails. One editor reported getting a hundred e-mails an hour, all of them substantively the same.[4] The bombardment Morris had asked for turned into a deafening barrage that brought the editorial departments at several newspapers to their virtual knees. Predictably, the blizzard of e-mails actually had the opposite effect that Morris had hoped for. The sheer volume made the message unintelligible. It angered the recipients. Bruce Dodd, editorial page editor at the *Chicago Tribune,* told a reporter, "It has quickly escalated to a nuisance."[5]

Gore conceded when the U.S. Supreme Court took away his options a month later. Morris's e-mail storm played no role in determining the outcome of that decision, and as far as the recipients of his messages were concerned, few regarded it with anything but scorn. Some might see failure in Morris's attempt at civic engagement. After all, nothing came of it.

What is clearly evident, however, is that at any time any of us may be only two or three forwarded e-mails from thousands of strangers—friends of friends—who, because of that link, may share many of our passions. Morris's tiny, thirty-name address book acted as a detonator that set off a firestorm of cloned messages within a few days and tens of thousands within a week. All of the ingredients were present: an incendiary political situation watched intensely by a whole nation, a few minutes on the computer by a man who wanted his voice heard, and an Internet that could speed his message along from point to point at light speed. Never before has such power to communicate, instigate, and inspire been vested in average people, and here we are, nearly all of us with online access, within a few keystrokes of the same breathtaking charge.

Writing letters to the editor is one of the many forms of civic engagement that have declined over the last thirty years.[6] Perhaps we just don't have the time, or we don't think anybody would read the letter. Maybe we think that writing a letter doesn't do any good; it's just one small voice calling out from the wilderness. But as Joseph Morris's e-mail campaign showed, the Internet in the hands of an average individual with a bone to pick is a powerful instrument. He didn't write one letter; he essentially wrote tens of thousands. His letters were not printed in the local editorial section, but his whole campaign was covered by nearly every major newspaper in the country. What should give all of us pause, and a sense of hope for the use of the Internet in civic engagement, is that Joseph Morris is just one of over 150 million Internet users in the United States today, and every one of them has a bone to pick.

The Short Circuit

It is quite natural to think of the Internet as a distribution medium such as film, television, radio, print publishing, or any form of mediated, one-way, one-to-many messaging. The World Wide Web, that part of the Internet most visible to the average Net surfer, is replete with graphics, text, audio, and video. It can and does look and behave like other media. However, the Internet is first and foremost a network that users employ for unmediated, two-way, one-to-one and many-to-many communications. Esther Dyson, founder of Edventure Holdings and former chair of the Internet Corporation for Assigned Names and Numbers, sees the technology taking society to a level the traditional media cannot. The Internet, she believes, "is the tool of the non-establishment" that will change the political power structure. "The Internet is a medium of conspiracy, a medium of people not heard. It is profoundly disruptive. It asks you to talk back."[7] Because of this fundamental characteristic, everyone on the Internet during the 2000 election was a coequal partner in a political drama, not just providers or consumers of content, as they were in other media.

Neither the media nor the candidates used the Internet effectively for *interacting* with voters, essentially short-circuiting any chance they had of truly connecting with the online electorate. The message to voters, quite often, seemed to be "don't interrupt." The media disseminated news and did a fairly commendable job of covering the campaigns; they provided links to additional, deeper bodies of knowledge and conducted online polls to obtain voter feedback. However, media sites did not provide a forum for real political discourse, and several attempts to fabricate public forums or online question-and-answer sessions were largely unsuccessful. It's possible that the media simply had no interest in promulgating online civic journalism, and so they put little effort into enabling and promoting public forums. In fairness, the public didn't readily cooperate when the media or the candidates did provide interactive opportunities. We logged in to a Webcast sponsored by Harvard's Shorenstein Center in Washington, D.C., which featured a panel of political reporters discussing the campaign. A chat-room designed to involve site visitors in the panel discussion was conducted concurrently, and the text-based musings of the Internet audience were displayed side-by-side on the Web page with the streaming video and audio. Even though the chat-room facilitator repeatedly urged the visitors to ask questions of the panelists, chat-room participants wandered, completely disconnected from anything discussed by the panelists, and vice versa. Neither group acknowledged that the other existed.

Perhaps voters were skeptical about traditional media sites' motives and suspicious of their methods or were reacting to the larger context within which such efforts were put forward. Voters may have recognized what scholar Rita Kirk Whillock chillingly suggests when she writes, "Political uses of the Web have deprived individuals of an effective public voice while perpetuating a voice that is of more value to the propagandist than to the group of individuals involved."[8]

Although the Internet originally was developed by the U.S. Defense Department, it was adopted early on by members of the counterculture who saw it as an excellent way to connect people with similar beliefs who were separated by time and space. Stewart Brand, who started the Whole Earth Catalog and was at the epicenter of several cultural revolutions in the San Francisco Bay area, was also founder of the WELL in 1985, the cybercommunity Howard Rheingold glorifies in *The Virtual Community: Homesteading on the Electronic Frontier*. Rheingold describes the WELL's early inhabitants: "The Whole Earth network—the granola-eating utopians, the solar-power enthusiasts, serious ecologists and the space-station crowd, immortalists, Biospherians, environmentalists, social activists—was part of the core population from the beginning."[9]

The counterculture's presence on the Internet even has scholars such as Andrew Calcutt debating whether the Internet will be the end of the nation-state, because of the way it empowers individuals, or the advent of Big Brother, because of the power of control that could potentially be exercised.[10] On balance, the Internet community continues to behave in an anarchistic, somewhat antiauthoritarian manner, even as its numbers swell with average, everyday people. What was designed as a technological marvel—one that can avoid downtime by routing itself around nuclear blasts—has become a cultural marvel in the way that it routes itself around corporate control, censorship, and even copyright laws.

Until a couple of years ago, anyone could purchase a domain name with somebody else's name in it. Zack Exley, a former union organizer from Boston, created the parody Web site gwbush.com and demanded $350,000 from the Bush campaign to sell the domain name back.[11] At one point during the campaign, people began offering to sell their votes to the highest bidder on e-Bay before they were stopped by California secretary of state Bill Jones. Gore and Nader supporters traded their votes over the Internet in an effort to prevent Gore losses in tightly contested races, while providing Nader with the 5 percent of votes cast nationally to qualify for federal election dollars. Even the millions of Napster transactions, most by ordinary music lovers, provide hard evidence that the Internet functioned as a platform for the unfettered exchange of messages, ideas, and private property.

David Legard, writing for the Singapore Bureau of the IDG news service, analyzed the Internet from the viewpoint of Eastern philosophy, ruminating on whether or not the Internet is a yin or a yang construct. "According to the ancient *I Ching* and *Tao Te Ching* texts, yin represents all that is informal, consensual, and flexible and yang represents all that is orthodox, formal, and rigid. . . . The Internet—anarchic, personal and anonymous—is pure yin," he said. "It is a perfect fit with modern Western notions of individual freedom superseding communal benefit, democracy before prescribed stability."[12] As hard as they tried not to be during the 2000 election, U.S. political institutions are hierarchical and inflexible, and they could not disguise their yang-ness.

All of these things taken together—the technology, culture, psychology, and even the soul of the Internet—may have contributed to a disconnect between the political institutions and the electorate. It is possible that the institutions misunderstood the two terms *Internet* and *World Wide Web*. If the Internet can be thought of as a superhighway, then the Web should be imagined as the signage. While the institutions covered the Web landscape with billboards and broadcasts, the electorate whisked by on their way to someplace else—usually to see each other. They behaved as Mitchell Kapor, the founder of Lotus Development Corporation, predicted to an interviewer: "Instead of a small number of groups having privileged positions as speakers—broadcast networks and powerful newspapers—we are entering an era of communication of the many to the many. And while there will still be editors and intermediaries and people who will be looked to for their wisdom or attractiveness, the nature of the technology itself has opened up a space of much greater democratic possibility. We must not lose the opportunity in this country to run that great experiment."[13]

Online Optimism

If the political parties and the media did not make the most effective use of the Internet during the 2000 election, what good is the Internet? More than 100 million people voted in the 2000 election. About 50 million voted for Al Gore. But only 6.5 million gave Gore's Web site even a passing glance on the day before the election, or about the average number of people who see a movie *every day*. Media sites had a few big days but cut back operations shortly after the election. If voters did not flock to the political and media sites to consume information and news about the election, what role could the Internet possibly play in reeducating and reinvigorating them? Compared with their reliance on other media, people did not use the Internet to become more politically informed. If that weren't sobering enough, the Pew Center found that people who use the Internet are not any more likely to be politically active than those who do not, at least in the ways that the Pew Center measured. Is there hope for the Internet in our democracy?

We turned our lens toward the Internet users—often barely visible among the elephant-sized institutions. Our study became largely qualitative as we began studying human interactions on the Internet and began measuring the social impact of this technological phenomenon. We believed we had to look past the survey data and page view audits. Without wading into the tangled and unresolved debates in social science concerning quantitative versus qualitative work, we found, as sociologist Alan Wolfe did, that in issue after issue "the data one obtains from surveys and the data one obtains from more qualitative interviews are not always the same."[14]

In a speech he gave to the Computer Science and Telecommunications Board (CSTB) in February 1993, Congressman Edward Markey recalled how Robert Kennedy, visiting Detroit twenty-five years earlier, after the riots, "spoke of the difficulty of measuring the wealth of a community by quantifying intangible assets or values."[15] Kennedy said:

We cannot measure national spirit by the Dow Jones Average nor national achievement by the Gross National Product.

For the Gross National Product includes air pollution and advertising for cigarettes, and ambulances to clear our highways of carnage. It counts special locks for our doors and jails for the people who break them. . . . Gross National Product swells with the equipment for the police to put down riots in our cities. And though it is not diminished by the damage these riots do, still it goes up as slums are rebuilt on their ashes.

And if the Gross National Product includes all of this, there is much that it does not comprehend. It does not allow for the health of our families, the quality of their education, or the joy of their play.

. . . The Gross National Product measures neither our wit nor our courage, neither our wisdom nor our learning, neither our compassion nor our devotion to our country. It measures everything, in short, except that which makes life worthwhile; and it can tell us everything about America— except whether we are proud to be Americans.

Markey compared Kennedy's remarks to the difficulty of measuring the Internet's social effects. He said, "Similarly, we can look at the speeds of our telecommunications networks, the millions of miles of cable, fiber, and copper, ascertain the processing power of advanced computers, and measure their memory capacities. . . . In the final analysis, we can tell people everything about the state and quality of our network except those things that make use of such a network worthwhile."[16] Like Kennedy and Markey, we felt we had to go directly to the people themselves to measure the wit, courage, wisdom, and compassion of Internet users and not rely solely on survey data or Web site page views to judge the Internet's value in the political process. We became convinced that if the Internet is playing—or can play—a role in restoring social capital, either in its old or in new forms, we'd have to find it by talking to ordinary people.

We interviewed more that two hundred people who had used the Internet for political purposes, and we discovered that the citizens themselves found the most appropriate political uses of the Internet during the 2000 election. The interviewees used the Internet in creative ways to deepen their political involvement, largely because the Internet made it possible for the electorate to participate in ways that were not possible in previous elections. In our case studies, they used the Internet to create meaningful relationships, to establish connectedness with others whom they did not know in the flesh (at least initially) but with whom they shared beliefs, a sense of identity, a course of action, or thought-provoking discourse. In several cases, their actions harkened back to the era of true grassroots movements.

One of the criticisms of so-called grassroots activism in recent years is that it has been captured by money. Corporations and well-heeled individuals can hire firms to generate this kind of grassroots activity—writing Congress, phoning, petitions, and so on—and make it appear genuine and spontaneous when it is not. What we once thought of as grassroots politics has become "Astroturf politics."[17] The Internet, used in the way we observed, offers the promise of letting individuals reclaim a piece of the Astroturf (perhaps the middle of the field if not the red zone and the goal line) and make it grass again.

The exchanges that occurred between people on the Internet showed evidence of honesty, trust, and reciprocity, and the individuals involved often expressed heartfelt attachments to each other. The resulting relationships yielded tangible benefits to both the individual and the group and in many cases had some notable political outcome. Since these relationships usually involved many people (in a few cases numbering in the thousands) we call them *communities*.

Cybercommunities

In the social sciences, there may not be two more elusive subjects than how to define community and whether the Internet is a medium that can support one. Everyone agrees that a community must be a place where the needs of both the individual and the collective are met. The collective provides for each individual an environment to reach potential as a human being, while each person provides the collective with a measure of individual skills, gifts, and talents. When they are functioning properly, communities that help the individual also tend to have individuals who work toward the betterment of the community in a spiraling, symbiotic relationship.[18]

The community, then, is the central square where social capital is invested and earns interest. No meaningful connection between social capital and the Internet can be established (aside from its use as a medium, which we have already discussed) without first determining if Internet-based communities provide an environment where individuals and the collective form mutually beneficial connections. Disagreement over Internet-based communities begins, though it is not limited to, the discussion of whether or not the *place* where individuals gather to form connections must be real and physical or can be imaginary and virtual. Can real connections be made in imaginary places?

One definition of community insists that the members coexist in time and space—that they interact in person. Another camp describes a community as any group of people who share a common interest or belief and who support each other for both individual and collective good, as in the gay community or the academic community. When this kind of community comes together over the Internet, it is referred to as a *cyber-community*.

Strong arguments are made by those who believe there can be no "out of body" community. It is impossible, they say, for people to form communities if they do not or cannot interact face-to-face in shared public space. There must be actions between them involving discourse, contracts, promises, or shoulder-to-shoulder heavy lifting. These are not simply symbolic acts but real acts of conjoined efforts that result in tangible accomplishments. The social theorist Ferdinand Tönnies, writing in 1887, used the term *gemeinschaft* to describe a type of community in which people live in close proximity with each other. They share "real and organic life" and common beliefs, needs, goals, and rewards for living and working together.[19] Earlier in the same century, Alexis de Tocqueville found the United States filled with communities such as this and marveled at how smoothly the American democratic system operated within them. The nostalgic imagery of the gemeinschaft is of older, simpler times, and both de Tocqueville's and Tönnies's ideas left a lasting impression on thinkers throughout the twentieth century. Modern political scientist Richard P. Hiskes says that such public acts are still necessary for the collective life to emerge. The essential public acts of democracy include all of those forms of social capital Robert Putnam sees declining—letter writing, running for office, voting—and extend to such things as "how we spend our time with our fellow citizens—their real presence, not their cyber presence in chat rooms; how we take the time to gather in all our public places."[20]

There are those who are certain that cybercommunities are full-blooded relatives of the real ones and meet the truly important criteria of community. Largely through personal involvement in or prolonged exposure to these virtual communities, writers like Howard Rheingold insist that cyberspace can be home to groups of people where both the individual and the collective grow and prosper together. Real community is described by Robert Bellah and his colleagues as "a context within which personal identity is formed, a place where fluent self-awareness follows the currents of communal conversation and contributes to them."[21] Rheingold and others *lived* in virtual communities where they formed their identities and contributed their gifts back to the collective.

There is also a school of thought that sits somewhere between the absolute critics and the true-believing cheerleaders of cybercommunities. First, their definition of community includes both the material type and the symbolic. Jan Fernback writes, "A community is a bounded territory of sorts (whether physical or ideological), but it can also refer to a sense of common character, identity or interests . . . as with the virtual community."[22] This idea of community turns away slightly from the rigid view enshrined in the gemeinschaft model and gives a nod toward theories that recognize times have changed. We are where we are as a society. Technological advances, especially those that have changed the way we communicate with each other, have made old forms of community very difficult to maintain while, ironically, shrinking the globe. Social, political, economic, and cultural goods flow back and forth through the airwaves and fiber now, and that means we have new forms of community that connect through those same channels. Steven G. Jones believes that the Internet can provide its users with connections for communities to develop. But he cautions that "the Internet is not a social world unto itself, a cyberspace divorced from other spaces, but . . . it is part and parcel of a [real, physical] social world."[23]

The debate cannot be resolved theoretically; it is an empirical question. We have researched and written an empirical book to try and untangle it.

We believe that cybercommunities exist. The remainder of this book shows why we think this.

The New Online Communities

We could have avoided confrontation by calling our groups of Internet users who bonded for political purposes something other than communities. However, we could not ignore the obvious—that the people whose Internet activity we studied displayed every characteristic of a real community except (though in some cases including) face-to-face meeting, which some scholars argue isn't necessary anyway. They grew and evolved as individuals and contributed to the collective. The collective, in response, rewarded them. In the process, various forms and degrees of social capital were created. We present them in the following chapters and leave it to the reader to decide if the people, their cohorts, and their activities described in the following chapters add up to community and whether these communities are involved in valuable forms of civic engagement.

Nearly everyone who has written about the Internet and the emergence of communities on it studied it before Election 2000. The people featured in their studies and analyses are now in the minority of Internet users. During the year 2000, the population of Internet users grew dramatically, not only in number but also in diversity.

Many ordinary people came online during that year, joining the technophiles, early adopters, and educated and affluent whites, who had dominated the online universe for some time. Mitchell Kapor, teaching at Massachusetts Institute of Technology (MIT), tells about how one of his students, a card-carrying member of the Internet cognoscenti, moaned about the onslaught of the masses.

One of the students remarked that he was a participant in an Internet discussion group in which a new user from AOL announced his presence. Emphatically the student said, "I knew he was going to say something clueless before he even posted two words." I replied, "Let me see if I've got this right. You believe that all America Online users are clueless. You know nothing about this person other than that he has an account on America Online. You haven't seen him write anything, but yet you judge him. Let me ask you a question: If you did this in the real world, not in cyberspace, what would it be called?"[24]

Kapor himself coined the term *domainism* for the attitude of Internet old timers toward the new online users, who are gradually nudging aside the natives.

During 2000 grandmothers were wired by their middle-aged children so they could exchange e-mail with their grandchildren. More school-children got Internet access from their classrooms. Wireless Internet be-came widely available, giving cell phone and Palm Pilot owners Internet access anywhere, any time. AOL Time Warner expanded its Road Runner service, bringing broadband to its cable customers. Inexpensive Internet-only appliances such as WebTV became widely available, so people who were intimidated by computers could go online from their television sets. Today's Internet population has a far more egalitarian profile than the privileged, elite, insular groups in the late 1980s and early 1990s. Even so, many commentators still describe the relationships that Internet users form in less than complimentary terms. There is a preconception that the moment someone gets access to the Internet, he or she adopts the antiso-cial behaviors that many early users (the subjects of early studies) made prevalent and that critics chastised.

Our study of election-year Internet users uncovered a diverse and in-teresting group of everyday people living in the social capital–deprived world Putnam chronicled. They lived their real lives where suburban iso-lation and sprawl, the pressures of the two-income family, the effects of electronic entertainment, and the generation gap had steadily shredded the connective tissue of their society.[25] Online, they were suddenly em-powered with the mechanism to stitch it back together. Studied before the Internet became a part of their lives, they may very well have appeared to be suspended in some sort of apathetic state. They may have been too busy with their careers to join the Kiwanis Club, too far away from town to attend a political meeting regularly, and too hooked on the TV sitcom *Friends* to read the paper. After the Internet, they joined more organizations or made associations with others online, because time and space became inconsequential. The desire for connectedness had been present all the time. The Internet and the election gave them the means and the reason to reconnect.

Some of our profiles feature people who joined together, over the Internet, with others with whom they shared an *identity*. S. B. Woo, a college professor, contacted a number of friends by e-mail to determine if they, like him, were interested in increasing the political clout of the Asian-American community. They were, and within six months Woo and his cohorts had organized a large and influential bloc of Asian-Americans, including some Republicans, who agreed to collectively support a single candidate—Al Gore. Still others organized around a common *belief*. Jeff Cardille, a student at the University of Wisconsin, helped people make contact with strangers over the Internet, with whom they traded their votes (Gore for Nader). Even though the legality and ethics of the transactions were debated, the level of political will and personal trust involved suggests a very strong commitment of social capital by the parties.

Many others we write about formed communities of *action* over the Internet. Zeke Spier was a nineteen-year-old college freshman when he became one of hundreds arrested for street protests during the Republican convention in Philadelphia. He became radicalized and thereby willing to take the consequences, almost entirely by reading about political corruption and government-sponsored misdeeds over the Internet. The Internet helped him connect with others who had reached the same conclusions and who wanted to express themselves in the same way—actively, on the street. Kevin Matthews put up a Web site where people could sign online petitions, which thousands used. The echo of that form of civic engagement turned into appearances on TV and radio talk shows, articles in newspapers, and other publicity that helped further his causes.

These are but a few of the examples that constitute the following chapters, which speak largely for themselves as models of civic engagement over the Internet. Many of the profiles have similar characteristics. The subjects were at the epicenter of some form of political action during the last election, and their deeds pulled others into that action. They all used the Internet extensively, if not exclusively, to accomplish their goal. The

Internet was more than a convenience for them. It was the engine that made their activity possible. In most cases, they were the first to use the Internet for civic engagement in precisely the way they did.

Notice also the variation in the profiles in terms of age, gender, ethnicity, wealth, geography, education, and political beliefs. And though we readily admit that many of these individuals were politically active and engaged before they became Internet users, many of the people they touched with their actions were not. They caught the attention of ordinary people on the electronic highway, not with billboards and broadcasts but with roadmaps and satellite positioning systems. If it is true that Americans have lost their way in real life and have become distant and alienated from each other, then perhaps they are becoming reoriented and directing their attention back to each other over the Internet.

6

COMMUNITIES OF BELIEF

ALL JIM CODY THOUGHT HE WAS DOING WHEN HE SET UP HIS Web site was connecting people with the same political beliefs—that George Bush would be bad for the environment and a generous friend to big oil and that he must not win the election. More than 5,000 people who visited Cody's site used it to pair up with each other and, in a demonstration of trust rarely seen in the flesh, agreed to swap their votes. Using Cody's site, Ralph Nader supporters in states where the presidential race was too close to call agreed to vote for Gore, while Gore supporters in states where Bush would be the clear winner or Gore was far behind agreed to vote for Nader, thus helping him toward the benchmark 5 percent of votes cast and a share of federal election funds for the Green party in 2004. Then Cody got an e-mail:

This letter is to formally notify you that voteswap2000 is engaged in criminal activity in the state of California. Your Web site specifically offers to broker the exchange of votes throughout the United States of America. This activity is corruption of the voting process in violation of the Elections Code Sections 18521 and 18522 as well as Penal Code Section 182 criminal conspiracy. These offenses are felonies that carry a maximum penalty of three years in state prison in California for each violation. The right to free and fair elections is a cornerstone of American democracy. Any person or entity that tries to exchange votes or brokers the exchange of votes will be pursued with the utmost vigor. I demand that you end this activity immediately. If you continue, you and anyone knowingly working with you may be criminally prosecuted to the fullest extent of the law.

Sincerely, Bill Jones, Secretary of State, California.

Suitably intimidated, Cody shut down his site immediately, and the fledgling community of belief seemingly dissipated with barely a trace. Except for those 5,000 votes.

As we have noted in earlier chapters, the four types of communities we found on the Internet are more readily distinguishable as conceptual entities than they are in reality. In virtual space, strands of belief, action, identity, and discourse necessarily intertwine. But together, they are woven into a general phenomenon that forms the central observation and argument of this book: that ground-level, bottom-up, person-to-person activity is where the real impact and benefit of Internet technology was to be found during the election and is also where most future efforts at Internet-aided political participation and civic engagement should be directed.

What we are calling communities of *belief* are marked primarily by points of view or political ideologies—organized sets of beliefs about the most important goals the nation should aspire to and what government should or should not do in order to best achieve them. In more traditional, non-Internet terms, the analogs for these communities would include challenge groups like those that arose in the 1960s, such as Students for a Democratic Society (SDS) and the Democratic Socialists of America (DSA), or more recently and toward the right on the political spectrum, the Christian Coalition and the Federalist Society for Law and Public Policy Studies. Communities of belief almost always lead to and encourage political *action* on the part of their members, but they remain anchored in particular beliefs.

The Vote Traders

Perhaps the most widely reported and discussed of our grassroots-based stories is that of Jeff Cardille and other Nader traders, like Cody. Nader traders rallied to the idea of exchanging votes between Gore and Nader, first on the Internet and then, and more widely, off of it. By seeing the group as one of our communities of *belief*, the reader gains a more critical and nuanced perspective on the fevered criticisms that were leveled against it, namely that it was engaging in illegal vote selling and that it was corrupting the electoral system. As participants in a community of beliefs, the individuals involved in the group were navigating what everyone engaged in a common cause must navigate: the forging of compromise in order to pursue a common end and the ongoing maintenance of trust. The Nader traders found and trusted each other out of a common purpose of action; this common purpose was political liberalism and a desire to avoid contributing to a Bush victory by voting for Nader in states where the election was tight.

Obviously, agreeing to switch votes is an activity requiring the highest levels of interpersonal trust. But although much of the trading that actually occurred took place between individuals who knew each other in real terms, the virtual beginnings were essential for the quick promulgation of the idea and for the original demonstration that it could work. If it could work on the Internet, then it could work elsewhere.

When James Madison and his colleagues at the Constitutional Convention in 1787 cobbled together the fragmented system of governmental structure we still live under today—a structure divided horizontally by the separation of powers and vertically by federalism, with its intertwining layers of local, state, and national government—they did not foresee the political and technological innovations that nationally based political parties would bring to the political system. In particular they did not anticipate the parties' ability to organize and unite geographically dispersed individuals for common national aims. The parties got around the roadblocks to national majoritarian rule that Madison and the other Framers had erected.

Perhaps by the same token, and on an admittedly much smaller scale, the Internet offers a similar way for individuals to get around the rigid structure of the current electoral system, with its winner-take-all selection process and its geographically based districting, which in turn supports the viable presence of only two major parties' candidates. Through the Internet, individuals created a virtual geographic base for Nader that extended across state lines, offering him the ability to compete nationally for liberals' votes. This is precisely what Nader trader Vic McMurray is getting at later in this chapter when she says that "we are smarter than the system we've been given."

"You're a 'Nader trader,' that's what you are. And everyone's going to know, because I'm going to spread the word."

So declared Jeff Cardille after a University of Wisconsin housemate walked through the door one afternoon around Labor Day and announced a breakthrough. She and her boyfriend visiting from Massachusetts had settled a long-running Al Gore versus Ralph Nader debate. "I've figured out my dilemma," Tanya Wagner told Cardille and the four others who shared the quarters. Wagner and her boyfriend were swapping votes: She backed Nader, but would vote for Gore in tightly contested Wisconsin; he supported Gore, but would vote for Nader in Massachusetts, where Gore was expected to win easily anyway.

PHOTO 6.1   Jeff Cardille

Cardille recalls how the deal was consummated between Wagner and her boyfriend. "He kept saying, 'You can't vote for Nader in Wisconsin; you need to vote for Gore in Wisconsin because it's going to be so close.' She said, 'I need to vote for Nader and that's what I'm going to do. You should actually be voting for Nader.' So they were at the bus stop one day and they thought, 'We can switch our votes.'"

Cardille was blustering about telling the world, but Wagner had struck a chord, and she had the house buzzing. Cardille was struggling with the same dilemma. A vote for Nader might hurt Gore, who needed every ballot in his neck-and-neck battle with Bush in Wisconsin and in more than a dozen other swing states where the race was close.

The vote trade idea simmered until the first of October, when Cardille decided it was just too good a notion not to share. He finally sent the e-mail that got the ball rolling on one of the first trade sites just two weeks before the November 7 election. And when he did, the curtain rose quickly on a national drama that illustrated how the speed and reach of the Internet can instantly transform any landscape, empowering the littlest people and shaking up the biggest. It would be several months before the participants themselves appreciated what had happened with such unprecedented speed in a political world where orthodoxy, money, caution, and conventional thinking rule, where innovation is as often punished as rewarded, and where little is done on the cheap or off the cuff.

Many Nader supporters were committed but conflicted as the election neared. Gore was clearly their second choice; Nader wasn't going to win. No one wanted to hand the election to Bush. Debate over what to do— and whether voting was a practical matter or one of principle—produced a coast-to-coast debate. The Nader trading inspired by the likes of Cardille, Steve Yoder, Jim Cody, Amy Morris, Jamin B. Raskin, and a handful of others thrilled those who believed their vote might otherwise be wasted. It troubled others, who recoiled at what they believed was un-American, immoral, and illegal. Several states—California most loudly— threatened lawsuits to stop the vote swapping that ensued. Some Republicans complained that it might cost Bush a victory. Gore suggested strongly that he would be hurt by votes cast for Nader; Democratic running mate Joseph I. Lieberman said outright that it would be damaging ("A vote for Nader is a vote for Bush"); and Nader himself condemned trading, saying on ABC's *This Week* that Bush had a "horrific record." Defeating the "bumbling Texas governor" should be a "slam dunk," Nader said. Minnesota's independent governor, Jesse Ventura, admonished potential vote swappers. He told ABC's *Good Morning America,* "Wasting your vote is not voting your heart and not voting your conscience."

Vote trading was perhaps the most intriguing flash of Internet influence in the election—a development that could be a teasing taste of the future. According to a loose tally and estimate for eleven of the sites, 16,024 swaps were consummated online, 1,412 of them in Florida. Nader partisans in the close states switched allegiance to Gore to help him there. Democratic swap mates—either in overwhelming Bush or Gore country—threw in for Nader, assured that they hadn't cost Gore a thing while gaining him a vote in a state where he needed it. The state-based winner-take-all system of the Electoral College has especially alienated voters in the states where the race has been lopsided. In all but two states, Nebraska and Maine, the top vote-getter gets every electoral vote from that state in the college. Margin of victory in a given state is meaningless when the president is not directly elected nationwide; in states where the likely outcome is generally known beforehand, each individual's vote means even less than it might have otherwise.

That is, unless the electoral stars are in alignment, and you can swap.

Democrats stuck in Bush strongholds were especially happy to vote for Nader to gain Gore a vote he would not otherwise have received in a critical race elsewhere. Two swappers were John and Margaret Morris, who live in Utah. They dealt with twenty-five-year-old daughter Amy, a San Francisco resident who created a trading site with just a week to go in the election. Although California was never in serious doubt for Gore, he did slip some in the late going and took heat for paying the state so little attention. Amy Morris voted for Gore and rang up two votes for Nader from her parents in return. Upset that threats of a lawsuit by California had intimidated Cody into shutting down his popular Los Angeles site, she started votetrader.org. "In Utah, if you voted for Gore, there never was any chance that Gore would win," said John Morris, a law professor who is also general counsel for the University of Utah. "Utah has the title for being the most Republican state in the country. So Democrats like us waste our votes in national elections. We were ideal candidates for this kind of an exchange." Says their daughter of her parents: "They're completely disenfranchised."

Because of many stories like the Morrises', Nader traders emerged from the election convinced that the mainstream media missed a big part of the story. The idea may have been born and fueled online mostly by younger voters, but it flourished offline and across generations and among voters who were anything but Web savvy. Nader traders believe thousands of people traded offline with friends and family, not blindly, faithlessly, and recklessly with strangers. It was common, they say, for people like John or Margaret Morris to trade offline with relatives or acquaintances they knew well. Indeed, Cardille's site— one of the first and one of the most popular—merely touted the idea of vote swapping. It did not offer, as some sites did, to actually match traders and help to connect them through databases, an idea that drew the particular ire of many state attorneys general who said the scheme was illegal.

"The mechanical swapping with strangers was only a small part of people who did it," says Cardille, who swapped offline with a friend from grad school who lived in Austin, Texas. "I directly know about twenty people who did it just personally among friends, and only one of them traded on the Internet. I definitely think hundreds of thousands of people did it. I've heard from enough people that I'm pretty convinced that it was really done by the kid who's always argued with his dad about politics. And the dad says, 'You're way too idealistic; some day you'll understand.' And the dad ends up voting for Nader in the election."

Still, the movement would have been nowhere without the Internet, which contributed its instant impact, lightning speed, and uncontrollable and unpredictable flourish in a two-week rush. Most who traded offline heard about it on the Internet or through the flood of media stories the Internet-spawned movement fed.

"I decided I was going to write an e-mail," Cardille remembers, thinking back to late October. "It looked pretty good. Then I realized that folks like something to click on to read more. So what I did was basically the same thing that I suppose other dot-com-type people do—look to see if the name is taken. I asked the Web thing to search for 'nadertrader,' and it wasn't there. So I looked in the Yellow Pages here and found Earthlink. I called them up and asked how much it costs to start a Web site. It was $70 to get the name ($35 a year). And then I had to pay for them to host it. So it was on the order of $200.

"My first thought was I ought to write an e-mail and send it to everybody. And then I realized that that might die out or mutate. But if the Web site was there, people would still be able to come back and see the longer, full idea. If you're like me, you probably get lots of forwarded e-mails, fragments of something that was a longer e-mail. I realized that somewhere down the line, it might be sort of unintelligible what the overall idea is. So I saw it in those first few days just as an information dissemination idea and Web site."

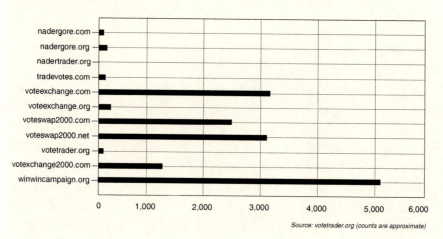

Source: votetrader.org (counts are approximate)

FIGURE 6.1   Nader trader vote-swapping results from a number of sites.

Just like that, nadertrader.org was open for business.

Cardille sent the e-mail to a handful of friends—somewhere between twenty and forty, he guesses—and did little more than paste it into the Web page address. The text laid out the concept of vote trading.

"All my site did was to distribute the idea. It didn't do any sort of mechanical swapping at all. No posting, no nothing. I didn't even have a feedback page or anything like that until much later. A few days after, on about Thursday or Friday, a couple of sites went up that did this, provided that mechanism for people to be able to swap their vote with a stranger. Mine was strictly the idea that you should create this community with people you already know. My girlfriend traded with her old college roommate. The other guy in my house traded with his old college friend. A friend of mine . . . swapped with his dad. I think the thing that gets the most attention is that you can connect with a stranger on the other side of the country who you'll never know, you'll never know what their face looks like. I think that's more appealing from a media angle. I think overall, though, it's a lot more likely that people did it with folks they already knew or with a friend of a friend. Like, for example, there's a case of a Unitarian church in Pittsburgh. A woman had heard about it through a friend and realized her parents in Indiana would be a way for her to connect all the folks in her church with all the folks in the Indiana church. So she set up a calling tree, where folks in Indiana, a Bush state, were paired with Pennsylvania, which was a swing state. So all of these Unitarians in Pittsburgh traded with folks there. None of that will register on any of the Internet-based Web sites. But it was through an idea that was registered through the Internet."

About fifteen church pairs traded votes, Cardille said. But Cardille is perhaps too swift to downplay the importance of the trading between strangers, for it is that phenomenon which illustrates most starkly vote trading's significance regarding social capital. It comes back to trust. It is certainly worth noting that friends and acquaintances, or even just acquaintances by extension through a common church, would trust each other enough to trade votes; but it is striking indeed that strangers could do this through the Internet.

Cardille himself busts the notion that online movements are started by and limited to technophiles. He's no computer whiz—he's never owned a computer—and his site wasn't fancy. "All I could figure out to do was put things in bold. No kidding. And to make the text bigger. So I just worked within those parameters."

The Cardille e-mail went out, and the site went up on Monday, October 23. Monday, there were zero hits. On Tuesday, the number leapt to 432. Wednesday logged 3,411; Thursday hit 10,448; and Friday, 22,963. By Wednesday, November 1, the one-day tally was a staggering 123,000. The final total: 429,000.

As is often the case with the Internet, there was a substantial measure of synchronicity. The idea of Nader trading sprang up in several places at different times, then flashed at once. American University constitutional law professor Jamin Raskin wrote an article that floated the idea of vote trading, and the piece appeared at 4:00 P.M. Pacific Time on October 24 in the online magazine *Slate,* the same day Cardille was drawing his very first couple hundred hits. Steve Yoder, a thirty-eight-year-old Washington, D.C., freelance writer, actually had had his site up since October 1 (vote-exchange.org), but by mid-October his message board arrangement had sealed just six matches. Cody, working out of Los Angeles, launched voteswap2000 on the 26th, directly in response to Raskin's column suggesting that a knowledgeable programmer could easily design a database that actually matched visitors; by the 30th, California's Republican secretary of state Bill Jones was talking about a lawsuit, and Cody was in retreat. That ignited even more media coverage and assured, in the minds of Cardille and the others, that the mainstream media stories would focus on the controversy and the questions about the legality of sites like Cody's that actually offered to help arrange online trades.

Yoder says Nader himself influenced Yoder's creation, which was not a database but simply a bulletin board. Potential traders connected by posting messages to the board, where they could pair off without ever making personal contact. (Later on, Yoder would require that posters include their e-mail address.) "I was listening to a Nader rally out in Denver in August," Yoder recalls, "and what struck me was that at one point in the speech, he talked about the need for Green voters to vote smart, to vote strategically. That planted the seed for me. Then I was arguing with a friend who is a Green voter. We were arguing whether in an election year like we had it was responsible to vote for Nader, and one thing led to another. That's what really got the ball rolling."

On October 2, Yoder e-mailed Steve Herrick, who was listed on the Green party's Web site as one of its three national coordinators. Yoder invited Herrick to visit his vote exchange site and to promote it if he liked the idea. Herrick e-mailed back the next day with an unequivocal response:

I'm sorry, I can't support this plan. Innovative as I think it is, I can't bring myself to encourage anyone anywhere to vote for Gore. What it comes down to is, I'm not afraid to spoil Gore. I'm quite content to watch the Democratic Party bite its nails before the election, and wonder where it went wrong afterwards. We Greens didn't come this far only to compromise and be co-opted. I understand your concern, but I don't share it.

All was quiet until the Raskin column appeared October 24. Yoder got wind of it and called Raskin, who immediately mentioned Yoder's site in a C-SPAN interview not much more than an hour later. Yoder also got a link to his site from *Slate*. Raskin, who employed interviews and commentary to champion Nader's unsuccessful challenge to be included in the presidential debates, said the idea of the Nader vote costing Gore the election was bugging him. "I am somewhat of a political realist, and I was getting increasingly anxious about the role that Nader's candidacy might play in facilitating a Bush victory. I was dreading the catastrophe that kind of happened. I remember clearly I stayed up one night tossing and turning, and this idea hit me that there's a way around it. All along in the campaign, lots of people, not just me, were saying, if you're a Nader voter in a swing state, you should think of voting for Gore. But that struck me as not a good deal. Nader was trying to get the 5 percent for federal funds for the Green party. And Gore was trying to get 270 in the Electoral College, and then it occurred to me because of the mechanics of the Electoral College that there was a way to make a deal.

"I woke up my wife, Sarah, and I said 'I really think this might be the way out. Do you think this is too cuckoo?' And she said, 'Well, it's a little bit out there, but why don't you go write it,' which is what I usually do, and I went up to my attic, and I wrote the article." Raskin, who often writes op-ed pieces for *The Washington Post* and *The Nation* magazine, contacted friends at *Slate* because there wasn't much time. The article was up within three or four days, on the 24th.

On the opposite coast from Raskin and Yoder was Cody, a freelance Web designer who was attending grad school at San Jose State and was inspired by the *Slate* article. Cody teamed with a business partner to put voteswap2000.com online at 5 P.M. PST on Thursday, October 26, forty-nine hours after Raskin suggested the idea in his piece for *Slate*. The Cody team's total investment was $35 plus the value of their time. Cody posted notices at about fifteen independent media center sites in big cities, online areas open to users. He chose cities in states where the race was either very close or very lopsided. "I posted just a little notice. 'Here's our URL. Here's what we're trying to do.' We started to see traffic in the hundreds the next morning."

Yoder started referring calls from the news media to Cody from his own site and even linked to it, advising visitors that Cody's creation actually had the software that could make matches. Friday was busy for Cody, starting with a call from Lisa Napoli, MSNBC's Internet reporter. *The Industry Standard* and Associated Press followed, as well as the *San Francisco Chronicle, Newsweek,* and CNN's *Burden of Proof.* Cody, Cardille, and Yoder all were in touch, and the group settled on Cardille to chat on Sunday with National Public Radio, because he was most comfortable with the media.

At Cody's site, visitors were asked what state they were from. If the site could help them with a swap, they were asked to enter their e-mail address and where they were from, and the software matched them with a swap mate. Someone like Cardille, the Nader supporter, would be paired with a Gore supporter in a state where the vice president was either hopelessly behind or well ahead. "When the database found a match," says Cody, "it would automatically send an e-mail to each one of those persons telling them they had been matched." The site encouraged swappers to contact each other and talk. After promising anonymity at first, by Saturday Cody and his partner decided that was a bad idea; they began to require visitors to provide their e-mails to the partners the database provided. By October 30, 5,000 people had been paired in 2,500 matches. This aspect of the vote trading illustrates how the Internet can stimulate and facilitate connections that are pursued offline as well as online.

Cardille remembers that for him "media attention was through the roof. I did a thing on our local ABC nightly news, which got picked up by ABC national. My cousin in Denver called my mom and said, 'Jeff's on TV, what's going on?' There were articles in *The New York Times* a few days later, on CNN's Web site, and all over the place."

The questions began coming. Is it moral? Is it legal? Is it right? Cardille, a thirty-three-year-old getting his Ph.D. in environmental studies, says he can't remember ever taking a class in politics in his life. But he is politically well versed. His earliest political memory is the Watergate hearings that interrupted *Sesame Street* when he was a six-year-old. "Nixon is a very bad man," he remembers his mother telling him. The youngster went on to develop a nuanced sense of political values. "Clearly," he says, "in this country, we have a secret ballot, and any informal agreement that a person makes on how they're going to vote is, in a legal sense and in my opinion, no different than the typical campaign strategies that all candidates do. 'If you vote for me, I will try to improve your life.' It's a trade in a legal sense, and in my opinion a First Amendment right of a candidate to say they'll do their best to do something for you without giving you a written contract. This is the same kind of verbal agreement, in my opinion."

Raskin says people were hung up on the idea of trading, a word he avoids. "My language has always been 'I have decided as a Nader supporter in a swing state to vote for Gore in the explicit hope that there will be Gore supporters in Mississippi or Texas who will vote for Nader and vice versa. As a Gore supporter in Texas or Mississippi, I've decided that the best way to promote Gore's chances and the progressive coalition is to vote for Nader and to hope that Nader supporters in swing states will vote for Gore.' And this is to me just core, protected political activity in the form of coalition building.

"I spoke to the campaign manager for Nader, and I told her I was going to do it, and she had no [reservations]; she didn't want to stop me in any way. But the campaign was clear that their position was 'Vote your conscience.' And whenever someone said to me, 'Well, we support voting your conscience,' I said, 'Fine, but some people's consciences are a little more complicated than that.' In other words, some people's conscience told them to do whatever they could to stop Bush and put Gore in office, but also get Nader the 5 percent. And I think it was a strategic blunder on the part of both the Gore and Nader campaigns to keep their distance from the effort. I think Nader hemorrhaged probably half of his vote in the last twenty-four hours because there was so much pressure on progressives and liberals not to let Bush get in. And had they gotten behind the vote-trading effort, they could have cemented that support and gotten something for it. They should have embraced it. And similarly, Gore should have gotten behind it and instead of forcing people to choose between A and B, Gore should have said, 'There's this creative alternative that's come up.' Total win-win. We were able to determine that several thousand Nader supporters vote traded in Florida—that is several thousand votes that went to Gore, and if they had gotten behind it in Florida and 10,000 people had done it rather than 5,000 people, then Gore would be president today."

Raskin said he wasn't surprised the established political hierarchy couldn't deal with the idea. "I knew that in the heat of a campaign, the campaigns tend to make knee-jerk decisions, and I think both of them did. They are so focused on getting people to vote for their guy that anything that appears to depart from that agenda is anathema. So I wish there had been some cool strategic heads either in the Gore or Nader camps, because we almost changed the course of the election with a grassroots effort that was resisted by the Gore campaign, the Bush campaign, the Nader campaign, and then all of these Republican state officials who did everything in their power to intimidate people and scare them away from it. The radicalism of this effort was its completely grassroots character. There were no party bosses behind it. There was no big money behind it."

Cardille says he recognizes that the whole idea was "more difficult" for some people who saw trading as a moral question. "It brings up in a way I didn't expect very deep questions about what it means to vote. We've been told all our lives, in civics class and high school, what our vote means. We'll learn something like a vote is the way you express your will in a democracy. And that's been true since the beginning of the country. But this is a case where you might be able to cast your vote in a way in a different sense of the word *cast*—you'd be able to move that vote and take it from one place to another. There were some people who didn't feel comfortable with that—either because they didn't support both candidates, so it seemed illogical to support both candidates, or [because] they felt that, because it's a right, you should not give that right away. I know two of my friends here in town, two of my old housemates who lived in the same house a couple of years ago, they were very much offended by the idea."

Yoder says the Web sites "were doing nothing more than facilitating communication between voters and allowing people to do what our policymakers do at the national level all the time. And it puts more power into the hands of individual voters. And if that undermines the clout of big money and big media and all the other huge forces that are swaying people's decisions—if it's actually putting the decision and the clout back in the hands of individuals—I can't see that as anything but good. How is individuals trading between one another different from a political party making promises during election time? There's no more of a commodity being exchanged by those individuals than by a political party. I have talked to people, and my mother-in-law is one of these people, who say 'Your vote is your vote. You cannot trade it.' That's just a core belief of hers, and I respect that."

In his piece for *Slate,* Raskin suggested that the phenomenon is *very* American and not the least offensive to U.S. senators, for one, who are regular practitioners of "vote pairing." On Capitol Hill, senators who know they are going to miss a key vote strike gentleman's agreements with colleagues on the opposite side of the issue. When both agree to miss, the theory goes, no harm is done.

"This plan is not for everyone," Raskin wrote about Nader trading.

Some people regard voting as primarily moral and expressive—not political and strategic—behavior, and they will recoil at the thought of ever pulling the lever for someone who is not their first-choice candidate. I cannot convince them. This is a plan for people who regard voting as essentially strategic behavior that requires us to focus on real-world political outcomes and meanings. But if it is immoral to vote strategically, the campaigns should stop trying to convince people—Nader voters, most prominently—to change their votes.

He continued, "Finally, it might be argued that there is something irresponsible about this kind of massive vote-trading. The point is off-base. It is the highest form of democratic politics to consult your fellow citizens about electoral choices." The practice of vote trading, Raskin said, "is the essence of legislative log-rolling in Washington: You vote 'yes' on my highway bill, and I will vote 'yes' on your tax bill. We compromise to arrive at mutually workable solutions."

California and Oregon disagreed. Both e-mailed Nader trade sites and warned them that they were violating state laws. Cody immediately shut down his Los Angeles–based site when he heard via e-mail from California secretary of state Bill Jones. It was about 5:00 P.M. PST on October 30 when Cody read the e-mail that opened this chapter.

Things might have been different had Cody had the time, money, and confidence to push it. He did not. "I was in shock," he said. Five thousand people had been paired on the site. "That's three years [in prison] for each count, and there were 5,000 counts." Further, his partner wanted nothing to do with a lawsuit. And Cody said he looked at it with a Web designer's mindset. "When you find out something wrong with your page, you stop doing the thing that's wrong and fix it." But when he called William Wood in the secretary of state's office, he hit a brick wall. "What he was telling me, because he was using the word 'brokering,' because he was considering the promise to vote a certain way to be something of value and therefore in violation of the law—it seemed to me there was no way to fix this. Or the only way to fix this would be to hire a lawyer and we really didn't have the money to do that." The conversation ended with Cody promising he'd make things right by sending out an e-mail to everyone the site had matched, telling them, "You're not in trouble; it's just us."

Raskin calls it calculated political intimidation. "If the Democrats and Greens did not properly understand the breathtaking potential of vote trading, the Republicans clearly did. It scared the daylights out of them. There was a very concerted effort by Republican state officials to crack down on this and to get newspaper articles out telling people it was illegal. It was almost as if they were saying it's criminal to vote for someone who was not your first choice. They were very intimidating. I got a bunch of calls and e-mails; some people were afraid to talk to me because they were hearing that I was somehow the ringleader of this nationwide conspiracy."

Cody said that, in the meantime, reporters were telling him that federal officials thought the arrangement appeared legal. "My initial reaction was shock and embarrassment that we had apparently violated the law. As the days went by and I thought about it and I read the law and heard from other people, I realized that, the way the law was written, there was no way the writers of the law could have anticipated this situation, and therefore, it's very difficult to believe it actually applies the way they said. At that time on that Monday, from the tone of the letter, I didn't realize that Bill

Jones would have to go to the state attorney general to enforce anything. I fully expected, at eight o'clock the next morning, to have the state police knocking on my door and carrying off all my stuff. Even that by itself would be disastrous to me because that's how I make my living. I cannot afford to have all my computer equipment impounded for months and months waiting for a trial.

"After the days passed, I began to think why this was done. I didn't know anything about Bill Jones, then I began to realize this guy is a Republican officeholder; he has a political reason to do this. I don't know Bill Jones still. I don't know what kind of person he is. Maybe he believes he was doing what was best for the state of California or maybe he was just doing something cynically because it served his political party that way."

Cody and his partner also heard from the secretaries of state of Oregon and Minnesota, and the partner continued to feel any legal resistance was trouble for their business. But Cody was angry and frustrated and felt he had been bullied. "At the time, it was like, 'When is this going to end?' Were we going to get them from all fifty states, or what? I was feeling threatened and exposed because I was being threatened by various state governments, and I wanted legal representation. Personally, I was starting to get angry. My feeling is, I don't know Bill Jones and I don't know what his motivations were, but if his motivation was to just push us around because it served him politically, I feel that's reprehensible. It angers me personally. If I can do anything to stop somebody from getting away with something like that, I'm inclined to do it."

In San Francisco, Amy Morris was so inclined—and not at all intimidated. Morris, who works for the Goldman Environmental Foundation, had already dealt her vote with her parents back in Utah. "I started getting excited about ways to do that on a larger scale. I was really struggling personally with this Nader versus Gore issue. I personally relate more to Nader's politics, but of course I didn't want Bush to win. So it was sort of being stuck in that idealist versus realist argument. This seemed like a place I could focus my energy, a place where I could compromise."

Her father, John Morris, fifty-seven, said his daughter was determined to vote for Nader and he was happy to switch, recalling in his own youth "a really formative experience for me. I was in law school in 1968, and I voted for the Peace and Freedom candidate in California instead of for Hubert Humphrey. I've forgotten the name of the candidate—that's how insignificant it was. The dynamics were exactly the same. The issue was not around domestic politics but around the war. But the perception among people—I was living in Berkeley at the time—was that Humphrey was not sufficiently pro-peace on the war issues and that, even though Nixon was a complete asshole, people just couldn't support Humphrey. It wasn't the 'pure' thing to do. And that was a very close election. I don't know if anyone has done sophisticated analysis on how that vote went state by state and whether it affected the outcome, but given what happened in Nixon's subsequent career, I just ended up feeling really crappy about it. So I came away from that experience just thinking that I was not going to make any more votes in my lifetime based on some sort of notion that I had to cast my vote for the candidate who was the purest when that candidate (a) had no chance of winning and, more importantly, (b) could end up being a spoiler, which actually did happen in this election. People can do what they want, but in my view, it was the worst political decision I ever made. So the ingenuity of trading was very attractive to me."

Moved to action by her own convictions and her conversations with her father, Amy Morris started inventing and typing in domain names for her own Nader trading site and quickly came across Yoder's and Cardille's. But neither provided the kind of database matching envisioned by Morris and two of her friends, one in New York and the other in the Bay area. The threesome moved ahead, purchasing the *votetrader.org* domain name on October 26. Morris contacted Yoder to chat. He mentioned Cody's site out in L.A. "When we found out that that site existed, we decided that we weren't even going to post our site, because we hadn't developed our database yet and it seemed like it would be redundant. So we ended up just sending out a lot of e-mails to friends about that site." But by the close of the day that Monday, Cody was pulling the plug.

The threat by Secretary of State Jones riled Morris. "It seemed so outrageous that he would be saying that these were illegal because it seemed so clear to us that it was political free speech." She contacted the American Civil Liberties Union (ACLU) and the National Voting Rights Institute for advice and support, and she and her partners posted their site November

4; they took care to specifically label their site as not brokering votes, language the state of California had used in its complaints about other sites. Time was short, but Morris says it was important to make a statement in California. "That's definitely what was generating our interest at that point because we realized we weren't going to get tens of thousands of hits in a couple of days before the election." The site ended up being responsible for at least one hundred swaps, and Morris estimates that ten or so were swaps that gained Gore votes in Florida. "And who would think that was a number that actually [could] make a difference?"

Her father actively promoted vote swapping among the university community and figures that perhaps a dozen of his and his wife's acquaintances traded. "What I did was, as the developments occurred, particularly right before the election, I kept forwarding e-mail to people about what the current situation was and what they could do. We thought it was the right thing to be doing."

Morris stressed that he has no expertise in election law, but as a citizen, thought the trading seemed "perfectly appropriate." "There's no fraud involved. People still retain the right to cast their vote however they want. I would distinguish this from someone being paid for their vote, which is clearly illegal." Trading, he says, "clearly is in part a reflection of the distortion of the system imposed by the Electoral College system. Most people thought Bush would win the popular vote and, if Gore had a chance, it would be with the Electoral College, and I would have preferred that result, but I still would think the system stinks."

Raskin said he heard from many people just like Morris in a flood of e-mails after the *Slate* article appeared, five hundred in the immediate aftermath. "People were saying, 'This is the first time I've felt any political hope in this campaign.' Some people were saying they hadn't felt any political hope in decades. There was a family of Democrats in North Dakota who said, essentially, 'We've been disenfranchised from presidential elections for generations, and now suddenly our votes can mean something.' I think they were Gore supporters, and they said, 'By casting our votes for Nader here in North Dakota, we can contribute to Gore's momentum in some swing states.' Suddenly people were feeling not imprisoned by the Electoral College but liberated in it."

The National Voting Rights Institute challenged Secretary of State Jones in a California lawsuit that continued into the summer of 2002. It takes the Raskin line, says Gregory Luke, an attorney with NVRI. "The only people who are going to access a Nader trader site and then enter into some discussion about some concerted political action are people who already share a political commitment to two basic principles: One is that they're willing to support third party candidacy in an effort to gain 5 percent of the popular vote to qualify for funds; and two, a preference for one of the two major party candidates. And all that's discussed or decided when two people get together about this is what's the most efficient way for those two people to try to achieve both of those goals that they both share. It's a misnomer to call it trading or vote swapping or any of those things. It's concerted political action, in the same way people would talk about party building. And I feel about this very strongly in the sense that this is the same type of activity that people do within a state except they're doing it across state boundaries now and responding to the way our political institutions are structured constitutionally."

Days before the election, NVRI sought a restraining order to muzzle Jones, but Luke said there was too little time to assure voters or Web sites that they wouldn't be prosecuted. The injunction was denied the day before Election Day. "What we were hoping to do," Luke says, "was to get an order from the judge that we then could go back to people like Cody and other people and have them post on their Web sites and tell people 'Hey, this is not activity for which you can be prosecuted. Keep going, everybody, do what you need to do. Communicate what you need to communicate.'"

Luke hopes the courts won't dodge the issue, but they may, waiting for a new election, a new time, and a new case. "We want to see if we can resolve this very important issue about technology and the use of technology in a profoundly democratic manner, want to make sure there is at least by the next presidential cycle an opportunity for people to make these kinds of political communications across state lines again using this technology. The technology is not going to go away. The third parties are not going to go away. Close contests between the two major parties are not going to go away. Whether it comes up in 2004, 2008, it's going to come up again." Indeed, Luke says, the plaintiff in the ongoing case being pursued by NVRI already has registered *voteexchange2004.*

Cardille was nonplussed when the state of Oregon dropped him an e-mail and challenged him, he recalls, "on the grounds that I was having undue influence on the election. I called a friend who is a civil liberties attorney in Washington [D.C.], and she got them to rescind their accusation and back down very quickly. It was very exciting, actually very flattering." Cardille also had a low-key contact from the state of Wisconsin. A spokesman from the Department of Agricultural Trade and Consumer Protection wanted to drop off a copy of the state election law. "I said I didn't think there was anything I was doing wrong. If they had a particular thing they wanted me to change, we could talk about it. But otherwise, I said I didn't think I'd necessarily be there if they came by the house. He came up with a compromise of 'maybe I can read you the number of the election law that we'd like you to read.' And I said, 'Sure, you can read me the number, but I'm not sure I will have time to read it.'"

Cardille's site did not have a mechanism for swapping votes, as Cody's did, and that gave Cardille an edge, he figured. "I felt the only way the idea could be [quashed] was creating a crisis of confidence where average people were afraid of the idea. So I thought early on, when it was up a couple of days, that I would be sure to keep up my site no matter what, so that, if it involved changing a few words, that would be fine. If I needed to recommend that people engage in political discussion with their family members, that would be fine. But that it was clearly protected under free speech and there would be no reason for me to feel intimidated or frightened at all."

Ultimately, some people no doubt were chased away from the sites by the talk that they were illegal, whether that was right or wrong. Still, Cardille says, "I think [the accusation] didn't intimidate most people. I think that most people looked at it and said, 'First of all, it's politically motivated. And second, who's ever going to know [I swapped]?'"

Cardille himself says he'd have some reservations about trading votes with a stranger, reluctant to make a deal until they'd talked on the phone "five or six times."

Cardille was curious to hear others out on the question of voting, and vote trading, and not just via online. "We have a farmer's market in town in Madison on Saturdays, and people gather around the Capitol building. I put up a little Nader trader sign and had people come by all day long and tape-record their feelings about the idea. Folks had a really sophisticated sense of what it means to vote. Some people said the idea of voting is to affect an outcome. 'I am trying to do something that is practical. I want a result.' So they were looking at it as result based. But there were other people who were just as passionate in saying, 'This is something that is more inherent to me as a citizen. Whether or not I get the result I want, voting is not related to that issue.' And I can't say that those people are wrong.

"There were some people who came up and said, 'I actually feel better about my vote than I had before,' and I thought that was really interesting. I'm thinking of this woman, Vic McMurray, who ended up facilitating trades for about forty-seven pairs of voters between Madison and Wyoming, and all through phone lists, not over the Internet. It was a huge network. She came up to me and said she and her friends were meeting for dinner the next day, which was the Sunday before Election Day. She said, 'We've all given ourselves the challenge to come back with as many names as we can,' because at that moment she said she didn't have anyone to trade with, and she said she absolutely was going to vote for Nader unless she got someone to trade with, that she wasn't going to compromise her principles on that.

"She said, 'I feel we are smarter than the system we've been given. We've been given a system where you've been told you have to vote this way. And we've actually outsmarted the system in a way that's evolutionary. You can think of that [trader] community as a step forward that people are making together. And it's neat to think of ourselves as being smarter than the system.' I heard that and thought it was great."

Morris supports an instant runoff or vote-ranking system, a national popular vote in which voters would rank their choices for president. If no one polled a majority, those voters who supported lesser candidates would have their vote count for their second choice. This, in effect, was what the Nader voters had a chance to do. "What we were thinking of vote trading as was a way to facilitate some kind of vote ranking within the current system. Obviously, those voting for Nader would rank Gore second," Morris said.

Cardille laughs that McMurray symbolizes the kind of trading that went on offline. "Vic is really bad at the Internet. She couldn't get logged on to see the site I had. She heard about it and thought it was a great idea but never went to it. I would tell her the list of swing states. The people she ended up trading with were sixty- to seventy-year-olds in Wyoming, retirees."

Cody is a strategic voter, too, and says he was surprised at the vigor of some vote swap opponents. "I was surprised in that I didn't really consider that people would think it was dishonest. I realized after the site was up, and those were some of the e-mails we got, that this was subverting the whole idea of voting. But to me, I've always voted that way. I'm originally from South Carolina, which is a very conservative state, just like Utah. So I totally understand the feeling of throwing votes away knowing the person I'm voting for has no chance at all of being elected."

Amy Morris says semantics are important. "The trick is to frame it. *Vote trading*—the words are a misnomer. We tried to word it on our site to make it clear you're not trading goods. You're not trading money. It's a different process than I think the people who wrote the laws were trying to protect against. As far as I'm concerned, it's just convincing each other to vote strategically. It's kind of basic political speech. The name *vote trading* or *vote swapping* pushed a lot of buttons for some people, got them excited for or against it. But it's a lot more subtle than that."

Her father says the idea of trust—that the person you traded with might change his or her mind or even be a fraud—was oversold. He would have traded online with a stranger and lost no sleep over it. "I would have done it even if I didn't have 100 percent confidence that the person on the other end would vote, because in our state here, voting for Nader or Gore, either way, is pissing your vote away. So even if I wasn't confident, I would have done it. I'm losing nothing by doing that."

Cardille and a number of other Nader-site creators gathered in Washington, D.C., the day before the inauguration to discuss what had happened and to make introductions. They gave a package of items to the Smithsonian Institution and reflected on the Internet phenomenon and what it meant to them all. In a comment that illustrates the Internet's trust-building potential, Cardille added, "None of us ever had seen each other's face, which is kind of strange if you consider it a movement. For a movement to not know what the other person looks like is pretty unusual."

Not every moment was a highlight, though Cardille says nine in ten of the e-mails he received were upbeat. "One angry guy wrote me, 'You should be shot on sight. You're the worst kind of traitor.' The one guy, I guess it was the worst, wrote, 'Just to let you know, we are not being vindictive, but I know where you live. You live at 1333 xxx, Madison, Wisconsin, your phone number is this, and we will sue you into the ground if you don't take your site down in the next hour.'"

Cody says that when the adventure ended, "I had a lot of mixed feelings about it. Our original impulse when we started the whole thing was to do something useful, something that people would find helpful. Not everyone is going to find what we did helpful. Certainly people who supported George Bush would hate it. We didn't expect anything else. Some people from the Green party hated it. They didn't like the whole idea of trading votes. That surprised us a bit. I guess that's something we didn't expect—the level of hatred. That caught us by surprise."

Raskin says that the next time around—if there is one—should be different. "It all depends on the political dynamics of the situation, of course. But I do think that the vote-trading forces will be much better prepared this time politically, ideologically, technically, and constitutionally. So I think all the Web sites will be carefully designed with legal assistance to make criminal prosecution as unlikely as possible. There are easy ways of designing Web sites to make any criminal prosecution absolutely ludicrous. Let me put it this way. I think anything short of people sending each other their absentee ballots is a First Amendment win in the courts. People have the right to persuade each other about voting and to form political coalitions. And that's what this is all about." He agrees there are no certainties, though. "Well, I can imagine a loss in the courts. The reason I say that is, I could only barely imagine the Supreme Court doing what it did in *Bush v. Gore*. I think it's a completely political court, and anything's possible. But if there is any First Amendment justice, the vote traders win."

Cardille avoids declaring that the face of politics has been or will be changed forever. "In this case, the Internet was perfect for this. It was an idea that needed to be distributed quickly and to everyone. It was able to be successful only because of the Internet. I don't know that that necessarily says something about the future. Like in the year 2004, will this same thing be used again?"

Cody says, "I'm still committed to the Internet and will be looking for things like the vote swap thing to try to look for good ideas and implement them. I hope there will be political uses for it in the future. This kind of scares the traditional parties. It's a different thing than they're used to. They're used to doing things in a different way. They have their hierarchy set up, their party hierarchy where they work their way up and become more powerful as they advance in the party. This is a runaround to the whole thing. It's a democratic thing. I like that about the Internet. It doesn't cost much to set up a Web site. Out-of-pocket expenses for us were $35. We generated way more interest than we ever thought possible. It allows somebody without any power, without any particular connections, to do something that means something to a lot of people. That's the opportunity."

Raskin agrees and even sees the potential for sea change. "Look, politicians and parties, unions, corporations have always dealt in large blocks of votes. What's different with Internet vote trading is that the voters themselves are engaging in collective political action without the intervention of political elites. The traditional political parties don't exist except as frameworks for recycling corporate cash into the political process. The Internet might be the vehicle for the re-creation of political parties or at least political coalitions and tendencies. A lot of pressure will be brought on the two-party system. And one reason I was excited about doing this is I was able to take a stand on principle about debate exclusion and also act strategically with respect to the ultimate election."

The People's Campaign

Though dedicated to action and anchored in discourse, the left-leaning political coalition known as the People's Campaign and the attendant stories of Keith Joseph and Kristina Bas supply a telling example of the Internet's value in building and sustaining communities of belief. The People's Campaign formed around two common purposes—the challenge to the established political order in New Brunswick, New Jersey, and the reliance on authentic, broad-based democratic political participation within the coalition. Bas's and Joseph's activities in the People's Campaign were informed by deeply held beliefs, which were in turn catalyzed and sustained by political action. Members of the coalition disagreed on some matters of philosophy and tactics—as the left is wont to do—but they remained connected through the basic concept and practice of democracy. In their case the Internet was woven into traditional local political organizing, and this organizing extended to those who were less well-off.

However, the Internet's role in the People's Campaign also suggests two deep challenges to effectively using the Internet to build social capital, which we have discussed in earlier chapters. First, the electronic discussions at times threatened to be only that: disgruntled individuals airing their gripes and exorcising their political demons. Second, the digital divide dogged the organizers. As Joseph trenchantly observes, the Internet inverts the political problem posed by traditional mass media: On one hand, representatives of the poor can easily place their point of view in the new medium, but the poor themselves have difficulty accessing it. On the other hand, the Internet did allow the coalition to discover and connect with a similar group in Florida and also helped the coalition to sustain itself after the local election, which it lost decisively.

In November 2000 twenty-eight-year-old house painter Keith Joseph ran for city council in New Brunswick, New Jersey, along with two other unlikely candidates in that hardscrabble college town on the Raritan River. Tired of watching the same political machine win election after election, usually unopposed and, in their view, always unresponsive to the working poor, Joseph and others formed their own political party. They used traditional forms of neighborhood canvassing, public events, raucous meetings, and the Internet to organize, communicate, and recruit. In the process, they formed an archetype of the community of belief. Existing partly online and partly face-to-face, the grassroots political movement labored through the pains of birth, growth, adulthood, and ultimately defeat, then lived on in cyberspace many months after its loss at the polls.

PHOTO 6.2A   Keith Joseph

PHOTO 6.2B   Kristina Bas

The new party—the New Brunswick People's Campaign—was a broad coalition of people who believed they had been systematically excluded from politics in New Brunswick. They accused the Democratic party of ruling for decades in an almost Richard Daley–like economy of political favors. The disenfranchised included minimum-wage workers, minorities, students, lower-middle-class renters, and the working poor. They had never lifted a collective voice during any of the previous elections. When they joined together, they were not always in agreement with each other on specific political issues and were often divided by race, religion, educational background, and even neighborhood affiliation. Nonetheless, they remained united by certain core beliefs and managed to pull together a fragile alliance, elect some officers, select their candidates, and raise funds. They chose as their treasurer twenty-six-year-old Kristina Bas, who wore many hats throughout the campaign.

"The Internet gave me the tool I needed to keep people who didn't live in New Brunswick, who lived in other parts of New Jersey or even other parts of the country, aware of what was happening in the campaign," said Bas. "And that is the advantage of the Internet for any grassroots movement." Underfunded startups such as the People's Campaign cannot afford the mass media or even mass mailings to spread their messages. But the Internet provides a low-cost, easily accessible alternative. "Articles about the campaign would appear in the newspaper and then on its Web site, and we would e-mail that article to all of our supporters," said Bas, describing one of the several ways the campaign used the Web. The Internet also gave the challengers the opportunity to debate their views on the key campaign points online asynchronously and reach something like a consensus long before face-to-face meetings. "The Internet gave the people in our campaign a chance to discuss where they were coming from, why they thought things should go this way or that way. So that's why I think the most successful stuff was our e-group rather than our Web site," said Joseph.

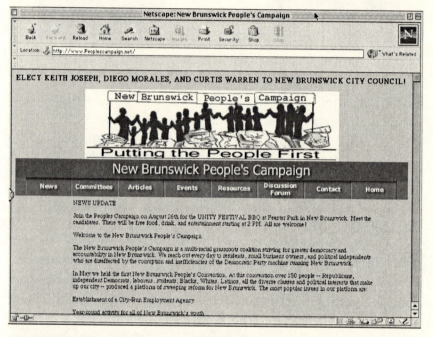

PHOTO 6.3   The People's Campaign Web site. Insiders found that the site was not important to the campaign. The online bulletin board was.

The fact that people had discussions online is not new or unique. The fact that the Internet played a key role in helping people form a new political party, that those involved did not agree with each other from the outset, and that none were paid political professionals *is* new. The major political parties—in fact, most national organizations of all kinds—haven't enjoyed that kind of grassroots organization and participation in a long time. We long ago became a nation of dues-paying but not physically active members of civic organizations. And many critics of the Internet have said that politics is too local and the Internet too global for the two to meet. But there it was, a key tool for the alternative-voiced underdog in what would be a long, hard campaign in a small city.

Candidate Keith Joseph grew up in a typical working-class home in Parsippany, New Jersey, and sometimes sounds a little like Sylvester Stallone on the phone. The image he conveys: a truck driver who reads Keats. His parents were strong proponents of education and had the newspaper delivered every day to make sure their kids kept up-to-date on current events. They were politically active but tight-lipped about it. His parents never talked about politics around the dinner table and didn't even tell each other who they voted for. "They were afraid to find out that they had canceled each other out," Joseph explained. His father, a painting contractor, had had only one year of college, where, he explained to his son, he "took up space." Determined to see his children make more of themselves, he sent Joseph and his sister to York Academy, an expensive private school in Livingston, New Jersey. Joseph felt out of place there but persevered. "It was a pretty well-to-do place," he said. "And that contributed to my class consciousness. At York, I was definitely in the lower end of the class structure."

Joseph's grandfather had been a longtime union man, a lifelong member of the AFL-CIO, and a staunch Democrat. He told the young Joseph stories about the struggles of the working class and regaled him with tales about the union. "I grew up with that mix of working-class sympathies and the educational opportunities usually afforded to much wealthier people." His father, who died when Joseph was fifteen, was, by his own definition, a radical. Without the guiding light he had always known, Joseph was on his own to develop a political leaning. "They had clubs at school like Amnesty International, and they were liberal enough for me but not active enough." Some of the readings for classes, assigned for their contribution to the world of literature, actually helped frame Joseph's view of the political landscape. Joseph saw *Lord of the Flies*, for example, as an analog for the mess that the state can make of things when it steps in and tries to establish order. He laughs when he uses *Gilligan's Island* as a classic example of a functioning anarchy.

Treasurer Kristina Bas's upbringing mirrors Joseph's in several important ways. Bas was born in Bayonne, New Jersey, to two immigrants. Her working-class parents were not well educated but emphasized schooling for their children. They were born overseas and were more left leaning than many of their American contemporaries. "They were not blindly pro-American, and they hated Reagan," Bas said. "They taught us to be critical and to question and not to be blindly accepting of American life." While they were politically more liberal, they were socially more conservative than some other parents of the 1980s and '90s. Bas's parents, particularly her father, had a very fixed notion of the roles of men and women in society. "He wouldn't even let me play soccer," lamented Bas. "He said it was a sport meant for boys."

During Bas's childhood, the family sat down to dinner, and political discussion was part of the routine. "It was something that was a normal part of the family discourse," she said. "My father was not educated, but if he had been, he would have been brilliant." A largely self-educated man, he read voraciously and shared his thoughts with his children. From the time she was about twelve years old, Bas read *The New York Times*. She believes her parents' open-mindedness toward other cultures and other ideas contributed to her own development as a progressive activist. At the same time, they were "old school" about the roles of men and women, and Bas's fiery personality caused her to resent and rebel against the disparity in the treatment she and her bother were afforded. "He got away with a lot of things I would never be able to get away with." When she learned about feminism, she identified with it.

While in an all-girl Catholic high school, Bas was exposed to activities and ideas that empowered her as a woman. "The nuns were actually pretty forward thinking," she laughed. She was active in animal rights and environmental causes, and as she grew older Bas's sense of her female identity increased. Out of that emerged her awareness of the problems she faced in a male-dominated and male-defined world. At that time, though, she was only aware that these feelings were inside her. She internalized and personalized them.

Joseph went to Bard College for two years, a place he described as freewheeling and dedicated to the arts, full of very different people holding unusual views about things. Although he was comfortable with the easygoing, laid-back nature of Bard, there wasn't much to get the adrenaline flowing, and Joseph likes action. "I was just swimming there," said Joseph. He transferred to Rutgers, where he majored in philosophy. He took a very strong interest in politics when the university infringed on what Joseph considers his basic rights under the Constitution.

The university raised the tuition and that ignited student protests. The protests, in turn, prompted the university to institute a student code of conduct, "which, in my view, was in violation of civil liberties and the Bill of Rights," said Joseph. To him, the Bill of Rights had always been an abstraction, something that guaranteed certain liberties under conditions nobody would ever experience. It didn't apply to your life at work or your life at school. It didn't apply to anywhere that mattered. "It didn't even apply to you at the mall, which is private property," he said. Suddenly, the university passed a compilation of rules that pushed Joseph into the political arena. He decided to get involved in the resistance to the code of conduct and spoke openly and often against it. At a demonstration where he was permitted to speak, he experienced "a radically democratic moment," as he called it. But he also realized that it didn't matter. "We could talk about it and discuss it, but we weren't going to change anything. We weren't empowered to change it." The code of conduct was enacted despite all the rhetoric and demonstrations, but Joseph's interest in free speech was ignited, and he has remained engaged in political processes ever since. He began to read books about political theory and immersed himself in political culture.

"Originally, my anarchistic bent was also an anti-technology position," he explained. But in 1995 he bought a computer. Once he began surfing the Web, he was hooked. "I started using the Web to advance my access to political ideas," he said. "There are lots of Web sites devoted to Marx, for example. Lots of countercultural literature." Joseph would read, take note of referenced authors, and then look *them* up on the Web and in the public library, creating what seemed like an infinite tree of knowledge and ideas growing from a single source. "I used the Internet for information gathering. Sometimes it was old theory, like Marx, and sometimes it was new information, such as Gary Webb articles. I also go there for CNN," he mused, referring to a popular news source on the Web during the last election.

Kristina Bas graduated near the top of her high school class, but despite a glowing transcript, she wound up at her "safety school," Rutgers, and majored in political science. "In college I wanted to become a lawyer," she explained. "Interestingly enough, when I was in high school, I wanted to be a chemist." Like many college freshmen, Bas underestimated the course work her first semester and did poorly. She recovered by the end of her second semester but felt she had lost momentum. She got into a state of personal doldrums, well out of character. She was negative and stagnant—that is, until Rutgers did something that got her blood boiling and reawakened the activist in her. In 1994 the university closed down the Women's Center on the Douglas campus, which mainly served minority women from the community. This was a real and local affront to her.

Bas became actively involved with the group that formed to save the Women's Center, "and what I stumbled into was a huge community, a huge movement at Rutgers, that had existed for at least two decades." The community consisted of activist, socially conscious, minority, women's, and nonmainstream groups on campus and in the local community. "It had much I wanted and needed at the time," she said. "There was this huge movement with very diverse components. Latinos, African-Americans, environmentalists, gays and lesbians, and of course, feminists. It was unlike anything I had ever seen before." The group gave her ideals credibility and gave her confidence because here was a group of people who believed in the same things she did. "For me it was an extremely transformative experience." Her proximity to so many people with similar beliefs and similar goals, who had lived through similar experiences, made her realize that the problems facing women were systemic, not personal. "The broader development that I made was only possible because of these particular personal relationships that I developed."

The work to save the Women's Center gave Bas a chance to put her abstract concepts and theories about feminism and empowerment into practice. She became an organizer of the movement and learned many of the techniques on her own. "These are the practical things that they did not teach us in our classes," she said.

In those days of activism, all contact between members of the community was physical and face-to-face. "E-mail was nonexistent," she pointed out, "and most people didn't even have computers." They braved the rain and snow and attended meetings at members' homes or in public spaces. They failed to save the center but were successful at organizing and mobilizing a diverse group. It was an experience she would put to immediate use on her next big project.

After graduating with a degree in philosophy, Keith Joseph became, like his father, a house painter and continued with his political action work. Which was his avocation and which his life's work even he is not sure. As Joseph's general interest in politics increased and his theoretical underpinnings grew, he realized that New Brunswick's political landscape would be fertile ground on which to exercise his newly discovered passion for action. He began networking with like-minded people, and it was at this point that Joseph and Bas converged. Joseph and Bas each joined the New Jersey Freedom Organization (NJFO), a political action group composed mainly of college students, graduate students, and recent graduates. It undertakes almost every conceivable cause, from environmental protection to peace action to police brutality. "It was a story about a notorious police officer who maced a woman right on her front porch that got me involved," explained Joseph.

Like Joseph, Bas was drawn into the NJFO because it was a community activist group that believed in people's democracy. "It is democracy for everybody, not just rich people or corporations, which is what we have in this country," she said. She is passionate in describing the political and social structure of New Brunswick as she sees it: The aging blue-collar manufacturing town has lost its economic base, and what remains is a couple of all-powerful corporations, a standoffish effete university, and a single political party that has dominated for three decades. A large percentage of the population is African-American and Latino; many are noncitizens. "When I was a student, I didn't see it," she said. "Students live in a protected environment, don't walk down certain streets or shop in certain areas. We lived in fostered isolation from the reality of New Brunswick."

NJFO gave Joseph and Bas and many other students and former students an opportunity to organize in the New Brunswick community. There were many problems: understaffed and crumbling libraries, an educational system with poor graduation rates, deteriorating housing stock, skyrocketing rent, and poor police-community relations. NJFO saw downtown development efforts as designed specifically to clear out small businesses and make way for commercial franchises. Bas recalls a growing disenfranchisement of the poor, the working class, and the student community.

As time went on, NJFO members got a little older, a little bolder, and more confident that they could do more than meet and complain about local politics. The New Brunswick City Council would have three vacancies to fill in November 2000, and the group decided to work to fill them with candidates who would answer to the people, not to the bosses. In January 2000, they called a meeting and invited representatives from outside their organization to form a new political alliance. Joseph, Bas, and their group tried to run what Joseph called "a radically democratic election campaign, even in the way the campaign was organized."

"Initially, we had about forty or fifty people involved and a bunch of different organizations [at the first meeting]. This is a small number, but it grew exponentially in the next month," Bas said. "As we steamrolled along, more and more people got involved." About 150 people came to the first party convention. In an Athenian ideal, anyone with an interest in participating at any level was invited to vote for the leadership body, select the campaign manager, and choose the candidates. There would be no backroom meetings, deal making, or favoritism.

Joseph made a speech at the convention, emphasizing what he thought the party should stand for. "The main point of our program," he told them, "is democracy, anti-Bush mentality, housing rights, rent control, and other bread-and-butter issues. But I also told them that none of our candidates would be messiahs or saviors. We would all just be there to represent the people." The convention featured a pretty hotly contested selection process. There were three seats available on the city council, and there were ten candidates who wanted to run with support from the fledgling party, including a local Republican. In the end, the coalition chose Joseph and two others with working-class backgrounds—Diego Morales, a Latino bus driver, and Curtis Warren, an African-American van driver—and settled on a name, "The People's Campaign." To the organizers, they had made enormous strides by getting this far in the process.

According to Bas, the e-group discussion board that was set up for the new party was an important part of the early organizing success. The People's Campaign set up an online discussion group on the Web site egroups.com (since merged with Yahoo!). It had a moderator—a gatekeeper to maintain order and police the postings—but virtually anybody could join the e-group and send and receive messages through it. During the early weeks and months of the campaign, the site averaged about 120 messages per month, then dipped down, then up again during the tension-filled days just prior to the election. Bas explained that the e-group served two purposes: "It provided information about what was happening in the campaign to people who were not intimately involved," she said. "And it provided a forum for ideological and philosophical discussion about what the campaign should be doing, what direction we should be going." The coalition introduced a rich mix of controversial issues, and each interest group seemed focused on its own, such as housing, education, public transportation, or public safety. Much of the discussion about these items then took place on the e-group, where logistics and temperaments sorted themselves out, leaving the live, face-to-face meetings with more time to accomplish real objectives.

The People's Campaign e-group was a case study in group dynamics and community building. Unlike many discussion groups that are composed of people who usually agree with each other on specific issues, the People's Campaign group was made up of people who could be decidedly critical of each other. The ideological and philosophical discussions that Bas referred to often took on the tenor of a heated argument. Some members thought that the campaign embraced larger social issues and posted messages that lambasted capitalism, the two-party system, the police state, and so on. These drew the ire of others, who wanted to keep discussions centered around the city council election. They had an election to run, after all, and waxing poetic about class warfare was wasting time and energy. "One thing this brought to my attention is that there were people subscribed to the e-group who did nothing for the campaign," said Bas. "They became the hecklers. We said that they had 'e-mail muscles.'" These particular subscribers existed only in the cyberspace of the discussion group—they never appeared in person to canvas a neighborhood or work at a fund-raiser. "These people were destructive forces, always complaining and criticizing but never pitching in," Bas said.

Another problem with the e-group, at least from the campaign's point of view, was that it was an exclusive club. The discussion was limited to those with computer access—students, former students, and the better-heeled. It did not reach the very constituency the campaign was designed to empower—the working class. But in a serendipitous twist, the message board did attract the attention of unintended visitors. After the election, the group received an e-mail from another activist group in Florida, requesting that a People's Campaign worker visit and help *them* organize. "They were actually impressed with what we were doing on the Internet," said Bas, disbelieving.

When the e-group did work, it worked too well. Bas describes getting twenty or thirty e-mails per day during important moments during the campaign. They overwhelmed her, and she "wound up deleting a lot of them." In her words, "If you ask me if the e-group was the most stable, dependable, universal way to communicate, I'd say no, it was not. In this case, the handicap of technology was very apparent. If you wanted *everybody* to know something, there was no substitute for bringing it up at a general meeting," which was held every month during the campaign at the local public library. "The side effects of the Internet are still coming out," she added. "I don't think we know what they are yet. But I was able to keep together a network of supporters who never otherwise would have been able to know what was happening." As treasurer, Bas was responsible for fund-raising, and with the e-group and the Web site, she was able to advertise events and contact financial supporters directly. "We never had enough money to do what we wanted to do. It was easier to ask people for money if they knew what was going on and felt involved. The Internet helped me do that."

By the time Joseph decided to run for office, the Internet was an indispensable part of his daily routine. But during his campaign for city council, Joseph found the Web site failed to attract the voting constituency that the People's Campaign had targeted—the working poor and people living in the projects. However, "when we canvassed middle-class neighborhoods, people always asked, 'Do you have a Web site?' We did, but we never really put much into it." Although he and the party tried to run a campaign that would reach the middle class, they were fairly sure they wouldn't attract many middle-class voters no matter how hard they worked at it. Their message was targeted at others. While employing the Internet to reach his audience, Joseph experienced the digital divide first-hand. "It was good for our interorganizational work, but it wasn't effective for reaching our public," he said about the Internet. Most of the party activists were students, former students, and intellectuals. All of them had Internet access. The voters they needed to reach with their message of reform didn't. "[The Internet] is available at the public library, but it's not just a matter of it being available, it's knowing what it is and how to use it," he said. It is not a problem of access, it's a problem of cyberliteracy. "One of the things we need to do as a political organization is have computer literacy classes."

Joseph pointed out one of the great ironies of the last election, one that may dissipate as the next one approaches: "Everybody watches television, and if you want to reach the working poor with a political message, you can do it with TV. But only the richest campaigns can do that. The Internet is totally free and egalitarian. Any political office seeker can put a message up there. But only the privileged can get it. We did use the Internet but not as successfully as we would have liked. We had a Web site, but that wasn't where the action was. The real activity was on the e-group," he said.

The threesome lost in their bids for the city council by a 5–2 margin. "They had about 4,800 votes to our 2,200," Joseph said. "If we hadn't run, they would have won 4,800 to zero. I felt very positive that we had made a pretty good showing for the first time out." Indeed they did. New Brunswick has been ruled by the same political machine for decades. "They deliver turkeys on Thanksgiving; they have their hands in practically everything. All the parks jobs they have their people in, and so on," he said. "It's a tough thing to go up against.

"We learned a tremendous amount about politics. Some people who take these left-wing stances or even anarchistic stances are missing the tremendous experience of being involved in electoral politics. What's going on in Florida makes so much more sense to me having gone through this experience and having seen what can happen at the local level."

The election and the face-to-face meetings ended, but the e-group continued on its own momentum. After the three People's Campaign candidates lost their bid for the city council, one might have expected interest in the discussion group to have waned, but the number of e-mails exchanged on the e-group actually increased. Those involved in daily discourse about the campaign simply could not let go. In fact, eight months after the election, the e-group was exchanging almost two hundred e-mail messages per month. "There was so much activity on the e-group that we had to start another one," said Joseph. Most of the discussions were about the reasons the campaign failed.

They argued on the e-group, for example, about whether the candidates—Joseph included—should have shaved their beards and worn suits to political events. This volatile mix of differing styles may need to become less volcanic before an offline coalition can fully form. If this passion can be turned into constructive and productive opposition, they could clobber the Democrats next time out.

The Gunmen

How fitting and ironic that a group that would not seem to match one's likely first vision of a grassroots community would embody so many of the features of the Internet that we are extolling. Nevertheless, with John Caile and Have Gun Will Vote, it's almost all there—the Internet-based networking leading to deeper interpersonal connections, even friendships; aiding in unique ways people's ability to offer mutual assistance in political action; and greatly facilitating the gathering of relevant political information. Furthermore, though the group has a definite—and strongly held—point of view, it stimulated conversations across different sets of beliefs and party loyalties.

The ownership of a gun is, for Have Gun Will Vote, a feature so defining that arguably it should be a community of identity. Nevertheless, we have included its story here because it is a group born and sustained on the Internet that is united by a common belief about the sanctity of gun ownership. Its story, however, clearly illustrates the empirical challenge for us as authors of maintaining clear divisions between the four kinds of community.

Don't tell John Caile you can do better for him than he can do for himself.

Caile can repeat a months-old news commentator's observation—one that really got deep under his skin—as though it hangs as fresh as yesterday in the Minnesota air. And when he does, the story he relates is an apt metaphor about the Internet and why Caile finds it so powerful, and empowering.

"Well," he says, "I heard the most arrogant comment I've ever heard from a newscaster, and I'm saying it that way because there is no other way to interpret it. He was criticizing the Internet because, he said, 'The Internet provides too much raw information for consumers without the benefit of professionals like us to sort it out for them and give them the information they need to know.' . . . Well, thank you very much, sir, I didn't realize I needed you."

Caile, who lives in Minneapolis–St. Paul, is working with two of his three grown sons—commercial pilot Jason, who lives in the suburbs west of Chicago, and information technology specialist Sean, who lives in the same area—on an Internet-inspired and -enabled civics project that they say will help transform their frustrations, their opinions, and their cause into action. The URL of their work-in-progress Web site: havegun-willvote.com. Jason, thirty, is providing the design expertise; Sean, twenty-five, is the "computer guru." Their father will write.

Caile is just a bit of an online exception, perhaps, because in many ways, he does not fit the profile of the connected community builder. He is not young. He promotes an enduring conservative cause that is not of the classic online grassroots cut. He sometimes flashes the kind of sharp tongue, vigorously exercised, that people who don't know his sense of humor might associate with online "flamers." Yet it is the fifty-five-year-old Caile who has driven his sons to help build Have Gun Will Vote, a community of gun owners. Caile, who works as a freelance writer, is a well-known and authoritative voice on gun ownership who has testified before state legislative committees and been a guest on Minnesota Public Radio. He is director of communications for Concealed Carry Reform, Now: an all-volunteer group of 25,000 that has its own Web site and is lobbying to make it easier for Minnesota citizens to obtain permits to carry weapons. Caile is a familiar figure in the state

PHOTO 6.4   John Caile

legislature; he estimates he walks the halls for his cause as often as three times a week.

The Caile family trio is using the Internet as a tool to overcome time, distance, and the limits of regular citizens' modest resources, in a way that could not have been done before. The Cailes say they are out "to counter the 'antigun sentiment.'" But the story lies not in their cause; it is what the Internet allows them to do with their new enterprise. The cost is just a few hundred dollars. The real capital is their energy and belief in the rights of gun owners and their online community, which is literally a coast-to-coast web of contacts, information, and resources.

Sounding much like S. B. Woo of 80-20 (see Chapter 8), John Caile says the site will be "very political but nonpartisan. We will not be the marketing arm for any party. It is very clear what it means: 'I have a gun, and I will vote.' What happens next? You tell me. It's completely nonpartisan. We want the message to be very clear: If you are going to vote for laws that violate people's civil rights, I don't care what party you're in, you're in trouble with us. We will support a civil rights, gun owners' rights Democrat over a wimpy Republican any day."

Caile is as fervent a disciple of the Internet as he is of guns. He finds community online in many ways besides the planned online venture that nurtures his own, real family: comparing how the news plays around the country, even the globe, with other people in his online circles; sharing e-mails about ideas; writing to elected officials; helping strangers answer questions; even being his own press watchdog by checking out for himself the facts he hears and reads. He has connected in surprising ways with hundreds of people and built unlikely alliances as a result; he enjoys rattling off Internet anecdotes and a lengthy list of nationwide online associations cultivated in just the last half-dozen years.

Caile visits online bulletin boards and then later strikes up some conversations one-on-one, via private e-mails. He's seen comments he's made in one place show up in another, passed along on various Internet channels. He revels in the power of the Internet, the "ability to get in touch with other people in the state, find out information, go digging."

The Internet has shrunk the world, says Caile. "Let's see," he says. "There was a woman in New Jersey who wanted to know about firearms training, and she didn't even know where to start. She did a search on the Internet and she got me in Minnesota." The woman e-mailed Caile, and he posed her question to a former Chicago cop who does firearms training in Minnesota. Within hours—"that's hours, not days," Caile says—he had replied to the New Jersey inquiry to give the woman a local contact. It is not unusual, he says, to work this way, helping people he does not know and will never meet.

The Cailes hope that through their new Web site they will encourage more gun owners to vote. Gun owners are a rich target: They fit the demographic profile of the likely voter, and they can be inspired to vote if the issue is right and ripe.

"We're going to present our views," says Jason Caile, who flies Boeing 727-200s for Express One International, Inc., a cargo carrier. "Nobody's completely one way or the other, so some of our views fall on the Democrat side, some on the Republican side. That's the way it is. Hopefully, this gets more people to vote, especially in the next election. Obviously, having Bush in office is good for us. But let's make people more knowledgeable, get rid of some of the myths that are out there. That's my view. Getting more gun owners to vote is our priority, as far as I'm concerned. That is a big issue because they are a very large portion of the country that could swing an election."

The Cailes note that in Minnesota, there are 4.5 million people including 2 million gun owners. According to a Gallup poll in August 2000, 39 percent of American households have guns (an average of four guns per household). The National Institute of Justice reports that about 200 million guns are in private hands. Gun owners tend to be white, older, and middle class.

The Cailes repeatedly emphasize that their mission is not to tell gun owners *how* to vote or *whom* to vote for but that they *need* to vote. They say the site will provide online tools so users can track bills in the U.S. House and Senate, look up phone numbers, and send e-mails to each other and to elected officials. The site will link to other state legislatures and to directories of their gun laws.

John Caile is a particular believer in what the Internet can do for citizens who want to find and compare information for themselves. He does not neatly fit the stereotype that some Internet critics sketch of users who wall themselves off, orbiting in the same cybercircles of the Web universe that match their own strong views, to the exclusion of the rest. Indeed, one indication is in the voting booth: Caile voted for Bill Clinton in 1996, though he wryly calls it "the last time I vote for a Democrat in my life."

Caile and others—many of them established media critics—argue that it is the traditional news outlets that tend to look and sound more and more like each other, in part because of mergers and other market forces that punish news deviants. Some research suggests that many reporters and editors are out of touch with their audience across the spectrum: culturally, politically, and economically. CNN, Caile jokes, stands for "Clinton News Network." "There will always be a market for what people perceive as legitimate news," he argues. "It isn't just the Internet versus TV. People are not stupid. The Internet gives them choices. If the Internet becomes so politicized that you can't trust that Web site, then you'll go to another one."

Caile himself is not fixated on the gun issue; he sees the power of the Internet to build alliances and connections to be used for many things. A favorite example: bonding between motorcycle riders and gun owners. He calls this kind of thing "the next big step" online. "Motorcycle riders have traditionally had the same enemies as gun owners. Show me someone who wants to regulate and take away your firearms, and I'll show you someone who wants to make people wear helmets. So now we're sharing databases with motorcycle riders—cross-pollination. We're sharing voter lists. And when we meet with candidates, we now set up joint meetings, and the very look on the politicians' face tells you it's a good idea, because when both of us walk through the door, the candidates have dealt with one of us and know how strong *we* are, and they've dealt with the other and know how strong *they* are. They see you walking in together, and they have a 'Come to Jesus' meeting rather quickly."

Looking back, Caile says the Internet has transformed his political experience since he bought his first computer, primarily because he can access more "raw information" through primary sources and he can do his own research. "If you get a story on the TV or the radio, that's it. You get the story that that person decided you needed to know, whereas with the Internet, you can decide to do a search and find amazingly interesting background material and detail. The thing that the Internet gives you is the ability to go further, interactively. TV can never do that." And, he emphasizes, he does not need—or trust—media intermediaries to "separate hokey Web sites from legitimate information."

Caile, who calls himself a "news junkie," likes to spin the radio dial when he's on the road and spends a lot of time on public stations. Sometimes he goes on the Internet at home later—on the news sites or to trade a few e-mails—to see how different media outlets play the same story. As a news consumer, Caile does not fit the profile of the Internet user who is wedded to one of the brand-name news sites. He says he visits dozens of URLs. "I do specific, intelligent searches. If you go to one site to get all of your information, you're going to get one view. Forget it. It's just too general. I don't go to one site every day. There are dozens," says Caile, who notes that the Internet has allowed him to drop his newspaper subscription locally to what he calls the "Red Star Tribune." He calls the *Star Tribune* "agonizingly biased, almost painful" to read.

When he goes online, it's with a mission. "I don't play games online. I do e-mail, but it takes two minutes to write an e-mail. The most time I spend, I'm looking for information. Every month, there is more and more information out there. The search engines get better and better. No question, the Internet has made things better. Is it changing the way I vote? Not likely. But it allows me to get a better understanding. We don't have to depend on a candidate's rhetoric. We can do a search and see how they voted on this or find out about that, and it makes it very easy to do. I can go deeper, deeper, deeper."

Caile says that on occasion, he has sent a hundred e-mail letters in just two days. He receives fifty e-mails on a slow day, but typically at least a hundred, often from citizens in other states asking for advice on tactics that might work with their own legislators or other elected officials. "Without it," Caile says, "you'd have to walk the halls of the legislature and then stand around."

When he's online, Caile often votes in unscientific opinion and straw polls. He does not dismiss them, saying reputable sites are policing themselves tightly, and they often get it right. He believes in the intelligence of the online citizen. "Internet polls were absolutely dead on the money that [Governor] Jesse Ventura would win in Minnesota," he says.

"The Internet is the most underrated political force," Caile says, setting up another story. "I can tell you that politicians still don't get it." He recalls a debate among candidates for attorney general in Minnesota. Caile, who was in the audience, stood up as the candidates were mulling the consequences of making it easier for citizens to acquire permits to carry concealed weapons. It had been done in a number of other states already.

Caile remembers: "I got up and said, 'How many attorneys general from other states have you called and asked whether concealed carry has worked or not?' And they all stared at me. There was a long silence. And I said, 'I can see by the looks on your faces that you haven't asked anyone. Well I have, and they all have told me how well it's working.' They went on to the next question." Caile said he had contacted a number of states via e-mail—including Washington, Oregon, and Texas—and received detailed answers from them all, including some personal phone calls. Caile said he asked "for facts, not opinions," and mentioned in his e-mails that he'd like to talk with authors of concealed carry reform bills. In Texas he was connected with then-state senator Jerry Patterson, who wrote the legislation that passed there in 1995. Patterson is a retired Marine and Vietnam veteran. "We became friends," Caile says. "We've been talking three to four years now. We've never met in person, but there's a classic example of the ease with which you can research things on the Net, and you can actually start friendships with someone who lives 1,500 miles away."

Caile said he struck up online friendships with people in California, where gun issues have been hot, by starting with visits to chat-rooms. He made contacts, then moved the best connections to private channels, phone or e-mail or both. "It's really an intricate web. There's not a better word for it. I think each year, with each election cycle, the Internet will take on more importance."

Caile says he's networking online not just with gun owners. He's interested in education policy too. He's discovered that this same interest is shared by many people he's met online while talking about guns. A conversation with one woman about guns turned into a chat between the two of them, and she revealed that she worked in schools. She told Caile a story about taxpayer waste, building a whole new bond between the two and an entirely new set of e-mail and online contacts to share and to swap.

Caile's own experience is that Internet access has mushroomed among others in their fifties. "I don't know any who aren't on the Internet. My age bracket is very much in tune. It's just a matter of time before more and more people get on. It's going to happen. Five years from now, it won't even be an issue. It'll be like the telephone."

The Cailes illustrate one of the first principles of political involvement: If it's ingrained in the parents, it's in their children. Children whose parents are civically engaged tend to follow along. John Caile recalls himself as a fourteen-year-old growing up in a very politically interested and connected Chicago family. His own father took him to party caucuses when John was just eight. "He wanted me to see how real politics works. He was a Republican, my mom was a Democrat. He took me to both parties' caucuses. When I was fourteen years of age, during the 1960 election, I was in a room that had a bunch of tables set up in a horseshoe with coffee and donuts while about twenty guys filled out ballots. It's absolutely a true story. I can sit here now, and I can see that room, and I remember thinking, 'How come they have stacks of ballots?' These were party regulars. They were filling out multiple ballots. This was ballot box stuffing in the great tradition of Chicago."

John grew up with guns too, learning to shoot a BB gun at seven or eight; his father took him pheasant hunting with a shotgun when he was twelve, but John says he never got one. "I first learned to shoot a .45-caliber pistol at around age sixteen. I often went to a local gun range *by myself* to shoot, riding my bicycle to and from the range with my father's pistol in a gym bag." Today he owns a .22 target pistol, a 9mm pistol, two .40-caliber pistols, and a Colt .45 pistol, a pump shotgun, an AR15-type carbine, and a Browning heavy-barrel, precision Varmint rifle with a 10-power scope.

Today with the Cailes, it's a bit of a reversal, as it is the older Caile who has set his footprints in the Internet, leading the sons. This venture was his idea. Jason—a sports shooter but not a hunter—grew up with his dad's guns at home, and now his father's later-in-life enthusiasm for the Internet has him caught in the political undertow. "My father's been around guns, and I grew up with them, too," says Jason, who owns a Browning .308-caliber rifle, a single-shot 12-gauge, and a number of pistols. On the Internet, he's carried over his interest in painting into graphic design. He's also contributing his personal e-mail list of three dozen or so of his best contacts, in Florida, Texas, California, Washington state, and Wisconsin.

Although the positions in the gun debate may seem intractable to some, Jason says he still believes a site like the Cailes' could make a difference in attitudes, not just turnout. "What we're after is borderline people, people who need some education. If they can see our point just a little bit, if they can see having a relaxed concealed weapon law does seem to lower the crime rate in cities where they have brought those about, then people will begin to see the light a little bit."

Sean Caile works "more than full time" for a medical insurance software company in the Chicago suburb of Schaumburg. Though swamped at work, he was still shoehorning in from two to four hours a night on the family Web project as the calendar turned 2002, working on the $2,000, Windows-based home-built computer he'd set up in his apartment. Sean—the hardware and software brains of the effort—said the project was set back when everyone agreed to scrap the entire layout and start over, trading ideas via e-mail at all hours and every day as they worked to make the debut product perfect. The goal, Sean said: utility and interactivity, so that visitors to the site could find what they wanted on the home page or via a link and easily go offline to strike up a conversation about any of the news pieces or commentaries.

Sean was uploading everything to a server run by an Internet service provider (ISP) in Schaumburg, and he estimated that monthly maintenance costs to reach thousands of users—a seemingly modest and instantly achievable goal given the potential audience and the Cailes' contacts—would run no more than $200.

A target shooter since the age of twelve who enjoys twice-a-week visits to a range, Sean describes himself as a "conservative working guy" who voted for George Bush. He hopes someday to find the time to be as deeply involved in politics and civics as his dad because, he says, "gun owners *can* make a difference if there's something that's important to them. I think my dad will be able to convey that on the site, and myself and my brother, in a manner that people will respond to. We'll give people a place where they can write to their representatives. That's a feat in itself for people who are aren't super Internet savvy."

How to get the voters out is the question, John Caile says. "We've been very successful here in Minnesota. You have to find the hot buttons. The Internet makes for that. If you send an article to gun owners in Minnesota about how they just passed a law in California that now makes every deer rifle classified as a dangerous sniper rifle, that suddenly gets people's dander up. That's no longer an idle threat. You tell them, 'That's already been done. And if you want that to happen here, keep your fingers in your ears.' That's an example of using the Internet to convey information to bolster a point and to motivate someone to action. People don't ever act unless there's some motivation that seems immediate and severe enough that they think, 'I'd better do that.' According to the ATF [Bureau of Alcohol, Tobacco, and Firearms], there are about 80 million gun owners in the country. That's about as many people as voted in the last national election. So gun owners could control every election if they voted as a bloc. The problem is most of them are not aware. A good portion are hunters who tell themselves they don't have to worry about [gun laws] because that only applies to gun owners with handguns. 'I'm just a duck hunter. I don't have anything to worry about.' So I've always said gun owners are like the frogs in the water. If you drop them in boiling water, they will come out instantaneously. They will react. If there's a local issue that scares them, they come out and vote ruthlessly, and they're one of the groups that will absolutely, instantaneously step across party lines."

The Cailes will promote havegunwillvote.com through their e-mail lists, and they hope to link to some gun manufacturers that would link back. John Caile does not expect to carry any advertising. But if there is any at all, he promises it would be just to cover costs. "This is meant to be an informational resource linking lots of people with common interests and directing them to sites that will give them more specifically what they want and at the same time editorializing on the need to vote and how to vote and how to contact your legislator."

Caile is not a classic online multi-tasker, and he likes to use all of his senses. He knows online can miss nuance, context, and your own human-ity. He watched the presidential debates but did not go online at the same time. "I want to just watch and pay attention. I come from a long line of poker players, and we read body language, so we keep our eyes glued to the person who is speaking."

That said, Caile is a true believer in online communication. "There is no question that if it weren't for the Internet, I couldn't be doing all of this," Caile says about havegunwillvote.com and his new brand of ac-tivism and networking. "Or, I would probably be doing it but in a much less efficient way. I would have less efficient ways to gather information and less efficient ways to express an opinion to people."

7

COMMUNITIES
OF ACTION

ZEKE SPIER SAT DOWN IN THE STREET AT THE CORNER OF SOUTH Broad and Spruce in Philadelphia and momentarily blocked traffic, an act that would normally provoke car horns, irate epithets, and perhaps a digital display of anger from a discomfited commuter. However, his was a political act, there were 150 more protesters like him, and the police were nearby and ready to end their display forthwith. He was lifted off the pavement, shackled behind his back with a plastic tie strap, and placed on a police bus with seventy companions. Anxious to keep order and control during the Republican National Convention, Philadelphia police responded quickly to protesters who descended on the city during the unusually hot August of 2000. In all, 420 protesters were arrested in Philadelphia during convention week and charged with offenses that ranged from disturbing the peace to assault. Spier himself was charged with four misdemeanors, each carrying a possible sentence of five years, as well as conspiracy to commit the acts. His co-conspirators were a hodgepodge of activists from all over the country who came together for one week, formed a community of action, and gladly shared a ride to jail together for a cause.

Communities of *action* are obviously closely related to communities of belief. The actions their members undertake are for a belief-driven purpose, after all. But the groups that we label as communities of action are anchored in the doing and in making, changing, or at least affecting laws and policies. There are literally thousands of examples of non-Internet communities of action. Looking back into the nation's past, one might include the Populist party and the Women's Christian Temperance Union; more recently one might think of Greenpeace and Peace Action or the Lion's Club and Neighborhood Watch.

The Protester

Although at first it may seem to some parents of college-aged children to fit the contours of a nightmare, the story of Zeke Spier actually illustrates how the Internet can be a dream come true for communities of action. The many political communities that the Brown University student became involved with and in one case started through the Internet have long been familiar—communities protesting perceived injustices perpetrated against others and against the larger community as a whole, both nation and world.

The Internet did not produce a different kind of activity—the ultimate product of these communities was on-the-ground political action and civil disobedience. But it dramatically facilitated the communication of beliefs, strategy, and acceptable tactics. Its speed and lack of expense forged interpersonal connections more quickly, across wider expanses, and among more people than would have been possible otherwise. Indeed, it would not be an exaggeration in this case to say that, had it not been for the Internet, many of these groups would not have achieved the "critical mass" necessary to undertake effective action—the complicated logistics involved in collective political action by geographically dispersed individuals would have done them in. Many of the individuals may have taken to the streets regardless, but there would have been fewer of them, and they would have possessed less common understanding of their purpose and their tactics.

Note in Spier's story how the Internet is woven through his personal odyssey. It is instrumental in his self-education and awakening to social justice. It then gave him an easily navigable avenue through which to pursue his newfound passions at college and led to membership in groups devoted to causes he cared about. It facilitated his participation in and organization of actual protests and allowed him to congregate with people sharing the same views about nonviolence and arrest. And it is currently helping him to defend himself and others against what they maintain is unfair treatment at the hands of the legal system.

The most distinctive aspect of Spier's story vis-à-vis the Internet and social capital, however, is what it demonstrates about the trust that can be achieved through Internet connections. Pay particular attention to what happens in Philadelphia. These people were able to bank on what they learned about each other only through the Internet in undertaking real political activities involving the highest stakes—personal safety and legal prosecution. That kind of trust is hard to generate and maintain through any means.

This nation was formed by protesters; the First Amendment protects them, and folk ballads celebrate them. Not only is protesting an American tradition, but the exercise of the right of protest is the civic equivalent of lifting weights. It strengthens the American people even as it underscores the issues that divide them. People who have a squabble with the government are more likely to be civically engaged and politically active and to vote. Mayors, police chiefs, and the local chamber of commerce tremble at the thought of a street demonstration by passionate contrarians while their city is in a convention spotlight. It's a public relations nightmare. But there is no stronger evidence of a healthy democracy than the presence of vocal dissenters. They are the physical embodiment of the First Amendment.

And so it was in Philadelphia on August 1, 2000. Hundreds of demonstrators from all over the country shadowed thousands of Republican National Convention delegates as they descended on the City of Brotherly Love for a week of speeches, rallies, caucuses, and celebrations. The delegates settled into a regimen of carefully scripted activities scheduled well in advance by the Republican National Committee. The agenda was set. The delegates gathered by states in their assigned areas on the convention floor. Speaker after speaker held the floor and methodically pounded down one campaign plank after another until the entire platform on which George W. Bush would run was soundly constructed.

Meanwhile, somewhere in Philadelphia, the demonstrators found each other, formed affinity groups, selected spokespersons, and reached agreement on the nature of the protests in which they would engage. Times, places, and topics were chosen. The level of civil disobedience was arrived at by consensus. Some protesters were willing to be arrested if that's what it would take to make their point, and those went to one street corner. Others were not, and they went to another. And so it went, block by block, until they ringed the convention center with a virtual picket fence of anti-issues: corporate control, the death penalty, the criminal "injustice" system.

Inside the convention hall, the television networks and newspapers did their best to make an inevitable outcome, foreshadowed by events totally lacking in conflict or drama, appear interesting. Internet news sites covered the proceedings with high-tech streaming video from Webcams mounted on the ceiling or carried around by online reporters, believing, perhaps, that the technology really is the message.

Outside the convention hall, as far as two miles away, protesters were captured on video by police who later used the tapes as evidence in some of the trials of more than 420 people arrested that day. Included in the roundup by Philadelphia police was a nineteen-year-old veteran of vocal self-expression, group protest, and civil disobedience. Zeke Spier, a Brown University freshman who had already traveled to Georgia and Washington, D.C., to march, was arrested with seventy-two others on the corner of Spruce and South Broad. Owing to the Internet every step of the way, his is a story of awakening to social justice issues. Using the Internet, Spier prepared himself for political engagement, organized a demonstration, and assisted in his own defense in the criminal justice system. For Spier, the Internet was the information, communication, and networking instrument that enabled him to discover his passion for social justice and to find the willingness to sacrifice his freedom to express it.

Growing up back in Portland, Oregon, Spier wasn't especially political, and his family, though regular voters, was not particularly active in civic affairs. He, his parents (both lawyers), and his two brothers rarely spoke about politics around the dinner table. But Spier kept up with current events by reading and watching the news. They always had the daily

PHOTO 7.1   Zeke Spier

newspaper, *The Oregonian,* around the house, and Spier developed the unusual habit (for a preteen) of getting up at 5:00 A.M. and watching the morning news shows on television. He speaks about world affairs with confidence and intelligence that belie his age.

In public high school, Spier was a good student whose main extracurricular activity was theater. "My first experience of expressing political thought happened when I began working in school with people who wanted to do more topical theater pieces," he said. "I read books about the theater, particularly about Russian and German theater." European theater and politics are much more closely intertwined than in this country, and he was impressed with the power of theater as a means of political expression. Spier and his theater friends wound up writing and producing a play about the teenage immigrant experience. While doing the research for the play, they found themselves immersed in political issues because "a lot of what these people face as immigrants are because of government policies." The more he dug, the more he came to see current events in this country in a new light. "Some of the things about the way things work in this country made me angry."

High school classes in social studies and anthropology, which exposed Spier to historical injustices, furthered his immersion in political thought. He remembered a class that covered U.S. involvement in El Salvador.

"This is stuff I was just outraged about," he said. "This is against everything I had been told about our country. Overthrowing a socialist in favor of a dictator." Eventually, this thinking led to exploring other spheres. He became a feminist by speaking with his female friends and finding out about their experiences. By the time he matriculated at Brown University, in Providence, Rhode Island, in the fall of 1999, he was already cast as a socially conscious, politically aware reformer.

Spier sought out classes and activities that would expand his ideas about social justice. He took a course called "Civil Rights and the Legacy of the 1960s," but it wasn't the academic work that drew Spier closer to the radical thoughts and actions that would eventually land him in jail; it was the personal connections he developed with like-minded students. Spier got on various listservs and e-mail lists at Brown that brought activists together. "One list led to another, and I started getting information about everything. Meeting updates, discussions, teach-ins, scheduled demonstrations, you name it." He started attending meetings and small, impromptu classes held by various professors.

By October he was ready for something besides dialogue. Someone sent him an e-mail about the annual demonstration waged against the School of the Americas (SOA), located at Fort Benning, Georgia. The U.S. Army runs the military school, and its students—military officers—come from Latin American countries. The left generally regards it as a training ground for assassins and military death squads that operate in Central America. Critics say some of its graduates have been responsible for the most gruesome massacres of civilians in El Salvador, Guatemala, and Honduras. When Spier heard of the demonstrations to shut the school down, he said, "That's for me. I'm going." He boarded a bus and, along with a couple hundred other students from Brown, joined 10,000 protesters who "crossed the line" onto federal property at the School of the Americas, risking arrest.

Spier wasn't arrested but saw what he called "the police resistance to protesting." "The police lied to us, they misled us, they did things to break us up," he said. He described how, at one point during a solemn march to mourn those killed in Central America by soldiers trained at SOA, the police unleashed an ambulance through the crowd, sending the protesters scurrying off the road. "It was a ruse. It just stopped and didn't pick up anybody," he sighed. When he first went down to Georgia, Spier thought he'd get a chance to have his voice heard, he'd be empowered, and then he'd go home. However, the behavior of the police toward the protesters alarmed and awakened Spier to the dark side of free speech. "It radicalized me," he said. About a month later, Spier followed demonstrations against the World Trade Organization (WTO) in Seattle, and the violent reaction of the police strengthened his resolve to protest again. "The adrenaline," he said, "was flowing."

"The first place I went to was the computer to find out about the WTO," he said. "I heard about the demonstrations in the mainstream media, and I did not think it was the full picture of what happened. I didn't trust them." The media, after all, did a poor job of reporting what he had just experienced in Georgia. "I went on a bunch of searches and found the Independent Media Center Web site (indymedia.org) in Seattle," a site he would rely on again and again as his thirst for participating in civil disobedience grew. He spent hours and hours on the site, looking at pictures and video, reading firsthand accounts, and constructing his own image of what occurred in Seattle.

He surfed the Web looking for other sources of information about the WTO and its activities throughout the world. He concluded that it is antidemocratic and antipoor. He could not be in Seattle, and he needed an outlet for his feelings, so he did an art project about the subject for one of his classes at Brown, but that was only a weak substitute for action. Shortly afterwards, the countercultural Web site indymedia.org announced a demonstration against the International Monetary Fund (IMF) and the World Bank in Washington, D.C., in April 2000. It was on the East Coast and an easy drive from Providence. Spier could hardly wait.

Spier used the Internet extensively to organize the trip to Washington among his Brown peers. "We advertised our organizational meetings on the independent media Web sites and on all the e-mail lists." These were often unmoderated lists. Somebody would set them up, people would register, and then the lists would take on a life of their own. Spier co-opted the sites for a time, monopolizing the discussions to build momentum for the action. He also found it necessary to learn more about the IMF, so he researched the organization. "About 95 percent of the research I did was on the Internet. I visited the IMF official Web site, then I would go and do a search to find all the protest groups—twenty or thirty groups. I wanted to make sure I was informed enough, so I went after the facts, myself. It's more than a passion, it's an intellectual exercise." When April rolled around, Spier went down to D.C. with about one hundred other students by bus.

In what Spier described as "a halfway futile attempt to shut the IMF meeting down," he and his band of demonstrators were assigned an intersection to blockade. Other groups did the same to establish a perimeter around the building. "We woke up at 4:00 A.M. one day, went to the location, and sat down in the intersection at 18th Street and I. Some of us handed out information, others chanted," he recalled. The police did not bother his cadre, but Spier saw others who had been hit with pepper spray stumble by. "That helped radicalize me further," he said.

For the first time he caught a glimpse of a group called the Anarchist Black Bloc, built on a tradition, he says, that came from Germany, England, and Italy. These protesters dress identically in black, both as a statement of their political beliefs and also as a tactical effort to avoid being singled out by the police. "People in Europe are more militant than they are here," said Spier, "and it's pretty common in Europe for somebody to turn over a car or set something on fire." A black-clad militant can melt into the similarly dressed crowd and avoid detection. The Black Bloc idea was used by some WTO protesters in Seattle and then again in Washington, D.C., during the IMF protest. "The American version [of the Black Bloc] didn't destroy property. They acted as decoys to attract the police and lure them away from the peaceful protesters. I actually saw them position themselves between a line of demonstrators and the police who were approaching. I was really impressed by that. They were the reason I didn't get pepper sprayed."

According to Spier, the Black Bloc is so loosely organized, the participants do not even know each other. They simply share a radical, anticapitalist view. They find each other, and plan their civil disobedience, entirely on the Internet. Infoshop.org is one Web site that features news and information for Black Bloc types. It provides the latest headlines for demonstrators looking for the next chance to protest. "Of course, they keep things very vague because they don't want the police showing up where they show up," he laughed. A big misconception about the Black Bloc and many other anarchist and protest groups is that they actually have a "membership." "They are simply a group of people who decide to use the same particular tactics during one particular action," he said. "It's not something you're in or not in. It's just something you choose to do or not do. And it wouldn't be possible at all except the Internet gives all of these people a chance to organize and not get caught."

To Spier, more important than not getting caught is actually making a difference. By the time he was sitting on the pavement at 18th and I, he had traveled about 1,000 miles to two different protests, had spent hours on the Internet indoctrinating himself, and had spent days away from school in strange cities. That morning, he had gotten up earlier than any self-respecting college freshman ever does and had barely escaped getting pepper sprayed by the Metro police. Did it matter? "I went into a sandwich shop just to take a break, and sitting there was this businessman. We started talking, and it turned out he was a delegate to the IMF conference from Europe. He couldn't get in because we were blocking the way," Spier said, with a bit of surprise in his voice. "We actually got into a decent dialogue about the protests and about the IMF. It was a marvelous exchange. I actually think he learned more from me than I did from him. He hadn't thought about a lot of the concerns that people were raising. I didn't change his mind about anything, and he didn't change mine, but it was a terrific discussion."

Four days later, Spier was exhausted and tired. "We slept on the floor of a Jewish community center, but actually got very little rest." He took a bus back to Providence. He finished his freshman year uneventfully, bought a car in June, and started back home to Portland by himself. "I had already heard over the Internet, on the listservs I was on, and on all the sites I usually go to that there were protests planned for both the Republican and Democratic conventions," he said. He planned his road trip so he could be back east, in Philadelphia, by the end of July.

For Spier the Republican convention offered an opportunity to protest a number of the party's policies with which he takes issue. His big three were the degree of power that corporations exercise over the party, George Bush's record with the death penalty, and the drug war, which Spier described as "a war on the poor, and in particular black people." "This country just went over 2 million people in jail. That's more than Iran and China. All of these issues, and the proof behind them, are on the Web site that you can go to, to learn about the protest. It's all there, as well as links to many other Web sites," he explained. "I don't automatically believe that everything on these sites is true, but there are levels of cross-referencing that I go through to get at my final sense of the truth. There are levels of trust, and I trust the ACLU, for example, and Amnesty International." Spier was convinced he was on solid ground when he decided to exercise his free speech right in Philadelphia later that summer.

During his road trip to and from Portland, his only contact with the Philadelphia protest organizers was by Internet. "I stopped at public libraries and checked the updates on the convention, how the organizing [was] going, any updates on the police, whether permits had been gotten for any of the marches, and so on. It ended up that I was able to get [to Philadelphia] on July 27, and my first stop was the public library. I got on the Internet and looked up where the convergence locations were." Convergence locations are places where teach-ins, training, and gatherings take place when protesters come in from out of town. "If it weren't for the Internet, I don't know how I would have found anybody," he said.

What he found, once he got oriented, was an affinity group that fit his particular beliefs—a group whose protest goals matched his own. In protest parlance, this is a group of from five to twenty-five people "who establish a consensus-based structure of like-minded individuals to participate in an action." Spier explained that in affinity groups, which is an old countercultural term with European roots, "people have different roles—a support person, a media person, somebody who can interact with the police." Eventually, each group chooses somebody to represent them at a "spokes council," where the entire protest is planned. In this way, directives come from the bottom up instead of from the top down. "The idea is to arrive at a level of involvement that everybody feels comfortable with, but to maintain a level of independence," Spier explained. "And another reason is to avoid being infiltrated by the police. At the affinity group level, you know everybody.

"Without getting into fuzzy legal areas, what with my trial pending, people in my group took part in a protest at South Broad Street in Philadelphia. About 100 to 150 people protested there, and that's where I was arrested." Spier had coorganized the protest, which focused on the damage caused to young people because of some Republican party policies. One issue he singled out was the party's support of mandatory sentencing in the criminal justice system and the adverse affect it has on the children of men and women incarcerated for minor offenses. Most of the protesters were young. Spier estimated the average age was between seventeen and twenty. He was quick to point out that they were not necessarily supporters of Al Gore and in fact intended to protest in exactly the same manner at the Democratic convention the following week. He wouldn't make it.

When the police arrested Spier and about seventy of his fellow protesters they were shackled, hands behind their backs with plastic tie straps, and loaded into buses. "I was charged with four misdemeanors," he lamented. "Usually, somebody arrested for protesting would be charged with a summary offense, spend a night in jail, and that's it. That didn't happen here. Each charge against me carried a five-year prison term." Spier and nearly all of the others arrested at Spruce and South Broad that day were charged with obstructing a highway, disorderly conduct, resisting arrest, and conspiracy to commit the other three misdemeanors. During his arraignment, Spier exercised yet another form of protest—perfectly legal and used by many in mass arrest situations like this one—of not giving his name. The practice is known as "jail solidarity," and it usually causes havoc for the arresting party, which winds up with a jail full of John and Jane Does. For the strategy to be effective, everyone arrested must agree to refuse to provide his or her name, something that requires that everyone trust each other. Spier became a John Doe and joined a number of others who refused to identify themselves to the court. He was unable to come up with $10,000 bail.

Little by little, others capitulated and gave their names to the police. Eventually, the solidarity eroded and after nine days in jail, Spier gave in. He gave his name to the police and was released on his own recognizance. The Democratic convention, which had been his next target, happened without him. Many of those arrested with him worked things out on their own or went to trial like he did on September 23. At Spier's trial, he was one of forty-three codefendants who were brought up on charges. The district attorney presented a case against only five of them, including Spier, while charges against everyone else were dismissed. The most damning evidence against him was a video shot by the police that showed Spier sitting in the street. He was found guilty on two counts, obstructing traffic and conspiracy to obstruct traffic, and is out on appeal.

Spier never went back to school and instead took a room in a house with several other young activists in Philadelphia, "where it's really not expensive to live," he said. He signed on with R2Klegal, an organization set up before the convention to support and coordinate the legal battles of anyone arrested during the convention. Anticipating that there would be at least some arrests during the protests, R2Klegal had arranged for some private attorneys to work on behalf of the protesters pro bono. However, more that 420 (by some accounts) were arrested, far more than the private lawyers were willing to defend for free and adding significantly to the coordination of the legal struggle.

The private attorneys were joined by public defenders, and the two groups worked closely to share information under the umbrella of R2Klegal. Spier did legal support for those arrested, helping them in court, dealing with the lawyers, doing press conferences and other media work. A significant part of the defense effort is over the Internet, using the organization's Web site, R2Kphilly.org, as the base of operations. "We also have a listserv of the defendants, and we keep everybody informed about court dates and other updates," said Spier. "The Internet is the main way we communicate with everybody involved." Spier isn't the Webmaster—the young man who is, also was arrested and was found not guilty—but he does post messages on the site.

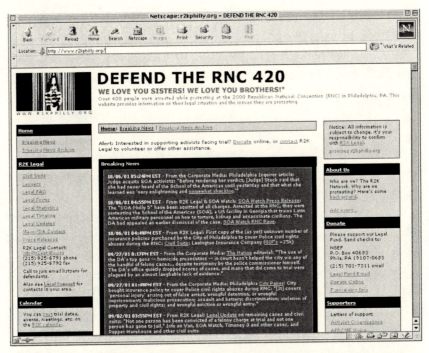

PHOTO 7.2   R2Kphilly Web site. Of the 420 who were arrested at the Republican convention, only three were still facing trial by February 2002.

About fifty-five defendants still had trials pending on January 20, 2001, even as George W. Bush's inauguration occurred two hours south on I-95. The majority were college students who hailed from thirty-five states, and keeping them informed about rescheduled court dates, new evidence, new witnesses, and other matters is a daunting enterprise for a grassroots operation like R2Klegal. The Internet provided the group with its only viable communications and networking tool. It is cheap, fast, and dependable.

Sean Nolan and Meg Flores are two public defenders who were assigned to about three hundred cases stemming from the demonstrations. Typical of public defenders, thirty-seven-year-old Nolan and twenty-nine-year-old Flores are hardworking, idealistic, and committed. Both come from the suburbs of Philadelphia, where they were raised by politically active, liberal parents. They share a passion for defending the poor, as well as many of the political beliefs of their clients. Perhaps because of that and their professionalism, they have gone the extra mile in their defense of the convention protesters.

Nolan and Flores were accustomed to handling individual cases, not a large number of clients whose arrests occurred on the same day in various places throughout the city. They had to find a new way of coping with the logistics presented by the huge caseload. They adopted the Internet to conduct their own investigation and develop a defense strategy. "There are still several felony cases we are handling. These people were charged with assaulting police," explained Nolan. "We think it happened the other way—they were themselves assaulted."

To gather evidence, Nolan and Flores visited the indymedia.org Web site, where photographers had posted pictures of the demonstrations at the convention, some of which seemed to contradict the police account. They contacted the photographers by e-mail and got additional pictures and statements from the photographers who had witnessed the arrests. The network of contacts grew from there until the attorneys had a file thick with affidavits and eyewitness accounts.

"Trial dates get changed, we file tons of motions, and we've been able to use the Internet to keep in touch with our clients. We just do mass e-mails," explained Flores. Most of the clients Nolan and Flores usually represent are indigent—they don't have e-mail addresses, or real ones either—but the convention arrests were primarily students, and they all do. Not only were Nolan and Flores able to keep the defendants informed, but as Nolan described it, "It's been helpful to them as well, because they are all trying to act in solidarity with each other, and they have been able to keep in contact with each other." "They are an extremely committed group of individuals," added Flores.

Zeke Spier is more than committed. He became, as he willingly admits, incorrigible. While awaiting retrial in Philadelphia, he heard about another protest (again, over the Internet) in November 2000 in Cincinnati, Ohio, against the Transatlantic Business Dialogue, a conference for the top two hundred CEOs from the United States and Europe. "This time I was arrested completely illegally," he says. "I was arrested for chanting."

The Petitioner

Perhaps no story better illustrates the potential for establishing communities of action through the Internet than that of Kevin Matthews and PetitionOnline. Born out of Matthews's educational experience resembling New England town-meeting democracy, PetitionOnline mixes local, national, and global political concerns with grassroots political activity to create a rich virtual blend. Along the way it establishes bonds of friendship and political solidarity around meaningful public questions, ranging from how people who share a set of political views should cast their votes in a presidential election to specific issues before city councils.

The communities formed by PetitionOnline have led to more traditional forms of political activism—writing letters to representatives and editors, voicing opinions through other media, and so on. But they have also been active communities that achieve important objectives, and maintain their connectedness, *online.*

Perhaps most important for the concerns about social capital, the communities of action fostered and sustained by PetitionOnline appear to enhance the participants' own sense of political *efficacy*; that is, a feeling of having power and effectiveness, of mattering. As measured by political scientists, this sense of political efficacy has declined significantly over the past forty years.[1] The decline of efficacy has been a principal culprit in the decline of social capital more generally.

But as Matthews puts it, PetitionOnline taps into "latent" political communities that might exist but presently don't, because not enough people can connect with each other through traditional means or because their views are unpopular in their own offline communities. In an influential work in social psychology, Elisabeth Noelle-Neumann has identified a "spiral of silence" at work in public opinion, through which a view held by a substantial number of citizens may nonetheless never be voiced—or heard—because it appears deviant and because the holders of the view fear the social isolation that they assume will result from expressing it.[2] PetitionOnline has helped to break this spiral of silence for many individuals by letting them discover that others share similar views.

PHOTO 7.3   Kevin Matthews

Kevin Matthews is a Renaissance man, typical of the forty-somethings who have led the Internet revolution over the past decade. Those intrepid individuals who adopted early defined the Internet for the rest of us. As entrepreneurs, technophiles, and visionaries they continue to find the most creative and stimulating uses of the Net—uses that go well beyond the narrow thinking sponsored by the lumbering, Johnny-come-lately media conglomerates. Matthews is all three of those types, and he managed to find a use for the Internet that provides him not only a nice return on investment but also a means to promote his own political agenda and sense of social justice.

Matthews and his wife, Donna, an attorney, are the founders of PetitionOnline, a company that hosts online petitions. Their company has hosted over 2,500 petitions taken by over a million Internet users in the last three years. About a fifth of the petitions are political, and the rest run the gamut from petitions to keep certain soap operas on the air to ones to prevent strip malls in residential neighborhoods. Some are local, others national. One asks for clemency for a condemned woman in Bahrain.

"PetitionOnline is a social experiment on the Web. An experiment in free speech and political community and communication and how you use the Internet for political organizing," explains Matthews. "We've had all kinds of people use it for everything from saving their favorite TV show to de Tocqueville–style splinter issues." Folks who want to create and circulate a petition can go to the site (PetitionOnline.com), author their petition, and then promote the Web address to their friends, who may then forward it to others. "We realized that, when somebody makes a petition, they are doing that because they are passionate about a cause. They take the initiative to promote that petition to their own community." Petition authors can retrieve their database and deliver the list of signatures to the petition's target—a city council, perhaps. "Our biggest problem has been unverifiable names, sometimes accompanied by scatological invectives." Indeed, a cursory glance at one list of petition signers included someone called "Earth Mother," whose comment line said, "fuck you sierra club [*sic*] you miserable failures." No return address.

Matthews himself has used his company's service exactly twice, both times for political purposes. Both times he got something he didn't expect. Without really trying, Matthews formed bonds of friendship and community with those who found his petitions to be enabling, ennobling, and enriching. The online petitions gave the signers a chance to have a real impact on an important issue, often in situations in which they had felt powerless and voiceless. Matthews talks with pride and a bit of glee when he relates how his online business (one of the few with a real revenue stream) turned into a forum for social networking, discourse, and action.

Although currently living in Eugene, Oregon, Matthews is a New Englander by upbringing and political leaning. His father is a physicist, his mother a social worker. It isn't lost on him that his high-tech company—one his father would be proud of—provides a platform for social good that his mother would admire.

To fully understand Matthews and how he got to where he is, you have to go back to his high school days. "I was sort of an outcast," he says. "I got the highest test scores of any male ever, but my grades were just average. I was interested in people, theater, and politics—not the stuff the other kids were into. I read *The Nation* every day. I was the only kid who knew Richard Nixon was a felon." He has always been stubbornly independent, interested in getting to the source of information, and making up his own mind. The Internet provides him with the resources he wants and needs to find and create his own body of knowledge, not the predigested form served up by the media. "The Internet helps me build my worldview on a pure foundation," he says.

After high school Matthews migrated West to attend one of the world's smallest accredited liberal arts colleges, Deep Springs College, located in a high desert mountain valley on the California-Nevada border. "It definitely had a contemplative feeling," he explains. There, the emphasis was on a strong liberal arts foundation, with a healthy dose of cow poking. All twenty-four students studied the classics while contributing some manual labor to the working ranch. Matthews's contribution was blacksmithing, which he found combined just the right amount of New England craftsmanship with being a Western frontiersman. The entire student body functioned as a student government, and Matthews was deeply involved. It must have felt to him, at the time, like what town meetings were like in the earliest days of New England's experiments with democracy. The experience of living, working, and governing within a small and close community, isolated from the rest of the world, had a profound effect on Matthews's sense of social networks.

When Matthews left Deep Springs, after only two years, he became a "starving artist, hand to mouth," in Santa Cruz, California. He utilized his experience and skill with eighteenth century–style ironwork to create his art but in the middle of what was even then shaping up as the heart of Silicon Valley. He attended the University of California–Santa Cruz (UCSC) part time, continued at UC Berkeley, and eventually earned a masters degree in architecture. After work on a few big projects propelled him into the big time, his reputation earned him an appointment to teach architecture at the University of Oregon in 1990, where he stayed for seven years. During this stretch of time, Matthews founded the Internet software and publishing company Artifice, the mother ship of PetitionOnline. It grew and became commercially viable, taking him away from the classroom. The freedom afforded by his company's success enabled him to get more involved in nonpartisan local politics. In a wonderful and ironic shift of fate, high technology sent Matthews back into low-tech grassroots organizing. He was even elected head of his local neighborhood association in Eugene. And that's what motivated him to author his first online petition on his own company's Web site.

"My first petition was to Ralph Nader, asking him to honor previous commitments he had made to not campaign in swing states, to peaceably coexist with the Gore campaign, rather than targeting and undermining the Gore campaign." The petition came out of real personal experiences Matthews was having with his social and political circles in Eugene. He's deeply involved in local environmental and land use issues, and Eugene, as he puts it, "is one of the ground-zero places for Nader-style environmentalists." Even though, according to Matthews, the number of Americans who define themselves as environmentalists had fallen from 75 percent to 50 percent during the 1990s, the decline is not evident in the Northwest, least of all in Eugene, where people wear the label as a badge of honor. Matthews found it difficult and uncomfortable to hold his own political beliefs (he's a strong Gore man) and still function, socially and politically, while surrounded by "really visible, boisterous Nader supporters."

He once attended a Nader rally. "It was huge. Everybody I knew from my overlapping environmental groups were there, and I was totally turned off by the whole thing. I was also personally intimidated by that," he recalls. He was convinced that it was important for Gore to beat Bush, and Gore needed these people who seemed to be irrational and intractably devoted to a candidate who had no chance of winning. He mulled it over for a few days and then started asking around to find out if others felt the same way. They did. Many people who had attended the rally and gave strong visible support to Nader admitted that peer pressure had caused them to be there but that they actually supported Gore. "The risk in Eugene is that you'd be branded as a sell-out or not a serious environmentalist," Matthews lamented. In an open letter, Nader himself had called environmentalists who supported Gore "spineless lackeys." Matthews had to do something.

"Here I am in a swing state, and here is this direct problem. So I thought, why don't I make a petition that will let people make their feelings about Gore visible, in a way that has the power of numbers uniting together but doesn't cause people to confront their friends over the coffee table." Matthews came across an open letter written by Carl Pope, executive director of the Sierra Club, that encapsulated everything he wanted to say to Ralph Nader, which was basically to stop jeopardizing Gore's chances. He got Pope's permission to use the letter as the basis of his online petition. Matthews put the petition up on his site ten days before the election, and without a preexisting mailing list or a Web site to promote it but just a small number of pump-priming e-mail contacts, more than 16,000 people signed by midday on Election Day.

Matthews's voice softens as he recalls what happened next. "I got so many thank-you letters, e-mails, and phone calls. So many people were watching the petition. There were people reading every signature. There were a lot of [pro-Gore] Nader hecklers, and if one of them signed I'd get two or three e-mails telling me about it. It became a huge community." Matthews was shocked by the petition's success, even though it had no direct effect on the election's outcome. It had demonstrated to him that this technological marvel he had cooked up in the backroom at the office could actually fly. Its second combat mission was only days away.

"I was looking forward to the election being over so I could fix up the rest of my life, and then there was the debacle in Florida. I can't just watch this happen without putting my oar in. I need to make a petition," he said, and within two days of the election he posted "Trust the People." This one urged George Bush to concede the election to Al Gore based on the popular vote and the unlikely resolution of the final Florida tabulation. He used a slightly larger e-mail list to get it started and within a few days had over 20,000 signatures. "There was a point of view that I thought was invisible in the national discourse. I thought there was a latent community of people that I could turn into a virtual community of people. That we could put our voices together and show up on the national applause meter." It worked. The petition itself attracted the attention of the national press.

Matthews wound up on a half-dozen talk radio shows around the country, including the Alan Colmes show on WEVD News Talk 1050 in New York City. On that show, heard internationally over the Internet, Matthews went one-on-one with Richard Viguerie, the nationally known conservative activist and fund-raiser whose Web sites include ConservativeHQ.com and ConcedeNow.com. It was a battle of dueling online petitions, with Viguerie claiming he had 30,000 signatures demanding Gore concede. During the show, one caller from Matthews's e-mail community got through and articulately defended the petition. "He was so excited, he e-mailed me the next day and asked, 'How did I sound?'"

Matthews could hardly believe where his brand of political involvement had led him. "I used the Internet petition to visualize an under-enunciated viewpoint, built up a community of people around the petition, publicized the petition to the media and got on the talk shows and other media channels, and then used e-mail to invite the community to participate in the talk shows, which they did." This last point illustrates how it is possible to create political communities and avenues for civic engagement that weave in and out of virtual and real space in a mutually reinforcing way. Each iteration builds on the past one, adding to the bank of social capital.

Although neither petition had a measurable political effect, both had what Matthews called a strong psychological effect on the petition signers. "It was satisfying for them. It involved people in the discourse, and when they signed it, they became co-owners of that petition." Many signers of the Nader petition took their enthusiasm to the streets. They wrote letters to the editor, talked to the media, called into talk shows, and contacted elected representatives and key players in campaigns around the country. "Trust the People" was still online months after the Supreme Court decision that awarded Bush the election, and a dozen or more people signed it every day as a form of personal protest.

One of the oldest and most sacred rights of the individual in a democratic society, in fact, any society, is the right to petition. It is one form of political participation that is measured by social scientists and used to determine the health of our civic engagement. Every month for more than twenty years (1973–1994) Roper surveyed thousands of Americans and watched every form of political involvement decline, including what had been the most common—signing a petition. That gauge dipped 22 percent over the twenty-year study. Unfortunately, the study ended just as the World Wide Web was born, and years before PetitionOnline.com powered up. Before the Internet made it possible to reach a national audience instantly and cheaply, circulating a petition took time, sweat equity, and dedicated volunteers—three things that the two-income, suburban, commuter families of the 1980s and 1990s simply could not contribute. People aren't refusing to sign petitions; it's just that nobody is bringing them to the door anymore. Matthews may be helping to solve that problem with his software, energy, and social consciousness.

The Expatriates

One of the more intriguing examples of an Internet-based community of *action* is that of Democrats Abroad and the story of Maria Mancini, the head of Democrats Abroad in Italy. Here the Internet was instrumental in realizing a twofold increase in the number of registered voters among expatriates as compared with past elections. It allowed more effective and less expensive advertising of the group and the information it provided and greatly facilitated the actual process of registering to vote. There is evidence in this story to suggest that the Internet's facilitation actually instigated political action among those who ordinarily would not have bothered—the Internet thus leading to increased political initiative. In addition, through e-mail contact, disparate expatriates learned for the first time of fellow expatriates living nearby. Thus the Internet also helped to foster more traditional networks of connection overseas.

All of this is a far digital cry from Mark Twain's *Innocents Abroad*. Expatriates are now able to share and spread detailed political information not previously available to them and more effectively engage in the American political process from a distance. In the future, the movement begun here in the 2000 elections could blossom into more sustained involvement in American politics between elections and lead to greater inclusion, through virtual means, into political communities of various kinds back home.

One day in early June, three young Americans ambled down into the Italian village of Carrara from their camp in the mountains outside of town. The trio, two men and one woman, are artists and live in this area of northwestern Italy because of the renowned marble caves that mark the countryside.

In town, they pick up a copy of the *International Herald Tribune* and find an advertisement for Democrats Abroad (DA), a group affiliated with the Democratic National Committee dedicated to organizing Democrats living outside the United States. The advertisement offers absentee ballots to any registered American voters living in Italy by contacting Maria Mancini, DA's country campaign chair for Italy, in Milan.

PHOTO 7.4   Maria Mancini

Lacking a telephone, the three locate a small Internet café and e-mail Mancini. Mancini, perched in front of a computer in her Milan villa, replies minutes later and directs them to a printable version of the application for an absentee ballot on the Federal Voting Assistance Web site. During the next twenty minutes, through three e-mail correspondences, the artists in Carrara download, print, and fax their applications for absentee ballots to Mancini. One week later, their absentee ballots arrive at the same café where their inquiry started, enabling them to vote in the 2000 presidential election.

"These people who were working in a cave in Carrara, would they have even cared what was going on back in the United States if they couldn't somehow have an impact?" Mancini asks. "[Without the Internet] I don't think they would have even been interested. They would have been on the outside looking in; but with the Internet they're on the inside."

Unlike any other election year, 2000 illustrated the overwhelming power a single vote can have in determining the outcome of a presidential contest. Most of the attention about the Florida recounts focused on disputed districts, confusing ballots, and all varieties of chads. Less news emerged about a voting bloc of American citizens overseas: 6 million men and women with unfettered access to absentee ballot materials over the Internet, and with that the power to swing the election for Al

Gore or George W. Bush. The raw numbers tell the tale: The 537 overall vote differential in Florida between Gore and Bush represented a mere 14 percent of the 3,733 overseas ballots received in Florida within ten days after Election Day. Given the number of Americans abroad, the odds that those 3,733 voters represented all or most of Florida's voting-eligible expatriates, especially given the state's large military population, are slim. A large number of registered overseas Florida voters likely went untapped in 2000, an oversight that will have profound implications.

Would the 2000 election have ended differently if more of the 6 million Americans abroad had voted? No one can say. But in future elections, the efforts toward more voter registration by Maria Mancini and Democrats Abroad could ensure that overseas U.S. citizens have a greater voice.

The three friends in Carrara represent voters who previously might otherwise have slipped through the net of Democrats Abroad because they lacked the convenience of e-mail. As the three artists in Italy demonstrate, online technology is connecting Americans living overseas to U.S. politics where other, more traditional measures have generally failed. And because of the legal wrangling in Florida, many are taking notice of the overseas vote for the first time.

"You'd never think that the people doing voter registration abroad would ever get this much attention. When I volunteered to do this I thought, 'Sure, no problem,' and now the whole world is looking at us," says Mancini. "Everybody's like, 'You know, those absentee ballots out there? What is that all about?' So I'm getting a million e-mails a day on press releases, what to say, and of course about what's going on."

Democrats Abroad's voter registration formula prior to 2000 relied on equal parts hard work and luck, quite unlike high-profile get-out-the-vote efforts found stateside, supported by well-funded activist groups or political action committees. Democrats Abroad used an all-volunteer staff with few mechanisms besides newspaper advertisements in the *International Herald-Tribune*, phone canvassing, and word of mouth for getting their message out. Getting Americans overseas registered to vote was hit or miss. Democrats Abroad would reach out with newspaper advertising and word of mouth, hopeful of motivating people to register. There was rarely any direct, meaningful contact with the eligible voters. They were scattered and difficult to locate. So handicapped, voter registration initiatives overseas had little success in mobilizing the 6 million Americans abroad.

One who worked on past voter registration efforts with Democrats Abroad is Gilbert Wells of Sintra, Portugal, who founded with his wife a Democrats Abroad chapter in Portugal in 1986. "The last time they did it [voter registration], four years ago for the last presidential election [1996], I got two telephone calls," he says. "One was from a person in the north country that was a tourist passing through, and the other was some lady from Spain because there was no DA in Spain. For all the money they [DA] spent, it was a total waste of time."

This was the situation when thirty-five-year-old lawyer and Los Angeles native Maria Mancini volunteered for Democrats Abroad in 1999 and became one of the thirty country campaign chairs working on overseas voter registration. She went to Milan to work for a client and worked for DA pro bono. Mancini was lucky enough to come into DA on the cusp of the information revolution and quickly learned what the tools of the Internet and e-mail allowed her to do that her predecessors could not.

"Because of the Internet, it changed everything for us. We were able to register people and get the info to them instantly instead of telephone calls," says Mancini. "You can blow out [messages to] hundreds of people at the same time. With e-mail, you can give detailed instructions on how to register to vote and how to vote. Four years ago, it just wasn't possible. Without e-mail . . . Democrats Abroad would not be the great success that it is today."

Mancini's results in the first overseas voter registration drive underscored how important a role new technology played in reaching new voters. The introduction of e-mail into DA's traditional voter registration techniques resulted in a 200 percent increase in the total number of Americans in Italy registered to vote in 2000 versus 1996. But Mancini says that number fails to take into account the people who e-mailed her from countries close to Italy without Democrats Abroad chapters for whom she facilitated receipt of an absentee ballot. In particular, Americans living in the former Yugoslavia turned to her as their connection to the American voting process. "We're attributing that to our combination of the advertising we did this time that we couldn't afford to do last time and in large part [to] e-mail," she says. "We had thirty reps in thirty countries around the world just doing voter registration. And everyone had a really successful go at it for those two reasons."

With e-mail making the world a smaller place in 2000, it became easier for one person like a DA country campaign chair to find, communicate with, and involve Americans abroad. In previous elections, registering to vote in a foreign country involved finding the nearest American embassy or consulate, filling out paperwork, and then waiting for the ballot in the mail. It boiled down to an individual's desire to vote; many Americans either found the process too hassling or lived too far from an embassy or consulate to make it worth their while to register. Even in Election 2000, the traditional methods of voter registration failed, while online modes achieved great success. "I did that [traditional voter registration drive] for the community Fourth of July party [in 2000]; it rained in Lisbon," Gilbert Wells says. "Only three people came in to vote. We set up a table right at the entrance where the people were coming in to the party, and only three people did."

Although physical paper registration will continue as a method of signing up American voters overseas, its status as the primary method quickly gave way to the Internet and e-mail campaigns during 2000. Besides the ability to download or fax an absentee ballot application and direct e-mail communication, easier information dissemination to Americans abroad and the availability of political information on demand for any voter registration coordinator also added to the indispensability of Internet and e-mail. The same Internet sites Americans at home depended on—like CNN.com, MSNBC.com, and nytimes.com—reached voters in the remote corners of the world as well. Maria Mancini also worked hard to get useful political information and absentee ballots to Americans in Italy, as well as to recruit new voters.

"My job was to look at information, evaluate it, and then pass it on. But I also had to let the people that I pass it on to know what the source was and why I thought it was worthwhile," she says. "I tried to do a combination of many news sites. I tried to pick out what the main issue of the day or week [was] and focus on that. The [Web] sites I was directed to that came from the Democratic National Committee, such as their page and Al Gore's page, I knew were checked and rechecked every day. Being an attorney, you have to go on instinct; you have to evaluate the source always."

The pipeline of information provided by the Internet flowed both ways. As the Internet allowed Mancini an easy way to keep Americans on her list abreast of political developments on the home front, it also afforded other Americans living abroad easy, direct contact with her—something that had been lacking in previous years. Mancini found that, increasingly, Americans abroad took the initiative to contact her to get information on absentee ballots and political involvement, in part because she was only an e-mail message away. In many cases, she said, she would receive e-mails from Americans living only a few kilometers apart in certain areas of Italy who knew nothing about their fellow citizens living so close. In one such instance, Mancini united several families living in Tuscany that all contacted her about voter registration information.

"I had noticed toward the end of the summer that a number of calls for voter registration were coming from the same area in Tuscany. Most were from Americans who fell in love with the region while on vacation and decided to either buy a summer home there or retire there," she says. "A number of calls were from little tiny towns in between Siena and Arezzo [two towns in the Tuscan hills]. Some towns had population of less than one hundred and others were just nestled in the middle of nowhere. Some people lived in old farmhouses and ran country inns for American tourists, some conducted wine-tasting tours, and some were just enjoying life. Most of the persons were only a few miles away from each other, but never realized that there was an American neighbor just on the next hill."

To unite these families, Mancini made a master list of their e-mail addresses and sent it out to everyone living close to one another. She says now they talk to each other about the United States and give advice on cutting through the red tape of the Italian bureaucracy, among other things. "It's pretty amazing," she says, "and totally impossible to do without the Internet or e-mail."

The spread of the "global economy" is increasing the numbers of Americans who will work and live overseas, underscoring the importance of

DA's services. Mancini, though very positive about her success in 2000, thinks more can be done to incorporate more American voters overseas into the political process at home. The procedure for requesting absentee ballots is one area where she sees room for improvement.

"Only 65 percent of states permitted the online version of the application. We have to have all fifty states allowing the online version of this request. Some states allowed you to fax the request back. Not one state allowed you to e-mail the application back. You had to print out the application and send it to the *county* where you're registered to vote," she says. "Some states didn't allow fax machines. You had to mail it. They really need an e-mail version of that request."

Even though its promise is far from realized, Mancini sees the increase in overseas voter registration during the recent election cycle as a positive step in a general reordering of the democratic process. The online absentee ballot application, e-mail, and online information all contributed to the success of Mancini's efforts. Although Mancini left DA to return to her law practice in Los Angeles, she is certain she helped lay a solid foundation for future political involvement by Americans abroad.

"We're getting a lot more attention, and the more attention we get, the better. I got a lot of calls from people who didn't even know who we were, and we've been in Italy for twenty years. We're streamlining. It all came together at the same time; it's actually very beautiful. You're only going to be able to do this if you've got the technology," she says.

"There are 6 million Americans living abroad. That's a lot, a lot."

The Overnight Expert

The story of David Enrich and Matt Grossmann and their Web sites, truedemocracy.org and votewithamerica.com, is an interesting example of a community of *action* that came into being literally overnight, as the election returns showed a Bush victory in the Electoral College (subject to the battle over recounts) and a Gore win in the national vote. But their overnight success was only partly the product of luck in the election's incredibly unusual outcome. Their success was also the product of a long-standing political interest and effort by Enrich, which he pursued through the Internet. Had it not been for the Internet, he would not have been able to "publish" his point of view in the first Web site, would never have been sought out for his opinions by the traditional media after the election, and certainly would not have been in the position through the second Web site to catalyze and enable the political effort to persuade presidential electors to change their votes to Gore.

Part inspirational piece, part cautionary tale, their story illustrates the Internet's unique ability to connect the one with the many, to democratize the power of influence, and to enable the many to act.

It's summer 1998, and a teenage college intern at Citizens for Tax Justice in Washington, D.C., fidgets. Bored, with time on his idle hands, he decides to put up a Web site devoted to the issues he cares about: low voter turnout, the Electoral College, campaign finance reform.

He creates "Citizens for True Democracy." And just like that, the Internet provides national voice—and some instant, though uncertain, credibility—to a young man who is just turning old enough to vote in his first election in the coming November.

Over two years, the site attracts some interest, and then a little more traffic as Election Day 2000 approaches. The reason: There's talk that in a race this tight, one candidate might win the Electoral College vote but lose the popular count, just the scenario "True Democracy" decries. Few people really think it will happen. But it could.

By now the fidgety intern—David Enrich—is a twenty-one-year-old senior government major at Claremont McKenna College in Claremont, California. It's November 7. Sometime after midnight, he turns to roommate Matt Grossmann as Peter Jennings drones on the set of ABC.

"My God," Enrich says. "I can't believe it's happening." It really does look like Bush could win the electoral vote but lose by a half-million or so ballots nationwide.

Enrich's phone begins to ring off the hook. Calls tumble in from newspapers, radio, TV, all seeking comments from the young men, as the media reports on the fly, trying to make sense for viewers of a complicated, too-close-to-call election. Hits soar on the Enrich-Grossmann Web site. David Enrich becomes Internet-age commentator, activist, celebrity, scourge.

PHOTO 7.5   David Enrich

Enrich and his roommate were a two-man band: Webmasters, copy writers, and election analysts and a voice for Gore supporters who were upset that their candidate seemingly had won the popular vote but not the White House. Meanwhile, reporters trolling the Net in the hours after the election found Enrich's True Democracy Web site and called, anxious for knowledgeable voices on the arcane rules of the Electoral College and what might happen next. The reporters had assumed that the makers of this Web site *had* to be the experts.

The media's interest spiked when the pair (Grossmann was identified as "deputy director for grassroots organizing") upped the ante through a link to a site they called votewithamerica.com. There, they posted the names of 172 Bush electors in eighteen states and as many addresses, e-mails, and phone numbers as they could find. The information proved a great resource for Gore backers, and they used it to full effect. Bush electors said they were flooded with calls and e-mails from voters urging them to be "unfaithful" and cast their electoral vote for popular-vote winner Gore, not electoral winner Bush, on December 18.

Some Bush electors complained that they were being harassed; a handful said they received nasty e-mails and even a death threat or two. The two Webmasters—who'd spent hours scouring the Internet and making long-distance phone calls at their own expense to compile the elector list—refused to take the names down. They targeted four Bush electors in particular who had been identified by the *Wall Street Journal* as possible defectors. Two switches would have created an Electoral College tie, and three would have put Gore in the White House. In the end, their vigilance (the electors might describe it as vigilantism) did not pay off, but they demonstrated that two college students with a Web site and a phone book can provoke a considerable disturbance in cyberspace.

Enrich, who moved on to work in the D.C. bureau of the States News Services, was surprised that a number of reporters didn't probe to find out more about him beyond the rather lofty proclamations on his Web site. The site does not mention his age or that he is a college student, though he said he was always up-front with the media about who he was and what he did—if they asked. The Citizens for True Democracy (CTD) Web page described Enrich as the "founder and director," as an expert on voter participation and electoral reform, and as a tax policy analyst. "David manages CTD's media outreach and coalition building in addition to researching voter participation, the Electoral College, and campaign finance reform," the site said. But he admitted in an interview the effort was in large measure a vent for his interest in declining voter turnout and not the kind of think tank some presumed it to be.

"I was, in my idealistic way, disturbed that so few people bother to vote, whether they don't see a stake in voting, [the] high costs of voting, long lines at the polls, whatever, so I was interested in examining why people weren't voting and ways to get them to vote," Enrich said. "And how important it is in our democracy for people to vote. Prior to the election, there were a good number of people coming to the site who typed in 'Electoral College' on Yahoo and our page would pop up. So, we had a decent-sized mailing list of people. Once in a while, I'd write something out and send out a newsletter. There wasn't a whole lot going on until a little before the election, when we got some people in Claremont involved and we started writing more." Their stories and analysis appeared on their Web site, which in turn caught the attention of information-hungry reporters from the mass media.

When the Electoral College became *the* story, Enrich was fielding an estimated fifteen calls a day from newspapers, TV and radio, even Voice of

America. Eventually, stories appeared in the *Los Angeles Times* and *Washington Times,* the *New York Post* and *The Washington Post,* the *Wall Street Journal,* the *Boulder* (Colorado) *Daily Camera,* and literally dozens more. He did radio appearances via telephone on shows in St. Louis, Pittsburgh, New York City, and Los Angeles, among many others. A mention by cable networks MSNBC and Fox News caused a huge spike in Internet traffic to the Web site. The Web site–mass media relationship became symbiotic, each benefiting from the other's attention.

"The phone started ringing early in the morning [November 8], and I'd stayed up all night watching this nonsense unfold on TV," Enrich said. "We'd developed a contingency plan, and of course we were expecting Gore to come out on top, but this idea of Congress and the electors had crossed our minds. There was a small chance of it happening." Of course, it did happen. The election results were so close that every state, not just the big ones, counted. "Both candidates needed every electoral vote they could get. The fact that Gore had won the popular vote but needed Florida to win the electoral vote caused every pundit at every news outlet to ponder the scenarios. So the phones started ringing, tons of media asked what we thought this meant for the Electoral College. They just wanted a quote from us." Enrich provided quotable quotes, and his name appeared in story after story about the possible outcome of the election and the Electoral College's role in it. His harsh criticism of the Electoral College, a body few people ever thought of during the mostly one-sided presidential victories of the past forty years, brought attention to both the process and to himself.

"I think the majority of people in the beginning had no idea, and we really didn't have any interest in letting on. . . . I don't think it crossed their minds that I could be a student," he said. "I'd say about half asked [about my pedigree]. It was interesting looking at the stories people wrote afterwards. They had no idea."

The story shifted from the Electoral College conundrum to the electors themselves when Enrich and Grossmann posted information on how to contact them. They used the Web—of course—to bird-dog addresses, phone numbers, and e-mails, putting in a series of eighteen-hour days. "Astronomy class got the shaft," Enrich admitted. In some cases, finding information about individual electors was surprisingly easy. "A lot of these people are kind of high up in their state party systems, and so you could go to their state party Web sites, and a lot of them would have e-mail addresses with the Republican party," Enrich says. Others were buried a little deeper in the files, but none of it was classified. "We also figured party activists were likely to have contributed money, and the FEC [Federal Election Commission] has your home address on the form, so we found a lot of home addresses that way."

Once Enrich had published the electors' names and contact information, all hell broke loose. Newspapers nationwide wrote stories about local Bush electors who said their phones would not stop ringing or their e-mail boxes have been shut down (in a case or two) due to hundreds of e-mails from Gore supporters. Enrich suggested text for e-mails or what to say in phone calls. With one click, an e-mail could go to the set of fifty-four electors for whom CTD had gathered e-mails. There was even a feature that directed visitors in how to make free phone calls over the Net if they had the necessary software. Enrich not only had used the Net for savvy political purposes but had also included some fairly sophisticated technical features to make political activism easier.

The results were effective, but not in terms of the outcome Enrich had hoped for. Enrich did manage to raise the consciousness of voters and encourage them to become active, engaged participants in the process. Frances Sadler, a Bush elector from Ashland, Virginia, called the two college students to say her voicemail had been disabled by a wave of calls. This was bad for Frances but a positive sign that voters were taking action. She asked Enrich to take her phone number down, but he declined. "We told her to just hang in there for two more days," Enrich said. An elector from Florida said she had received threatening e-mails, but in another case the effort initiated some civilized political discourse. An elector from Missouri conducted a day-long debate via e-mail that Enrich enjoyed and recalled as "substantive and civil." The office of Maricopa County, Arizona, sheriff Joe Arpaio, a Bush elector, reported receiving 2,000 calls the weekend before the Electoral College voted.

Turnabout was fair play. Bush electors were also getting a lot of e-mails from Republicans telling them *not* to switch their votes. "We actually got a bunch of e-mails from Republicans saying, 'Ha-ha, we just used your e-mail feature to send e-mails to Republicans,'" said Enrich. "We knew that was going to happen. We were fine with it; we just wanted people to be able to get in touch with the electors and let them know what they thought." Enrich's partisan efforts actually mobilized the opposition to new forms of engagement. If he had been unhappy with voter apathy before the elections, he could not have been more pleased that he was providing a boost to both sides of the aisle.

Enrich said he never regretted posting the electors' phone numbers and e-mails, despite the pressure and criticism. They are, after all, who voters really elect. "I don't have any qualms about being a pain in the butt for the electors. Their argument that they don't deserve to get contacted was pretty offensive to me. We don't vote for president. We vote for presidential electors. And these people are not supposed to be mysterious people without a name who just show up." Enrich's Internet-based campaign to disclose the workings of the Electoral College, and his more partisan campaign to force it to change its preordained decision, contributed to the national discourse and threw a spotlight on a lightly regarded but perplexing quirk in the American election system. The debate continues offline even now.

"I think a lot of these grassroots efforts were fanning the flames against the Electoral College, which is definitely what we wanted to be doing," Enrich says. Enrich, who voted for Nader, characterizes the call to abolish the Electoral College as nonpartisan. He does admit that if the tables were turned—if Gore had lost the popular vote but had won the electoral race—he would have been conflicted. "I would have had a much more difficult time asking people to vote for Bush than I would for Gore, and that's not something I would have admitted prior to December 18. However, I think we might have done it. I would have had to think a little harder."

Enrich would have had to face the enmity of his grandmothers, who supported Gore and were already giving him a hard time about voting for Nader. To them, he had wasted his vote and had helped cost Gore the election in the process. "I would have felt a little bad in principle going the extra step and asking the Democratic electors to vote for Bush. I don't think my grandparents would have been happy with that."

Enrich estimates he received 20,000 e-mails himself from Election Day through the Electoral College vote and had to develop a stiff upper lip. "We were getting literally thousands of e-mails a day by the end of this, and some of them were threatening. The majority was very angry. I think people are more inclined to send an e-mail when they're upset about something than when they're happy about something, which is why a lot of the electors were getting e-mails. We got angry e-mails from people ranging from 5,000- or 10,000-word arguments as to why the Electoral College was good and what we were doing was unethical, to racial slurs, to people just swearing at us. People told us to watch our back—we have your address. We were called communists a lot. In terms of the really threatening, really derogatory ones, [they were] quite easily 4 or 5 percent of them, which doesn't sound like a lot. But when you're talking thousands of e-mails, there were quite a few." The whole exchange sounds like a town-hall meeting gone awry, except that the participants were thousands of miles apart and venting their spleens soundlessly, but not any less effectively, over the Internet.

Enrich appreciates the Internet's power. "We wouldn't be doing this were it not with the Internet. This just would not be a feasible thing for us to do. On the other hand, the Internet has not replaced traditional media. I've read a lot about people spouting nonsense about the Internet is revolutionary. It's not revolutionary in the sense that it's not about to replace traditional media, not about to replace books. To some extent it's supplementing what people already read in magazines and newspapers and [see] on TV but it's not about to replace them."

What Enrich demonstrated with his own Web site, e-mail campaign, and petition drive is that the Internet is a completely different artifact that offers unique potential for civic engagement and social capital. As he simply puts it, "I have been really impressed with the number of people who are online and are putting time into something and organizing. There's a lot of value in being able to get in touch with a large number of people really easily. And I think it's cool that people can get in touch with the electors, even if they don't.

"I think it's really good for people to be able to get in touch with the source of information. I think it was good that people who were pissed off at me could e-mail me and tell me I'm a communist and get in a debate about it with me. The Internet does facilitate people sending stuff that really doesn't have much value. But it is interesting to read other people's perspectives. People do put a lot of thought into what they're writing, and it's been definitely an educational experience for me." Prior to the election and the serendipitous emergence of his Web site, everything Enrich knew about how things worked in the electoral system was theoretical. Book knowledge. The Internet and its power to connect people who agree and disagree, and to do so in ways that spark emotions and motivate people to action, provided Enrich with a real-life experience he'll never forget. "I've read all about the Electoral College in my textbooks and learned all about it in my government classes, and I've done a lot of thinking about it on my own. But I've definitely been introduced to a lot of new perspectives, all sorts of people—professors, high school teachers, and high school students." And not a few members of the Electoral College.

8

COMMUNITIES OF IDENTITY

ON NOVEMBER 30, STILL TWO WEEKS BEFORE BUSH WOULD finally win the election, Joe Bogosian typed out an e-mail to his local list-serv. It was 3:19 P.M. at his office in Washington, D.C.

The e-mail read:

The [Bush-Cheney] Transition Team is collecting volunteer contact information to use as the need for volunteers develops. While the McLean [Virginia] office is open, it is still being furnished with desks, chairs, phones etc., and will be moving to D.C. at some point in the near future. For this reason, mostly what they want currently is contact information. If you are interested in volunteering, please e-mail to me your 1) name; 2) phone number(s); and 3) email. I will forward these to the Transition office and you will receive a call as they get up and running.

The office will need volunteer staffing from 8:00 A.M. to 8:00 P.M. with at least seven volunteers at all times. The one immediate need is for volunteers to work this coming Wednesday and Thursday (December 6 & 7). If you send your contact information to me, please signify if you can work on those days. Otherwise, just send me your info and the Transition office will contact you as they develop the need.

Thank you.

As Bogosian chatted on the phone with a caller just a couple of minutes later, the audio alert on his e-mail started to ping and ding. It continued to provide a slightly distracting electronic chatter in the background for most of their thirty-five-minute call. Finally, his friend asked, "What is that?"

Bogosian explained that his e-mail was on fire and that almost every one of those pings was an instant response to the message he had just sent, replies from the area chapter of the YP4W (Young Professionals for "W") community, which he had formed. They were answering his e-mail, ready to help and fill the ranks of the Bush transition team.

"How many have responded?" the caller asked.

"One . . . five . . . nine . . ." Bogosian was counting. "Forty-five in thirty-five minutes," he said with genuine surprise at his own success.

"This is a pretty neat, incredible thing you've done," the caller suggested.

What Bogosian had done was create a virtual community of identity, in this case young professionals in the Washington, D.C., area who supported George W. Bush for president. He had organized them largely online, though after a while they gathered face-to-face for social events. They identified with each other because of their shared youth, professionalism, political beliefs, and willingness to work for a cause and eventually because of a connectedness to each other that transcended those things.

Communities and groups usually produce shared senses of identity through their actions, whether those actions are simply socializing or organizing members, fund-raising, or protesting. Some communities, however, also initially form around a shared identity and are primarily sustained by that identity. These identities are often based on ascriptive traits (ethnicity, sex, sexual orientation), either by themselves or in combination with certain beliefs or a certain focus of activity. The Log Cabin Republicans, a group of Republicans who are also gay, and the gay activist group Act Up! are two good examples. Other kinds of non-Internet analogs for communities of identity might include the Knights of Columbus, the Elks, and the 4-H Club.

The Asian-American Club

Although it also clearly implicates political *action*, the story of S. B. Woo and 80-20 is most notable for what it tells us about the communities of political *identity* that are forming on the Internet. This is the story of a geographically dispersed group that has come together around its shared ethnic identity and has built a supportive network dedicated to concentrating, and therefore raising, the political impact of Asian-Americans.

The participants did not have a preconceived set of political beliefs or policy positions that motivated them; rather, they were united by their common ethnic bond. And they apparently mattered. Through a representative process, the group deliberated and decided that it would back Al Gore in November. Consider for a moment that in 1992 and 1996 Asian-Americans gave Bill Clinton only 36 percent and 47 percent of their two-party vote, respectively. In 2000, however, Al Gore received 57 percent of their two-party vote.[1] Indeed, Asian-Americans were the *only* major ethnic group to switch their party allegiance between these elections. The importance of this fact for social capital formation is that this sea change in actual voting behavior suggests that 80-20 may have been successful because it effectively generated and undergirded political *trust* among its members; in this case, trust in each other to do at the polls precisely what its smaller representative group recommended.

This identity-based group continues to be instrumental in both uniting geographically disparate individuals and politically socializing many individuals who heretofore have not been politically active. Its basis is a common identity, which is strengthened, nurtured, and maintained *virtually*. It is a community that exists *through*, and indeed *on*, the Internet.

It's the last weekend in August 2000, and thirty-three Americans pay their own way to Los Angeles to discuss a proposition: Who is the best candidate for president?

There is perfect partisan symmetry at this gathering: eleven Republicans, eleven Democrats, and eleven independents. These delegates, elected via an online, nationwide nominating process, pepper reluctant representatives from the Gore and Bush camps with questions for a weekend, and then they vote. The verdict from the University City Hilton: It's Gore, 26–7.

There is no Associated Press story filed from reporters covering this convention, no live TV report from the hotel lobby. But several hundred thousand Asian-American citizens are awaiting word of the vote in their homes and offices, and the outcome is relayed to them via e-mail. When the weekend began, they didn't know whom the L.A. gathering would endorse. But most of them had already agreed that, whether it was Gore or Bush, they'd go along with the endorsement in November, even if it meant voting against their personal choice for America's forty-third president.

"We had a lot of arguments," remembers Yu-Chi Ho, a Democratic convention delegate and a professor who teaches applied mathematics at Harvard. "These people honestly put community interest ahead of themselves, their own loyalty." Two years ago, University of Delaware physics professor S. B. Woo, Ho, and five others hatched a plan to get the nation's Asian-American community on the same page politically and to help put the 1996 campaign finance scandal to rest. The rallying point: the 2000 election. The concept: Get 80 percent of voting-age Asian-Americans— who typically split their vote between Democrats, Republicans, and independents—to vote as a bloc. The tool to make it all happen was e-mail, from conception to D-Day in L.A. The engine was Woo, a man a bit startled by his success but hardly overcome by it. He created the 80-20 Initiative, and today there are 250,000 names on the group's e-mail list, two times the 142,000 in John McCain's hands when he bowed out and equal to the number Al Gore had on Election Day. Woo plans to hit 1 million and then 2 million, a number that would represent 20 percent of the 11 million Asian-Americans nationwide.

There are 4 million Asian-Americans in California, 6 percent of the state's registered voters, and 1.5 million of them live in the Los Angeles area. Yet within this potential force, there is a great divide. There are some thirty different ethnic groups in the Asian community, none with much political muscle on its own. That reality makes 80-20's task daunting, and

PHOTO 8.1   S. B. Woo

its success so far all the more notable and remarkable. Chinese-Americans make up three of every four names on the current e-mail list, but the idea is to expand and bring more members in from non-Chinese communities.

There seems no reason to doubt Woo will continue to successfully employ technology, brains, political savvy, and confidence to capture the Asian-American community's e-mails and allegiance. And the timing is right for Woo. The Asian community was burned by scandal in 1996, when Democrats had to return money that may have been illegally funneled from overseas. The convictions of John Huang and Maria Hsai stung the Asian-American community. But that blight has been dimmed by the success of Woo, Ho, and the others. The 80-20 Initiative appears to be one of the most successful grassroots efforts to emerge from the 2000 political season, a community of trust where individuals agreed on the candidate who had done the most for "equal opportunity and justice" for Asian-Americans. It shook some conventional pillars.

On Election Day, exit polls showed high name recognition for 80-20, and there are indications that the group's nearly quarter-million members delivered on their promise on November 7. According to an independent survey sited by 80-20 on its Web site, 85 percent of its members who voted actually did choose Gore.

According to an exit survey by the Asian Pacific American Legal Center of 5,000 voters, 2,000 of them Asian-Americans, Asian-Americans favored Gore over Bush 62.3 percent to 34.7 percent. And the numbers indicated just the trend 80-20 worked to ignite: 17 percent of Asian Republicans across sixteen cities in Los Angeles and Orange Counties told pollsters they crossed over to choose Gore this time. Asian voters who said they were Democrats increased 12.4 percentage points, jumping from 36 percent in 1996 to 48.4 percent in Election 2000. "There's definitely been a shift," says Ho.

Whereas the Asian-American voice splits in the voting booth, the African-American vote lands on Election Day with a satisfying thud for the Democrats. In 2000, 92 percent of African-Americans backed Al Gore, even higher than the 88 percent Bill Clinton drew in 1996. Another model for 80-20 is the Jewish vote, half the size of the Asian-American bloc but extremely powerful and heavily Democratic.

80-20 increased its name recognition with TV, radio, and newspaper advertising in California, particularly a thirty-second TV spot that featured a mom and dad and their two daughters. The commercial featured the very technology that made 80-20 possible and viable. As the dad checked out the 80-20 home page on his computer, the daughters took a break from setting the dinner table to explain what the group was all about.

Professor Woo is no political novice; he was the lieutenant governor of Delaware from 1985 to 1989. He understands organizing and the new tool of e-mail. "It's not the Internet, it's e-mail," Woo corrects people who marvel at 80-20's success. "I really cannot imagine having this kind of expansion rate without it. It would have been way too expensive and too time-consuming. Imagine—I used to be a politician, so I ran campaigns—if you want to do a direct mail of 10,000 persons, it would take a lot of work and a lot of money, involving many, many volunteers. With e-mail, you just push a button. It's reliable, inexpensive, and speedy."

By the end of the campaign season, an estimated 4,000 80-20 supporters had donated $400,000 to the 80-20 political action committee (PAC), a per-donor ratio of $100 that rivals what the major candidates did with their own Web operations. "We didn't press hard," Woo says. "If we did, we could have gotten much more."

"We have only tapped the tip of the iceberg," agrees Ho, whose adult son also is involved with the group. "We want to demonstrate that we have potential and show we can swing a lot of votes."

Woo said 80-20 was not afraid to excercise muscle: It withdrew an offer to sponsor a $600,000–$700,000 fund-raiser for Gore when the candidate's team said it was too late for Gore to personally appear.

Ho, an 80-20 founder and the group's treasurer, spent an estimated twenty hours a month just filing FEC reports and tending to the other financial matters of the new enterprise. "It's occupied most of my extracurricular time." He says e-mail is vital for organizing Asian-Americans, and it has provided a tool and a means to do something that otherwise would not have been possible. He knows not everyone fits his politically active mold. A Chinese-American who emigrated to the United States in 1950 as a teenager, Ho, sixty-six, has voted in every election since becoming a naturalized citizen in 1961. "Asian-Americans are very backward in political affairs, from their culture and upbringing. We have come a long way, but there's a long way to go," he says. "It's a process of educating them. I can't speak for all, but in the Chinese tradition, politics is bad, and you're taught to keep your nose to the grindstone. We do things on an individual basis, not as part of a group. But, certain things can't be accomplished individually."

The 80-20 Initiative is nonpartisan and nonaffiliated, according to Woo. The group's independence makes the parties uneasy; they were reluctant to appear at 80-20's convention, but both did eventually show up. "Nobody likes the independent swing bloc of votes," Ho says. "If you are always for them, that's fine, they're happy. But we said we are not going to be in the pocket of any one party. And the best way for the parties to respond is to destroy that movement. What happened with the Reform party? Essentially they were destroyed. So if both the Republican party and Democratic party decided not to come to our meeting, it would make us look bad. But ultimately, they came. At the last moment, they all came."

Election by election, Woo says 80-20 will support the politician who promises and delivers the most. Parties will not be able to bank on 80-20's support from vote to vote, as they have with other ethnic, economic, and religious blocs that tend to ally with parties and then stick with them for years, as labor and African-Americans have with the Democrats and the

Christian right has with the Republicans. "We made it very clear," Woo says. "We aim to be a swing bloc vote. . . . It's strictly based on who can help me in the next election. Politics is never pleasant. If you don't want to take flak, don't be in politics. We want our community to enjoy equal opportunity in workplaces, equal justice in the least amount of time possible. Some of us will have to take some flak."

Ho and Woo agree that this virtual community has shaken up the traditional one. Ho says, "In some ways we pulled the rug out from under regular Asian-American leaders who are well-connected with one party or another. Particularly, I think the Republican party leaders are not very happy with us. The Chinese-American leaders used to be associated with the GOP. To some extent we bypassed them. We are going an entirely different route." Woo notes, with some satisfaction, that some Republicans attacked them, something he takes as a sign of success. "People don't waste time attacking insignificant, noninfluential groups."

He says 80-20 should get credit for the Republicans' decision to pull its infamous "daisy girl ad." The 2000 spot mimicked a controversial ad from 1964 in which Lyndon Johnson attacked Barry Goldwater, intimating that Goldwater would lead the country into nuclear war. The image: an innocent girl plucking daisy petals one at a time in a field while a countdown to a nuclear launch played in the background, in sync with each pluck of a petal. The 2000 ad was paid for by a Bush political consultant—but disavowed publicly by the Bush camp. The accusation in the ad: Gore-Clinton sold nuclear secrets to China in exchange for campaign money. "As soon as we learned about it," Woo says, "we immediately started a movement that the TV ad must be pulled. I called [GOP party chairman] Jim Nicholson myself and left him a message. We really didn't think he ought to broadcast something like this and demanded it be pulled. Within twenty-four hours, it was pulled. I don't know of any other group that requested the pulling of that TV ad. To my knowledge, 80-20 is the only group that made a big fuss over it."

Using the Internet, 80-20 encouraged members to send protest e-mails but especially to call and send faxes to the party leadership. "I was told the wave of phone calls into Bush headquarters and the Republican Committee was so big that they were kept so busy handling all the press questions regarding the daisy ad that they felt politically it was not sustainable any-more," Woo says. "And that was to our regret. They never said anything about the possible damage that's done to race relationships. They simply said, 'It's bad politics, so we're going to pull it.' I think they should have thought about the kind of damage they've done to race relations."

Woo built his e-mail community in the humblest of ways, first ap-proaching Ho and the five other fellow Chinese-Americans who endorsed the idea and then sending out an e-mail to thirty more. From there, the idea circulated among a group of about three hundred, winning more support. "Why don't we try it?" Woo asked the others. "If we don't try it, we will never know." From the core of three hundred, about fifty gathered for a West Coast retreat September 26–27, 1998, that finalized the project. They pooled address books and scoured resources such as Yahoo! and AOL, sifting for Asian-sounding names. With the list of three hundred to begin, targeting primarily fellow Chinese-Americans, they were ready to drop the first e-mail.

Would it be perceived as spam or brainstorm? How would the "targets" answer? The response overwhelmed the organizers. "We sent it to every-body and asked, 'Can you help us?'" Ho recalls. "We heard back from 98 percent who said 'Yes.' We asked, 'Can we send you six more e-mails ex-plaining our purpose?' And 98 percent said 'Yes' again. Eventually, 90 per-cent of those original people had either joined or were seeking more in-formation."

Ho says that, though issues such as discrimination are a concern for him-self and all Asian-Americans, the 80-20 effort was as much about organiz-ing and educating as it was about issues. In the future, 80-20's centerpiece goal is equality. A major initiative: congressional hearings to explore the glass ceiling for Asian-Americans. To that end, 80-20 sent regular e-mails to its membership during Clinton's final year, urging them to fax the White House to promote the name of Asian-American Norman Mineta for com-merce secretary. He got it. Bush named two Asian-Americans to his Cabi-net, a first, including Mineta for transportation. Ho sees it all as a matter of patriotism. "Government statistics show that we don't organize," says Ho. "I have always felt that Asian-Americans should be involved in the American Way." Then he adds, "I would not want to live anywhere else in the world."

Woo emphasizes that his online, and now very real, community is organized and disciplined and has adopted bylaws. "We have to have a good set of bylaws to provide internal tranquility. A good set of bylaws means we have to be democratic, . . . and we have to be known as an organization that is ruled by law so that any time there's a conflict, we can go back to the written words and say how we're going to resolve this. And I think we have to raise some big endowments because, to me, a big endowment is a magnet that prevents a group from splintering into pieces after internal conflicts. And there have been internal conflicts, human nature being what it is. But if there is a big endowment, the losing group is not going to pick up their marbles and go home. They say, 'Hell, I hate that son of a gun, and I'm not going to leave so he can call the shots over all that money. I may lose today, but I want to have my say in the use of that money, and I'm going to stay.' And pretty soon, when people stay working with each other long enough, I think it's like Democrats and Republicans in Delaware. There's no sense fighting all the time. We seek some compromise."

80-20 is not a neighborhood occupied solely by technophiles. The Internet is not the primary news source for Ho, for example. He goes to newspapers like *The New York Times* and *The Boston Globe*, though he does get an online news package in his mailbox and news alerts from the *Times*. He goes online to shop and, if he's traveling, to get maps. Ho believes in what e-mail and the Internet can do for his community, and he doesn't worry about the ill it could do, say, from backlash. "Our group is so small it cannot become a force disproportionate to our number. What it will do is get us on the radar screen. We never hoped to achieve this much this fast."

Woo expects they'll go further. What will they do next? "Organize, organize, organize."

The Young Republican

As a stimulator and coordinator of an Internet community of *identity*, Kevin McCarthy is the Horatio Alger poster child whom Republicans search for: Born to hardworking middle-class parents, he put himself through college through pluck, luck, and perseverance. First a successful small businessman and then a staffer for a member of Congress, McCarthy is now married and a father himself. But rather than inheriting his parents' loyalty to the Democratic party, he has aligned himself with the independent, entrepreneurial spirit that he locates in the GOP.

He has trained that spirit in himself onto expanding into virtual terrain a previously existing but limited community of young Republicans, the Young Republican National Federation (YRNF). In doing so he has given the organization the opportunity to become a national community of much greater political significance and of greater meaning to those within it by supplying it with two essential ingredients: a permanent, day-to-day quality, and a centralized place where members spread out all over the country can meet.

This story provides a powerful example of how the Internet can complement and enhance previously existing political communities and turn them into something much larger than they had been before, thus aiding the expansion of social capital and further stimulating civic engagement. For McCarthy himself, the involvement has been most gratifying—in recognition of his work he was made national chair of YRNF and was given speaking time at the Republican National Convention in Philadelphia. Ironically, another central character in one of our stories, Zeke Spier, was using the Internet in his own way to organize and participate in protests occurring outside the convention hall, almost simultaneously.

Kevin McCarthy is the only Republican in his family, which makes for some pretty interesting conversations over the holiday dinner table. The thirty-six-year-old fourth-generation Central Valley Californian is of Italian and Irish descent, so he can engage his two older siblings and surviving parent in some passionate debates. His parents may or may not have been unhappy that he did not share their ideology, but they must have been very pleased that he followed their lead in his level of engagement in civic affairs. His father, now deceased, was the assistant fire chief of Bakersfield. His mother served on various boards in the community and currently heads an anti-graffiti program. His parents accepted a leadership role in the community whenever asked.

McCarthy follows suit. More than a Republican by party affiliation only, he is chair of the Young Republican National Federation, a political organization for young Republicans eighteen to forty years old. One of three major Republican organizations—the College Republicans and the Republican National Committee being the other two—it has chapters in every state and a membership of over 65,000. The YRNF membership is young, affluent, well-educated, and politically active. According to the Commerce Department study *Falling through the Net,* the most thoroughly wired demographic group matches the YRNF membership; they are statistically the Americans most likely to have and use Internet access.

YRNF members socialize and network in their local chapters and in larger groups at national conventions or at special events. They work tirelessly on campaigns locally and nationally, but during the hotly contested 2000 election, McCarthy felt that something else was needed to galvanize the campaign efforts of these young doers. He saw the opportunity to create a national community that could last all day long, every day, rather than one that sprang up during the convention and then dispersed to the hinterlands afterwards.

McCarthy realized early in the 2000 campaign that the generation represented by his members "owns" the Internet. "My original concept was, why couldn't we start our own community. Look at all the polls and surveys. The majority of people online back in June of 2000 were Republicans. They all have the entrepreneurial spirit of the Republican beliefs."

McCarthy started to connect the dots. Internet users are young, ambitious, and independent. The government has been slow to make its presence known on the Internet. "I can do my banking and stock trading on the Net, but I can't see my own social security account," he points out. "With the parties really close, whoever can capture the Internet will have a leg up to be the majority party." He built a Web site, Young Republican Online Community Network (YROCK), to reach out to the members and draw them closer together. It has had the effect of giving the members, who are spread out all over the country, a single location to meet and greet. It caught on and attracted over 1.5 million hits a month.

He saw the Web site as a recruiting tool as well. "I called the site 'YROCK' on purpose. I wanted to connect it with music. Everything young people know about politics, they learned from *Schoolhouse Rock* or from *Rock the Vote.*" McCarthy found that getting young people involved in the Republican party is difficult. "There's a stereotype. Even though [young people] think like a Republican, they associate the party with old white males from the South with extreme beliefs. That's not who we are." McCarthy uses his Web site to project a different image for the party. The name suggests a hipness that resonates with young people, and the logo looks like a radio station. Once he draws young people to the site, "they read news and information about the party, compare that to their own beliefs, and realize, hey, maybe I *could* join this party," according to McCarthy.

He persuaded his friend Frank Lutz, a pollster, to help him out with a strategy to drive people to the site "where we could educate them on the issues," in his words. McCarthy describes Lutz as "a loyal Republican who would also challenge the party when it would not reflect certain voices in America." They filled the site with interesting and fun polls—the kind of content they thought would resonate with the intended audience, young people: From among the four leading candidates (at the time), "Who would you most want to be your best man?" "Who do you think is an alien?" The poll results got them free publicity on *Good Morning America*. Jay Leno and Don Imus referred to the polls. They created a chat-room and provided "insider news—things only the party functionaries would know." They teamed with election.com to provide voter registration. They even had a political careers job service.

Never one to do anything small if he can do it big, McCarthy created more than a mere site. YROCK is an Internet service provider (ISP) that generates revenue to keep itself afloat. After all, McCarthy is a businessman, and he had to think about paying for the site and sustaining it. It would not do for the Republicans to set up a dot-com and then have it tank like so many of the NASDAQ pretenders. He relied on consumer emotion to drive subscriptions to the service. "If these people are identifying with us, why would they want to use any other ISP?" The only other political entity to become an ISP was the Democratic National Committee. McCarthy's Young Republicans went head to head against the other party's first string.

McCarthy created the site in a "field of dreams" flight of fancy that if he built it, they would come. He is that kind of self-starter, and he credits his parents with giving him the mettle. They had met in high school, married very young, had kids. His father worked two jobs, as a fireman and furniture mover, while his mother cared for the children, setting an example for them about hard work, the roles of parenting, and relying on one's own initiative to survive and get ahead. They put down deep roots in the community. McCarthy looked up to his father and was devastated when he passed away at fifty-eight from cancer. "I recently wrote a column about the one thing that could unite everybody behind the new president. Like Kennedy said, 'We'll go to the moon,' the new president should say, 'We'll cure cancer.' That's one thing that would not be partisan, that everybody could get behind."

McCarthy has his own family now—wife Judy, six-year-old son Connor, and four-year-old daughter Megan. He and Judy also met in high school, but they dated for twelve years before he proposed. Unlike his parents, McCarthy went to college and earned a master's degree from his hometown college, California State–Bakersfield. He put himself through college by leveraging $5,000 he had won in the state lottery by first investing it in the market and later by opening, operating, then selling a successful deli. "The monthly income paid for my education," he recalls. His dad must have been proud.

It was this self-made-man self-image, inspired by his parents and lived out by providing himself with a college education, that got McCarthy involved first with politics and then with the Republican party. He got involved with College Republicans because he perceived it as advancing an independent, fend-for-yourself ideology. "Growing up I was taught you can be what you want to be. Self-responsibility. I remember my father saying, 'You made a mistake; it's your responsibility to clean it up.' I always thought the Republicans were the party that insisted you can succeed on your own." He also remembers being unable to get gas during the Carter administration and having a strong feeling deep in his gut that the country was not as great as it once was. "The first vote I was able to cast was for Ronald Reagan," he said. "Remember that Michael J. Fox character on TV? I identified with him. A Republican kid with liberals for parents."

While in the College Republicans, he moved quickly up the ranks and realized he could be a leader, not just a joiner. He was elected chapter president. "We put together a great team and outperformed CRs from other universities like UCLA and Stanford." He learned the tools of grassroots organizing, the value of teamwork, and the power of bringing people together. The result of his organization's efforts in voter registration drives was to convert his county from majority Democrat to majority Republican. After college, he joined the local chapter of the Young Republican National Federation so he could continue a high level of involvement. Again, his abilities were noticed and he was elected Kern County (California) YRNF chair, then California state chair.

As state chair of the Young Republicans in 1996, when the Republican convention was held on his turf in San Diego, McCarthy sprang into action. "I decided that we needed to have a bigger say. Young people—we can't go out and do fund-raisers, we don't have a lot of money. Our greatest strength is in our time, our commitment, and our manpower."

He also recognized the value of media attention, so he organized the "freedom train." The Amtrak left Chicago on its way to San Diego and picked up young Republicans all along the route. The party on board grew in numbers, and the press at each stop took a greater interest. "We had local newspapers waiting for us at 2:00 A.M. in some towns along the way," he said. When the four hundred passengers arrived in San Diego, they had jobs waiting for them working on the floor of the convention. He threw parties at Planet Hollywood, got MTV and *Spin* magazine to cover the convention from the young person's point of view, and generally invigorated the proceedings. The attention helped the convention, and that in turn got McCarthy elected as the national co-chair and eventually chair of the YRNF.

All during this time he has worked loyally, now as district director, for Representative Bill Thomas (R.–Calif.). "I started as an intern in his district office, while in college, figuring it would be a good way to meet people and be involved in politics." Eventually, they offered him a full-time paid position. "I don't know if I'd work for another elected official. I believe in the things that he does. We don't always agree, but his foundation of beliefs in good government—I respect that. He takes what he does seriously." McCarthy likes his job, especially helping ordinary people get through the bureaucracy.

McCarthy was invited to speak at the Republican Convention in Philadelphia on the first day. "My message was, we are not your grandfather's Republican party." He only had three minutes, and he spent some of it talking about Teddy Roosevelt, Abraham Lincoln, and Republican greatness. But he also talked about the Internet and the role it would play in maintaining and growing the party's greatness in the digital era, especially for attracting young people. "I am absolutely convinced that the Internet is the most effective way to get young people involved in the political process," he said.

McCarthy's tenure as national chair of YRNF is almost up, and he is ready to move on. "I want to focus on politics, grassroots organizing, and the Internet." The success of the YROCK Web site has gotten McCarthy hooked on its promise. Based on his track record so far, there is a good chance he'll be there, leading the way and bringing more young people together.

The Businessman

The story of Joe Bogosian and Young Professionals for Bush (YP4W) is similar in many respects to that of Kevin McCarthy but illustrates some different advantages the Internet offers to political communities. Rather than showing how a virtual community can complement a previously existing offline group, this story demonstrates how the Internet can help a community that begins entirely online grow into something meaningful offline. The members of YP4W already had their age and strong feelings for Bush's candidacy in common, but the Internet enabled them to connect and nurtured the early period of their collective action, through which they got to know each other better and deepened their mutual trust. It also provided them with an effective way to pool their resources—of both money and time—in a way that could not have happened as easily offline.

It's the spring of 1999, and Joe Bogosian, a thirty-four-year-old Armenian-American lawyer, mulls a question: He'd like to do something for the Bush campaign, but what?

For the first time since law school bills burned a hole through his bank account, the Georgetown University grad has a little extra time, money, and energy to contribute to a presidential campaign.

PHOTO 8.2   Joe Bogosian

He poses the question to a friend, Alex, a peer in their circle of young Washington, D.C., professionals. Alex created Young Elephants, a political action committee made up primarily of twenty-to-thirty-year-old Republican enthusiasts. "Is there anything like that just for Bush?" Bogosian asks his pal.

"No," Alex says. "We should do it."

"All right, I will," Joe answers.

And he does. Before, Bogosian might have scribbled his name on a check and mailed it. Now, if he wished, he knew he could log on, click the mouse a few times, and land on georgewbush.com, where he could stuff a couple hundred bucks through a fiber optic pipeline.

The Bush campaign was online and waiting: "Help elect George W. Bush our next president. Just click here to go to our secure server."

But Bogosian wanted more than an automated "thank you" and an invitation to be an "e-leader." He wanted to do more than fill cyberspace with spam or hog bandwidth with pass-along "e-updates" from RNC boss Jim Nicholson. ("Please share this with five friends," Nicholson repeatedly wrote in his biting regular edition of *Gore Line,* an online newsletter.)

Bogosian achieved more than he envisioned, working with no formal budget and no grand "e-strategy" and with no greater goal than to help. Through a modest Web site and the power of e-mail—what Bogosian calls "the magic of the Internet and e-communications"—he inspired a nationwide social and political network of like-minded contemporaries who gave not only their money but their time and priceless enthusiasm as well. Bogosian's idea blossomed into a local chapter of eight hundred like-minded Bush backers and eventually ignited a nationwide phenomenon, an estimated thirty to forty chapters of YP4W (Young Professionals for "W"). The Internet was a perfect tool: It is estimated that nearly 80 percent of young professionals have Internet access from home or work.

Bogosian began by recruiting two friends to nurture what was then a Beltway effort. The trio was serious and committed: In March 1999 they paid their own way to travel to the headquarters of the Bush exploratory committee in Austin, Texas, where they chatted with Bush advisers Karl Rove and Jack Oliver. "We had all been involved in campaigns before," Bogosian says, "and we know that certain things cause campaigns a lot of heartache. There's a lot of well-intentioned people who do things and don't realize they're causing more problems than helping. That happens in personal relationships, too. There's well-intentioned people who do things that don't always turn out so well."

The Bush team was understandably skittish and uptight about independent, citizen-run Web-based efforts that it could not control, whether it was Zack Exley's infamous parody site, which the Bush campaign hated and even feared, or the efforts of friendly but perhaps politically inexperienced cybercitizens. And there was another potential headache: Would the FEC eventually require the candidates and these supporters to put a value on their online efforts and count them as campaign contributions? (The eventual answer would be "no.")

But Rove blessed the idea. "They gave us the green light," Bogosian remembers.

Not long after, in May, Bogosian and friends got the effort off the ground with a modest e-mailing to friends, inviting them to a get-acquainted gathering at Capital Q Barbecue, a Texas-style joint in the District. Before he knew it, a surprised Bogosian had more than a hundred people signed up to attend. Among the responses: e-mails inviting him to his own event. "Some of my e-mails have come back to me in third and fourth generation," Bogosian marvels. "They've gone out from me, gone through two or three people, and come back to me saying, 'Joe, did you hear about this?' E-mail is a very powerful tool. E-mail has become the communications tool of choice. And really, that's why we came up with this concept."

YP4W was aloft. And as the membership swelled in the Washington area and then quickly to more than a dozen other chapters, Bogosian was especially struck by the social capital that was banked. Strangers met and formed friendships and did more than pass e-mails: They traveled hundreds of miles to get out the vote for Bush, spent personal time together, networked and found jobs, and even laid plans for the group to stay together and do social good after the campaign ended.

"I know people who met through YP4W who went on *vacation* together," Bogosian laughs, emphasizing the word to underscore the personal nature of the network. "Someone had one of those beach houses, and they got together. I see it over and over. There have even been people whose job hunts have been assisted."

Working through e-mail, the D.C. chapter helped connect volunteers into carpools of from fifty to one hundred volunteers who drove to a number of the primary states, including South Carolina, Virginia, Delaware, and New York. "They'd drive together to South Carolina, check in at the campaign office, and say 'We are YP4W volunteers. What would you like us to do?'" Bogosian says they sometimes startled local organizers. "Then we'd go in and do it. This was all on their own dime. . . . They'd put four or five, ten people to a room, whatever. And it's really two nights—Friday night and Saturday night—and back. They'd get together after work on Friday, carpool to wherever they are going, stay overnight, and come back Sunday.

"It took the campaign to the very human level of personal communication. What we were doing was facilitating. The thing that was driving people together was Governor Bush. I think the passion and commitment people felt toward him is the selling point of the group, the network. Each person knows a few other people who feel the same way, and they would bring those people in."

Bogosian says YP4W could be very important to the party. "Any group needs some sort of feeder system. Take your university. Your young alumni clubs are the feeder systems to one day develop your big alumni donors, the school's lifeblood." These weren't college kids or technophiles but a younger professional class that both parties need—note that the age of the average political contributor is sixty-four. The members of Bogosian's group were Washington, D.C., lawyers and other professionals who harbored realistic dreams of working in the White House themselves one day.

Although the campaigns could get carried away with their e-mails, Bogosian says his group was judicious, sending them out once every two weeks or even less often. "We tried to maintain some e-mail decorum because all of us know there is plenty of junk e-mail out there and, if you start getting too much junk mail, you're not going to read it; you're going to delete it."

Bogosian tapped a resource the parties seldom mine on their own. For them, it's a business decision. "We did a whole bunch of fund-raisers at $25, $75, $100, and $250" per person, Bogosian says. They were the kind of low-dollar events that build camaraderie but just don't offer adequate return to make them cost-efficient for parties to organize. "And that was one of the concepts of Young Professionals," Bogosian says. "We are all capable of contributing to a campaign. The way I described it was when you're young and you start getting politically active, all you can do is contribute your time. There comes a time when you can contribute beyond time, money. But you're not at that $500 to $1,000 level. And so we created this group as a way for us young professionals to take a stake in the campaign at levels we could afford."

Bogosian fit his work between legal briefs and research. There were no frills. Al Gore's campaign had GoreNet, with Gore's daughter Karenna in charge, and pictures from a campaign bus tour were posted to the campaign Web site. There was no YP4W bus. No jpegs of smiling Joe. No bandwidth and no streaming video.

In the early days, Bogosian would vet some of his e-mails through Austin. "We always wanted to be a net positive to the campaign, so we'd call up in the early stages and say to somebody on the legal team at the campaign, 'Here's an e-mail we're going to send out. Is it OK?' Or call somebody in the public relations office and say, 'Here's something we want to do. Is it OK?'"

Eventually, the Bush camp formally folded YP4W into its campaign, with a full-time staffer to oversee it. Inquiries had spread beyond the D.C. chapter's core (which included the D.C. suburbs), and fifteen chapters were on board by Christmas 1999. Bogosian called Austin for help, and a deal was struck. Bush headquarters incorporated Bogosian's brainstorm into the campaign, coordinating the national network and administering the Web site. Bogosian and his team continued to oversee activities of the local chapter and stayed in touch with Austin via weekly phone calls.

In the meantime, local chapters developed local personalities. "We would throw happy hours so people could just come together for social networking to meet fellow Bush supporters," Bogosian says. "There'd be a cash bar. Some other chapters were more heavy on the social networking and light on the fund-raisers. Some groups are heavy on the political volunteering and nonexistent on fund-raisers. Each chapter took on its own character. In Washington and New York, we were more likely to give and get involved in fund-raising activities. In Iowa, it was a YP4W chapter that was more geared to helping the governor in the primary."

Bogosian estimates that his own chapter probably was responsible for half of all money raised, an indication that, for most chapters, the glue was camaraderie, not money. A proud Bogosian remembers, "We took something that was completely grassroots and were successful enough with it where the campaign wanted it. We point with a bit of pride to GoreNet, because GoreNet is sort of a similar idea in the Gore campaign, but it was started by the Gore campaign and run by Gore's oldest daughter. For us it was truly a grassroots organization that sprang up because we all wanted to do something for Governor Bush."

Bogosian accepts with equanimity the frontier nature of the Internet, an element that spooks the parties and that they have not overcome. "I take an overall view on it. I've run across this on medical issues, where there are sites that look semiofficial that are dispensing medical advice, and somebody could be surfing and find it and take it at face value. There's really no way to sift through the good or the bad, the trustworthy or not. It's a buyer beware situation. You have to put the onus on the person who is surfing the Web sites. You are surfing at your own risk."

Bogosian said he did not share his local e-mail list with Austin. "We really tried to keep it as much a grassroots-controlled thing as possible. We are each chapter coordinators with our e-mail list and people who signed up with us. They want to receive a message from us. I don't want to take the right that was given to me and exploit it."

Meantime, chapter members have talked about perpetuating the effort beyond the election. "We want to do charitable, volunteer activities in the community, not political. We believe in the governor's compassionate conservative message, so we want to do a volunteer activity. I have met so many people. I've made friends I did not have before all this started, a few very close friends. Any time you bring like-minded people together to network socially, you're going to have friendships develop."

9

COMMUNITIES OF
DISCOURSE

SOME FRIGHTENING THINGS HAPPENED TO HUMORIST ZACK
Exley when he created the parody Web site gwbush.com and took on a
presidential candidate. "There's this way that professionals word stuff to
fuck with your head. I got this full-page, very professionally written death
threat through an anonymous e-mail, so there was no way to trace it back.
And I'd never gotten a serious, well-done threat. All the other ones have
been, you know, one paragraph, misspelled, 'We're watching you.'"

It was an eye-opening experience for Exley, who suddenly realized that
there might be a price to pay for exercising his First Amendment rights.
He had filled his site with parodies and comic attacks on the Bush campaign. He had some fans, but he also provoked a nasty backlash, apparently from misguided followers of the Republican candidate. "It's interesting because until you get involved in something like this and you get these
death threats, you realize that there could be a cost for participating in the
public debate. Until you decide you're not going to worry about the death
threats, you do worry about them. When the president calls you names
and you get threats, you realize there really could be a cost. 'What if somebody actually does something?'" Free speech, as we all know, has always
come at a cost, but the rewards manifest themselves in the form of a
stronger, more informed, and more open community.

Communities of discourse are the most difficult of the four groups to pin down as a distinct category. Here the primary focus is communication itself. Through the members' discussions with one another, the interests that they share can sometimes be forged into an identity that distinguishes the group, but the group remains primarily anchored as a community on sharing their thoughts with each other. Analogs in the non-Internet world might include book clubs, language houses in university dormitories, sports radio call-in shows, or the regular crowd at a neighborhood bar.

The Humorists

The next two stories, of Rich Taylor's "Sore-Loserman" and Mike Collins's "Spaghetti Ballot," illustrate a particular kind of community of discourse, which is harder to see at first glance: a community created by humor. Our connecting with each other through humor in difficult political times is an age-old phenomenon. Perhaps the most widely recognized and remembered image from World War II, for example, is the cartoon of the hands, nose, and eyes peering over a wall above the phrase "Kilroy was here." By sharing an image or thought that we find humorous, we can let out the pressure when it threatens to explode us, and we can establish an immediate connection when we most need it. We can also use humor to give us a way to say what we need to say.

To be sure, the immediate aftermath of the 2000 election carried with it no D-Days, but it nonetheless left the nation in some state of anxiety, by anyone's account. As they always do in such times, people responded with humor. The Internet allowed an almost instantaneous sharing of the best of these responses—and among the best were Sore-Loserman and the Spaghetti Ballot.

The two images came from different motivations and resulted in different outcomes for their creators. Sore-Loserman was derived from others' previous ideas and was the product of long-standing political activity with a point of view. It has since led to political and financial success for some others, but not for Rich Taylor. Mike Collins, by contrast, was just goofing around when he posted the Spaghetti Ballot; its instant success caught no one more off-guard than Collins himself. And now he is back to being a private citizen, albeit one who will make sure to vote in the next election (more on that soon). Because of both images, however, many of us in the nation were brought a little closer through sharing the laugh just when we needed it most.

It's a postelection November day, and Rich Taylor opens an e-mail as he sits in the office in Muskegon, Michigan, working at his father-in-law's insurance firm. "We need to create an image, something to illustrate the recount after recount that's going on in Florida," reads the message from an acquaintance whom Taylor knows only by the online screen name *Travis McGee.*

PHOTO 9.1   Rich Taylor

Taylor—a graphics wizard who often fields such requests—happily complies. His first stop: algore2000.com, where he snatches some high-resolution wallpaper from the candidate's site. Taylor paints in a teardrop to replace the star (they are, after all, a bunch of whining, crying Democrats) and plugs in "Sore-Loserman," a label that's already getting play among Republicans like Taylor who are regulars on the conservative news and discussion site, Free Republic.

Within twenty minutes, the speedy Taylor recalls, he posts a pair of images on a Free Republic forum, a message board, for fellow "FReepers" to enjoy. There's a banner with white letters on a blue background and an-

FIGURE 9.1   The "Sore-Loserman" logo designed by Taylor

other on white with blue letters. Within days, protesters are downloading versions of the Sore-Loserman creation from all across the Web, printing them up and toting them all over Florida.

TV loves it. Newspaper photographers love it. America loves it.

Taylor puts teeth in the cliché that on the Internet every person can be a newspaper reporter, publisher, broadcaster, town crier. His modem spanned the 2,500 miles from the snowy streets of Muskegon to sunny Tallahassee, Florida, where his creation gave political voice to strangers who didn't know his name but shared his politics and sense of humor.

Taylor posted the banner on his own Web site as well as on Free Republic, which claims 50,000 registered users. He figures, from these two sites alone, the banner jetted in cyberspace all across the land. Visitors to Taylor's site could click on the banner, directly download the image to their own machines, and then share it via e-mail. "I had literally tens of thousands of hits, and at least 10,000 downloads." At the same time, he says, "these images were passed around to the nth degree by people who were reading the forum, and that's the vehicle that I think created the huge presence of this image. It's 100 percent attributed to the Internet in terms of speed and in terms of providing a vehicle to express your opinion about things."

Indeed, he sounds a bit like a one-man media conglomerate. "I am someone who doesn't express themselves in writing. I just express my frustrations graphically. And the Internet, obviously, is a tool for me to express myself to people who are like-minded, quickly and within moments of news." Sore-Loserman—or rather, Sore-Loserman and the Internet—put Taylor on a stage where he's instantly and always accessible, the subject of a range of emotion from curiosity to adoration and indignation. He's gotten e-mail attacks and viruses enclosed in attachments, especially early on, when he estimates he was getting as many as two hundred personal e-mails a day. He couldn't empty his AOL mailbox, capacity 1,000, fast enough. He says he's not a writer, but he is a seventy-to-eighty-word-per-minute typist and he answers every serious e-mail.

"I've gotten [e-mails saying], 'If you're a guy, I've always been looking for a guy like you.' That type of thing. That, all the way to 'Do you have a Web page with more graphics on it?' Or normally, because mine's an AOL account, I cannot get online now without getting instant messaged, which is frustrating for me. And I'm not saying just one. All of a sudden, three or four will just pop up."

Taylor donated $8,000 from the sale of Sore-Loserman T-shirts to Free Republic to help the nonprofit site navigate a lawsuit filed by *The Washington Post* and *L.A. Times*, which claimed copyright infringement when FReepers posted the full text of newspaper stories on the site. He is not in it for the money, though he has profited from the sale of all the other Sore-Loserman mugs, mouse pads, and the like. Taylor—a conservative who supported Alan Keyes originally, then voted for Bush—says he grew up in probably the "most liberal home in America. My mother was Jewish and my father was an atheist-agnostic. And I'm neither." He and his wife home school their three children, ages ten, seven, and five.

He enjoys the online talk, for the most part, and the way the Internet has expanded his reach so far beyond Muskegon. It's a far cry from 1979, when he took out a $3,500 loan to buy his first computer, a 4K, PRS80 from Radio Shack. Via e-mail and instant message, Taylor says, "I've had people who want to seriously debate me over what Gore did in Florida, what took place." He obliges. "When somebody seriously wants to discuss issues, in a serious way, without name-calling, talking about the facts and the truth about what occurred, I will take the time and I will do it. I enjoy talking with people across the whole spectrum. And I'm saying people that know how to discuss issues, be they liberal, conservative, or what. I like to meet people. I like to discuss things with them. I like to learn and to grow. I think the only way you can do that is to expose yourself to different ideas and the way different people think about issues. It's an enrichment."

Without the Internet, he concludes, "there's no way I could possibly meet the spectrum of political thought if I was to just sit and talk or even walk door-to-door." Like a DJ working a wedding, Taylor takes requests from fellow FReepers online. He estimates he gets as many as twenty to thirty ideas a day to convert into graphics, and he does perhaps one of those, posting it alongside his own originals. His "Cheaties" box featuring Warren Christopher and William Daley prompted a phone call from Wheaties manufacturer General Mills, which advised that he not try to market it. "I'll do an image quickly in the forum for people. It's just that people have ideas, and they like them, and they'd like to see them become real, but they don't have the skills to do it themselves." It's another way the Internet empowered the many in Election 2000.

Taylor believes it is impossible to nail down where the Sore-Loserman idea originated. And he doesn't even know the real names of many people anyway; they communicate using their screen names. Taylor says "Cpl. Baum" had posted a grainy thumbnail image of a Sore-Loserman banner, and "FReepers" were crediting Baum with coming up with the phrase *Sore-Loserman* as well. But a search of Free Republic threads, Taylor says, shows "LN Smithee," a Californian, used it before that. "And if you do a search beyond that," Taylor says, "you'll find even [then] people were calling Lieberman 'Loserman.'"

Taylor says the teardrop was his own but then adds, "People were coming up with this at the same time. One other person came up with the teardrop: 'Mass Exodus.' My teardrop looks different. But the thing I think is interesting about this whole issue is, I've always heard when someone has an idea, nine other people have it. I think in this case, it was obvious that we had a sore loser, and when it all came about, if you go in the [Free Republic] forum and check the date and times, they were just an hour from each other. So I honestly believe it was a concerted effort. However, it seems like the images I posted were the ones that were the first that were quickly disseminated."

Though there is still an ongoing debate about who gets credit for the Sore-Loserman broadside, the story behind the "Spaghetti Ballot," which lampooned the famous Florida "butterfly ballot," is unchallenged:

PHOTO 9.2
Mike Collins

It's 9:00 P.M. in Elmira, New York, November 8, and Mike Collins enjoys a laugh and a "you've got to be kidding me" moment with his sister and mom. The threesome, watching TV downstairs in Mom's split-level, gets a kick out of a report on the famous Palm Beach "butterfly ballot," which is getting its first national notice. Before long, it will be a subject of national cartoons and jokes, Letterman and Leno monologues, newspaper commentaries, and the TV pundits' seemingly hopeless and endless arguments about whether the ballot confused voters.

Mike trots up to his room, thinking that the ballot isn't that mysterious at all. "Maybe I'll do a cartoon for my friends and give them a laugh," he concludes, talking to himself. Working with his Flash 4.0 software, he draws his own version of the Florida ballot: a straight line across the top connects directly from George Bush to a dot, but the rest of the candidates are a tangle. The lines look like spaghetti. A voter favoring any other candidate but Bush could be lost. They might back Gore but choose Pat Buchanan. It's an argument Americans will kick around for weeks. Collins hits "send," and his creation is on its way to thirty or so friends in his address book, all but ten or so of them Elmira locals. He posts it on his own Web site, taterbrains.com, where he has fun doing animated cartoons.

It's the first cartoon panel he's ever posted, just a "goof" to please his friends. He's dabbled in politics, but not much. He just had a little fun with the Elian Gonzalez mess, and that's about it.

Then he's to bed. It's 10:47 P.M. Collins's job at the Elmira Water Board waits in the morning—work that is shaping up as an interim between his bachelor's in psychology and a master's in what he's decided is his real love, graphic arts. He's anticipating a big day November 9: It will be his twenty-sixth birthday, and his sister is expecting her baby, too.

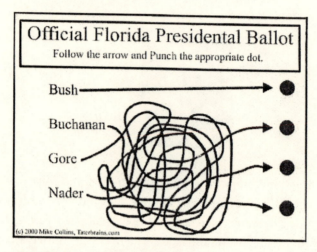

FIGURE 9.2   The "Spaghetti Ballot" that made Mike Collins famous

Twelve hours later, Mike Collins was famous, though he didn't realize it until a couple of hours after that. The Spaghetti Ballot blasted around the world, literally, in a half-day, shared at warp speed via e-mail first among friends, then among friends' friends, and then to strangers, and then, it would seem, to nearly everyone on the planet. Millions of people would look at the cartoon and laugh at it in the next few days. They would post it next to water coolers and on office doors. Some people chuckled; some felt outrage, sensing that George Bush was stealing the election and one way was by sowing this kind of confusion among Florida voters. Thousands of Palm Beach retirees—Gore supporters—were telling the national press that the "butterfly" baffled them and that they voted for Buchanan by mistake.

Collins's cartoon was the perfect bit of illustration for all media outlets reporting the story. Mike Collins's experience is a metaphor for the Internet, the tool available to Everyman, the tool that gives Everyman the same voice—in truth, a greater voice—than all the establishment media pundits combined. While the talking heads talked, Collins went over their heads, direct to the world via the Internet, rich territory for the humor Americans couldn't get enough of, and weren't given enough of, in the mainstream.

It's a phenomenon the young psychology major would come to appreciate deeply, but also regret. It's a story of a young man who only a half-dozen years before had been teased by his college roommate because he hardly knew a thing about computers, the story of a young man who, a couple of years later, self-taught, was so adept on the PC that he earned the title "engineer" at the Elmira Water Board, where he drew new maps with computer software and cataloged the city's infrastructure of pipes, valves, and hydrants.

The day after he'd spent some fifteen minutes drawing his famous cartoon, Collins, oblivious, was watching TV at the local hospital. He'd left work at midmorning November 9 to join his family at his sister's side; she was set to deliver baby MacKenna. "I wake up on November 9; it's my birthday," Collins recalls. "Also, I knew my sister was in the hospital ready to give birth. She was supposed to the day before, on the 8th, but they held her over, so I was pretty sure she was going to give birth on my birthday. So I was excited about that. I woke up, and I was like, 'Yeah, I'm going to have a new niece today.' We knew it was going to be a girl.

"I went to work. By 10:00, nothing had happened [with the cartoon]. I'm oblivious to any of it. I got a phone call at work about 10:30, so I left work and we were in the hospital until 6:00 that night. I was at the hospital with my family. We didn't have the TV news on. My cartoon was already on TV news, but I didn't know it. We were watching, like, soap operas. People had already seen [the cartoon on the Internet] and had made signs and were bringing it to the rallies or whatever they were and were holding signs up in the background." Having seen his new niece safely delivered, Collins went home to freshen up before hitting a few bars with friends in nearby Corning. Still oblivious.

"I got home. I checked my e-mail like I do every time I get home, because you never know who's going to write me. I do get some people from my site whom I've never met, so it's fun to check. Like I had a guest book that I like to read. Well, when I left in the morning, I had 17,000 hits on my site (since June 1). When I got home, there were 30,000 hits. . . . That day, I almost doubled five months' worth of hits. I was like, 'What the . . .' The first thought when I saw that was there must be a problem with my server or my counter's broken. I checked my e-mail. I watched the little bar that usually says, 'You're now receiving message 1 of 2, you're now receiving message 1 of 3.' It said, 'Now receiving message of, like, 170.'

"I read the first one. It says, 'Your Florida ballot thing was really funny, blah, blah, blah.' The second one I read is from my friend Dave, one of the original people to get my ballot. He says, 'Mike, there's people in my office receiving your ballot from all over the world. You're like an Internet celebrity.'" Dave, one of the few people in Collins's e-mail address book outside the Elmira circle, worked on Staten Island. "Friends in his office that Dave didn't even send it to were getting it," Collins said. "'Dave, look at this funny cartoon.' He's like, 'My buddy sent that to me last night. He made it.' Well, the third e-mail down was from the *Detroit Free Press*, wanting to publish my cartoon, sent out at 11:30 A.M., almost exactly twelve hours later."

Soon, Collins would add a "media" button to his Web site, for interview requests and for all the newspapers and magazines that wanted to publish the now-famous Spaghetti Ballot. The new celebrity started carrying his cell phone everywhere and telling reporters that his fifteen-minute creation was just meant to be funny; it wasn't a political statement, though he did support Bush. "I remember I looked at the ballot [on TV]," he would tell his interviewers over and over, "and then they showed all these old people saying, 'This was confusing, this was confusing.' Then they showed the butterfly ballot again, then they'd show some more old people, then they'd show the butterfly ballot again. I'm just looking at that ballot going, 'You follow the arrow. Come on, it's not that hard.' So I thought, 'Geez, the way these people are describing it, you would think it looked like this.' So I sat down and I doodled up this thing with squiggly lines all over it.

"That actually wasn't a political statement about the election itself, as everyone seems to think it is. It was more just making fun. I kind of viewed it like if I was a police sketch artist and one of the Florida voters came in and said, 'This is the ballot that was in question.' A quote I gave to *USA Today*, which my parents yelled at me for saying, but I said, 'I was just being a smart ass.' That's what I like to do. That's what I am all the time."

Collins estimates that the interviews he did and the reprint requests number "a couple hundred." He didn't keep track, but he remembers the biggies that will hold a prominent place in his scrapbook: *Time, USA Today, The New York Times, The Washington Post, The Baltimore Sun, The*

London Sunday Times . . . even *High Times*, the alternative magazine. The Associated Press, MSNBC, and the BBC, among many, sought permission to post the cartoon on their Web sites. He estimates the papers offered an average of $75 for a reprint; the London paper paid $200. By the end of 2000, Collins calculated he'd made about $2,700 from the reprints and from T-shirts. He was getting some banner ads on his Web site through a national company but hadn't seen any revenue from that. He was continuing to get about a thousand hits a day on his site, down from a thousand an hour at the height of his fame. "I didn't make a lot of money on this. Not as much as you'd think, considering how widespread it is. A lot of people ripped off my T-shirts."

Collins hooked up with a screen printer in the Syracuse, New York, area, but he never realized a T-shirt bonanza. What the Internet gave, the Internet took away. The T-shirt was ubiquitous, downloaded for bootleg purposes worldwide. There was no way that Collins could protect the copyright on his creation. It was impossible to keep up with his own, "official" version, though he did finally hire a lawyer to help him. "A lot of people . . . saw it, and took it, and made their own. We had an order for two hundred T-shirts from some store in Florida that called and canceled their order with us because they went with one of the bootlegs down there. They were closer, and they could get the shirts quicker. So that kind of sucked. You spend your whole life with this dream about becoming a successful cartoonist and getting your foot in the door and doing that for a living.

"This is what I'd love to do. To come that close and to know in your heart you have one of the most famous cartoons in the world based on this election, yet you've only made $2,500. Yeah, you've made $2,500 that you weren't expecting. But given the circumstances and knowing how widespread your design is and knowing you've only made 2,500 bucks, it's kind of a slap in the face. Because this could have been my big opportunity, and now I'm still an engineer at the water board. So I'm a little bitter about that, but at the same time I'm still getting a lot of traffic to my site, and I'm confident that something else could happen. This looks great on my résumé."

Collins estimates he added about 2,000 contacts to his address book, not counting media, from all over the globe. "I've gotten letters from Russia, Japan, Jamaica, Australia, Cuba. You name it, I've gotten an e-mail from there. It's kind of neat. It's exciting," said Collins, who pitched himself to Leno and Letterman but did not get a bite from either one. "Every time I check my e-mail, there's a new e-mail from somebody. I'm excited to see what they have to say. . . . I've answered just about every e-mail I've gotten. They're not often long answers. One or two words or one or two sentences. But at least I'm getting back to them saying, 'Hey, thank you for reading my site. Thank you for your kind words. I appreciate you visiting. I hope you come back.'"

Occasionally tucked away in the flood of electronic conversation—perhaps just twenty total—was some hate mail. Some were messages from people who were jealous of his success. "I've had a lot of people tell me I don't have the talent to make it and that I'm living a false dream." A few were angry that he hadn't even voted himself. He said that came out in a story in the local paper. Like everything else, word got around on the Internet. He says it wasn't the whole story, though. "The newspaper didn't say how devastated I was that I couldn't vote . . . and I have people ridiculing me saying my cartoon can't hold any credibility because I didn't even bother to vote and I'm not part of the democratic process to begin with."

Collins acknowledges he had not voted for president before, but in 2000 he researched the candidates, primarily on the Internet. He visited a site where he could punch in his own opinions on the key issues, in return for an assessment of how he matched up with Gore and Bush. He says his work confirmed what he'd assumed: his leanings were toward Bush (about a 70 percent match). "You want to know something silly about one of the reasons I didn't like Gore and Lieberman?" he confides. "This is just something totally off the wall and silly, but it's me. I'm an avid WWF [World Wrestling Federation] fan. I watch WWF, that's the only TV I watch, typically, during the week. I mean I watch news and stuff. But I know that Lieberman is either a part of or closely aligned with PTC, the Parent Television Council, which is avidly trying to get WWF off television. So right there, I don't like Lieberman, just based on that. I only watch two television shows a week, and this guy's trying to get them both off the air, so I'm not going to have any entertainment all week long."

Collins also visited the candidates' sites, followed the news pretty regularly through Yahoo!, and was excited when November 7 dawned. "I was all psyched. I was pumped." But the day took a nasty turn when he called the Board of Elections to locate his polling place. They told him he wasn't on the books, even though he says he was registered via New York state's motor voter provision ("I got my license right here in Elmira") and that he'd also filled out a form when he applied for college at State University of New York–Plattsburgh.

"I called them back at least twice to try to convince them to let me vote. I called Plattsburgh and asked them, 'Hey, am I registered up there?' I was going to drive six hours to vote. They said, 'No, you're not.' I called Radford, Virginia," where he'd attended a semester of graduate school, "and said, 'Am I somehow registered there?'

"But I found out that my mom wasn't going to vote at all. And you're allowed to bring anyone into the voting booth you want. So I dragged her to the polling station, had her bring me in the booth with her, and told her who to pick. So I got my vote cast because she wasn't going to vote otherwise. It was just cast under her name. I really wanted to vote. I hope that's testament right there that I wanted to vote. I was devastated. When I heard that I couldn't vote, I was literally devastated."

Collins is no political junkie, but he's gradually become more interested. "I would say I'm more interested just because I realize what a good source of humor it is. I'm not necessarily more interested in politics on a political level. I'm more interested on a let's-make-fun-of-them level. I do plan on starting to watch the news more, reading the news more, just to look for things to make fun of, things I'm sick of. That's mostly what my site is. I find things I'm sick of, and I figure people must be sick of them, too. George Bush will be good for my cause, I'm sure. Mispronounced words, misused words."

The Parodist

The story of Zack Exley and gwbush.com is another interesting example of a community of discourse built upon humor. Note in particular here the phenomenon of disparate individuals contributing on their own to

Exley's site and borrowing from each other in putting out their own messages. The individual Internet humorists engaged in mutual aid in the best anarchist sense by providing links to each other's sites. Thus, the Internet clearly facilitated their political participation. Furthermore, the use of humor led many of those originally searching only for a laugh to more serious avenues of political education and discourse concerning such issues as the death penalty and drug laws.

But what is more interesting in terms of the creation of social capital is how the Internet apparently influenced Exley himself, the creator of the gwbush.com site. First, notice how the ease of getting the domain name led him to develop very creative and effective forms of political action. But more important, Exley's trajectory of action is illustrative of the Internet's ability to cultivate a heightened sense of *political efficacy* so that, in addition to providing individuals with the opportunities for exercising political power, it can actually *empower* them psychologically. Pay attention to how Exley becomes emboldened to take on the most powerful people, largely by himself. Exley becomes the David to George W. Bush's Goliath. In perhaps the story's most fitting possible conclusion, Exley was in the end able to make his efforts pay off financially.

Zack Exley knows what a real death threat sounds like. The creator of Election 2000's most famous parody site, gwbush.com, remembers one e-mail in particular among the thousands he received. About one in four was a piece of routine hate mail. Examples included "Don't you have better things to do with your time?" "You must be a loser if you're spending all your time on this," and his favorite, since he's a former union organizer, "Go get a job."

But one anonymous e-mail dropped in Exley's in-box especially rattled the creator of the humor Web site that roasted Bush all campaign long for many things, particularly his tough stands on drug dealers and users. Exley's site was tough on Bush, hitting him hard on suspicions that Bush himself had used drugs, perhaps even cocaine. To Exley, Bush seemed a hypocrite.

The Republican presidential candidate responded to Exley's site angrily, telling the national press Exley was a "garbage man" and holding him up as the symbol of the "trash" out there. He suggested there "ought to be limits to freedom," spreading the sentiment among his 50 million partisans. Someone went overboard, and it made Exley's hair stand on end. "The one death threat was written very professionally. As a union organizer I used to read professionally written threats a lot," Exley says, though he had never gotten one himself. "Not only ones that would come to us but also the ones that would be written by the union busters to the workers in literature that they would send out."

Photo courtesy of FREEMANZ.com

PHOTO 9.3   Zack Exley

Despite the sobering reality that it is dangerous in the spotlight, gwbush.com was a thrill for Exley and the thousands who visited his site. It provided grist for the pundits, politicians, and academics still pondering the role and significance of the parodies.

How gwbush.com started, and the road Exley traveled, illustrates the dynamics of wit on the Web. It began as no more than a clever idea to wring a little money out of the Bush campaign but blossomed—or rather, metastasized—into a national resource of humor, news, commentary, and opinion; a target of anger; the focus of a community opposed to the drug war; and a kick for Gore believers. It was a phenomenon the communications theorists had never seen or analyzed before. One person threw the leading presidential contender "off message." One person sidetracked George W. Bush's legal team for months, testing alternate strategies of browbeating and pleading. Ultimately, Bush was spurned. The Federal Election Commission said it wouldn't waste its time with the Bush argument, that Exley should be subject to campaign finance laws because he was spending money to oppose Bush and operating as a political action committee.

Mom-and-pop parody sites flourished during the 2000 campaign, though none with the success and notoriety of Exley's. He had Bush to thank for that. Appropriately for an Internet story, Exley reserved gwbush.com for $70 "on a whim." He thought he might sell it to the Bush campaign eventually, and had no plans other than to wait for a call. Although Bush campaign director Karl Rove had bought up sites like bushsucks.com and bushbites.com, gwbush.com and gwbush.org, surprisingly, were still out there.

Exley bought gwbush.com, though he is not just a capitalist. He is also politically interested. He opposed the Gulf War ("If we'd had the Internet back then, I think we could have stopped it."), and he went surfing for available Bush domain names partly because he was offended that Bush wouldn't give a straight answer when *Newsweek* asked if he'd ever used cocaine. "*Newsweek* said, 'What if we asked you about cocaine in your past?' and he said, 'Then I would say that mistakes I made in my past are irrelevant, and I don't want to talk about them because I don't want to give kids the impression that anything Governor Bush did is cool to try.' He denied ever cheating on his wife. He denied being an alcoholic. So I was bowled over. I thought, this is going to be fascinating. I've always kind of been interested in the drug war—you know, over a million people in jail for drug possession or dealing—and so I thought this is incredible. How are they going to run this guy? This is going to open up a whole bunch of opportunities. But he wasn't actually running yet, so I went to see if he had set up a Web site, just to see how serious they were, how far along it was."

Exley, who calls himself an independent, waited for a call from the Bush camp. He was ready to sell gwbush.com for the right price, after having some fun. "I wasn't really intent on getting a lot of money, but I thought I could have some fun conversations with the Bush people. One guy who reserved one of these domain names just asked for a letter from

Bush. I thought I'd maybe ask him for all kinds of crazy things and put out a press release and get a little bit of press on that." He would get a lot of press.

Curious and a little puzzled because the Bush camp had not contacted him, Exley decided to prompt them. An amateur who did not appreciate how easy it was to copy a Web design, Exley worked together with a private firm specializing in corporate parodies. The firm copied Bush's official site and posted it for him, employing what Exley recalls as "conceptual weirdness." The Bush camp leapt, and attorney William Ginsburg threatened to sue. "I got scared of what the actual consequences might be because I didn't know at that time, if they just filed a lawsuit against me in Texas, just having to get to Texas and having a lawyer and all that stuff would have wiped me out. It would have been the end to my meager savings. It might not have been the end of the story, because it all depended on how much press it got. If it got tons of press, I figured people would support me and it would probably be fun. But I had no idea how the thing was going to play out. And they were threatening to sue over copyright infringement, and I thought, that's not very glamorous. It turned out they probably had a point on the copyright stuff. So I took down the copy site."

In an e-mail exchange that followed with Ginsburg, Exley goaded the lawyer: How could a free-market Republican and advocate of tort reform threaten a lawsuit? Why not just do the American thing and buy Exley out? "So he said, 'How much do you want?' And still having fun, I said, like Dr. Evil, 'One million dollars.' And he was like, 'What? You're insane.' So I sent him another e-mail spelling out, 'Of course it was worth this much. You obviously made a big mistake not having expertise on the Web like I do, and you reserved a very long URL to be your official site. Nobody's ever going to be able to find it. Everybody's going to type in *gw-bush.com*. That's, after all, how I found it, and you're going to miss out on millions of dollars in contributions because in this campaign, everything is going to be coming in through the Web. This could cost the presidency all because of your mismanagement.'

"But they took me seriously enough; it was kind of freaky. So I'm like, 'Geez, I came down to like $350,000, just an arbitrary number. What about that?' And I thought, 'C'mon, I'll make you a deal.' I would have done lots of good things with that money if I had been able to liberate some of the Bush campaign money. But they didn't accept it."

By now, word was getting out about the original threatened lawsuit. The press was interested, and Exley was getting some phone calls. He told them the domain name was not for sale anymore. "I told them, 'OK, look, it's not for sale anymore. Offer's off the table, and I don't know what I'm going to do with it.' But I realized what I was going to do was make some kind of informational or parody site. So the first thing I do is put up this one-page thing of a picture of Bush next to a picture of a famous drug-war prisoner, a woman named Dorothy Gaines. She gets brought up a lot when people are talking about the drug war, a real unjust story, a real bad story. I compared the two, and their pasts and their futures and their presents. She's in jail for, like, nineteen years. So that prompted their complaint to the Federal Election Commission."

Exley started cranking out press releases, "spinning it. I realized this was fun. I was in a position where I could learn a lot about spinning stories, talking to the press, participating in the campaign in that way." Meantime, the cocaine questions wouldn't go away, and the Bush campaign was telling reporters to call Exley. Exley, they said, was an example of someone who was peddling this idea and perpetuating it. It was a turning point for Exley; the candidate was condemning him but driving thousands of visitors to his site and dozens of reporters to the phones.

"He was giving them my number. He kept saying there were garbage men out there pushing this. So I think he gave them my site as an example of one of these garbage men. Like 'Look, these are one of the people, you're giving them attention. You're printing stuff for them.' Bush was screaming, 'He's a garbage man, and there ought to be limits to freedom, and you wouldn't appreciate it if this kind of thing was being done to you.' And when he was yelling all that, when reporters went and visited that day, there was a humorous site up that was just poking fun at him and also making points about drugs and stuff. Like, I had Bush turning himself in to prison for drugs."

The Bush harangue had backfired, even though Exley recalls that at that point it was a "toned-down site." The shots with Bush snorting coke via straws and spoons would come later. "So then the reporters kept calling. People kept doing stories. Every time it was about to die, Bush would go on the attack again." Eventually, Exley would need a lawyer. He contacted the ACLU, but Exley says it wasn't interested. Oddly, it was the conservative Rutherford Institute, the same outfit that represented Paula Jones in her sexual harassment suit against President Bill Clinton, that stepped in. Their argument: The Exley site was protected speech.

Exley pitched the idea that he was press, but Rutherford said "no." "They just said nobody is going to accept that these Web sites are press. But that, I think, is really fascinating because I think that's the whole significance of all these citizen-built Web sites, and there are thousands of them. We're back to the days of the two-penny press."

Eventually, Exley would be vindicated by the FEC ruling that said, in effect, there was not enough merit to the dispute to even consider it. In the meantime the dispute—and the bitter complaining by Bush—had built Exley a substantial and loyal audience of 5,000 to 6,000 viewers a day, ten times that number on days when the legal dispute was in the news. There were times the counter hit 70,000 a day on the front page.

The community that evolved sustained itself without any institutional coordination, guidance, or support. Regarding community building and social capital development, note that Exley spent perhaps an hour a day working on his site, building updates and new material on the back of contributions from his own visitors. "The picture of Bush with the straw up his nose, a lot of the good graphics, were done by a guy who wants to remain anonymous. He did the 'W dances' and the picture of Bush with the spoon up his nose. He did the Beverly Hillbillies page. He did a lot of great stuff that I never would be able to do. I wish he would take credit for it, but he has a business and he doesn't want [the attention]. He's a consultant. I get maybe ten or fifteen interesting submissions a day, and it's mostly graphics."

The parodists and their fans are literally and spiritually linked by the Web. "A lot of the Bush parody Web sites that came along after mine e-mail me and want me to put up a link to their site. I link to everybody's sites as long as there's nothing pornographic. We borrow each other's

PHOTO 9.4 Exley's site parodied the Supreme Court, showing clown faces on the five justices who stopped Gore's recount bid.

stuff, like I got a picture off Bush Watch and I put that on my site. The funny thing too is, sometimes you get these images and you don't know where they came from. Like the Supreme Court clown image. I saw it on one of the really small Bush Web sites that gets really no traffic, and it was just a one-page thing that somebody threw up. They asked me for a link and I visited their site to see if I could link to it, and I saw that. I said, 'Wow, great image, who did it? Can I put it up on my site?' And they said they took it off of somebody else's site. And then I went to that site, and they said they didn't know where it came from. It was amazing. Nobody knows who did it."

To Exley, the experience is much more than a hoot, a wild ride that he figures has cost him no more than $3,000 to $4,000 of his own money. He acknowledged at the end of 2000 that he was making enough money off Bush bumper stickers to make a living (though he will not say how much). His bumper crop includes:

George W. Bush, not a crack head anymore
How dumb is too dumb?
Born with a silver spoon up his nose
Impeach Bush and we'll call it even
Don't blame me, I voted with the majority

"'Hail to the thief'—that's a no-brainer. A lot of these slogans I get from a lot of different people."

The income is buying him time away from computer programming to write a book on his experiences as a union organizer. He's a political thinker, and he believes a lot of Web surfers are, too. He believes humor is important and that the independent small-time parodists played a vital part in the political discourse. A number of researchers think he may be right, and some are taking a serious look at the parody sites and how the Internet gave them a voice and an audience they'd never had.

"I always have been really political. I have a thought-out set of politics, but they don't really fit into any of the labels that are lying around right now. It has sucked me in. It has been sort of an involuntary thing because first Bush is screaming at me, then I'm in the paper, then it has this huge audience. So when you're handed a forum like that and you're political and you care about issues and stuff, it's hard not to take it up and use it." For Exley, it was having the voice that mattered. The future intrigues him.

Recalling his opposition to the Gulf War while at the University of Massachusetts–Amherst, he talks about the possibilities in future wars, though he did not get involved after the U.S. invasion of Afghanistan. "I have an idea for a site to prevent the next war. It would be a sign-up form, and you could go to the country that we're about to bomb and be a human shield." Whether any signers went or not, the point could be made just by expressing the sentiment. "If enough Americans felt strongly enough to go there and do something that drastic, it could cause a reconsideration of the policy, maybe. I think it would've worked with Iraq. Another idea, though, is to just do a fund and raise tons of money to prevent the next war. And you could do the two things in conjunction. Because before the Gulf War, if somebody had spent a few million dollars running an ad campaign that told the truth about what was going on, that could have prevented the war, too.

"I'm interested in the Internet's ability to allow small groups or large numbers of unorganized people to raise big chunks of money." Exley collected cash pledges during the 2000 election, hoping to buy TV ads to expose what he called Bush's hypocrisy. The $30,000 in commitments was nowhere near enough but may be an idea worth pursuing for another time, another candidate (or perhaps the same one). "The idea is, if you know your card isn't going to get charged unless the full amount is raised overall, you're not so worried about pledging a big amount. If somebody thinks, 'I'm only going to spend this $100 if this guy gets $2 million worth of pledges, then I'll be happy to contribute $100 to that effort because to see those ads running all over the country would be so fabulous.' But you know you're not contributing your $100 to a futile effort, which is only going to run one radio spot in Tucson or something. So I'm counting on that logic working. I'm going to actually register as a PAC now, which is what Bush wanted me to do. I have four years to raise money, and I have this steady traffic, and I'm going to try to do the programming so that, as we get closer to the goal, people will get e-mails saying, 'We're this much closer. Do you want to contribute more? Can you get friends to contribute?'"

Exley saw a shortcoming in how his own site evolved as a Bush parody. "I've sort of seen the disadvantage of this forum as being that it's all against Bush. I wasn't a Gore supporter. I'm sure Gore is a really nice guy and a wonderful human being, but I think he just didn't stand for anything politically. Everybody assumed I was just a Democrat going after Bush, so I thought the forum was very limited for that reason because the things I was criticizing about Bush could be said for Gore as well. Gore also supports mandatory minimums for drug sentences, and he's also a former drug user. Bush definitely is more of just blatant, shining hypocrisy than Gore.

"I thought the humor was a good way to engage Republicans and make them think about what was going on. I was raising topics like the drug war and Bush's hypocrisy on that issue, and a lot of issues, like the death penalty. The reason people were interested in reading what I had to say was because it was done with humor." Exley posted his phone number on the site at first to make it easy for reporters to contact him. But others were moved by what they read, and they phoned. People were touched. Educated. Some even perhaps changed.

"I literally got calls from people who were in tears, who were crying after reading the prisoner letters that I posted. Most people don't know about this, about what the penalties are for possession of drugs. So while the drug war parody was funny, I also worked in the facts about the drug war, and then they could go and actually visit real drug war sites and read these prisoner letters. With the death penalty page that I did, it was funny. It was making people laugh. But then they'd look down and see these pictures of these two people who were going to be executed that week, and they could go and click on their face, and it would take them to the Texas Department of Justice Web site, where they could read about prisoners, their last meal request, the details of their execution, what they said. This is like handwritten description of whoever's in charge of this whole thing. You read the minute-by-minute description."

It was Exley who created the countercoup.org movement, an online effort that called for national protests on November 11 to object to the Electoral College outcome. The ad hoc effort "was another one of those ideas, just like all the others. A month before the election, I put up a Web site that said, 'It looks like Bush is going to lose the popular vote and win the electoral vote.' And I didn't actually think that was going to happen for any reason. I just thought, if it did happen, it would be cool if I predicted it a month in advance. So with my friends standing around me saying, 'Why are you wasting your time?' I put that site up.

"I put a few protest locations in a few cities, and I said, 'Send in locations in your city, and let's all protest on Saturday the 11th if this happens. Let's prepare now in the event that this happens.' I sent out a mailing to a hundred people in my address book and said, 'Spread this around.' So the day after the election, people went back to the site, and the whole thing snowballed, and soon we had a list of sixty different cities. About 10,000 people protested in forty or fifty cities on the 11th. The biggest protests were, like, 2,000 people in L.A. and 700 people in San Francisco, 600 people in New York, 400 to 500 people in Boston. I got 1,000 e-mails the day after the election, and it became too much for me to handle, so finally I created a message board, so people could just do it themselves, to each other. People just got in touch with each other and just did it."

It was classic Exley, a man who insists, "I don't necessarily have a sense of humor actually. It's more the willingness to spend time on probably futile and bizarre projects. All of these things that I've done, including gw-bush.com, all my friends who I told about when I was working on it, all raised an eyebrow and said, 'What the hell are you wasting your time on this for?' I think probably all the people who do this stuff on the Web have this in common. They're willing to sink a lot of time into something that looks like it's probably going to be pointless."

10

THE FUTURE

"MAYBE I'LL DRIVE UP THE ROAD ONE OF THESE WEEKENDS soon to see Ed," Alan Kardoff mused shortly before Christmas 2000.

Gas prices weren't bad, and Ed Rudd's home in Gadsden, Alabama, wasn't that far from Kardoff's place in Melbourne, Florida. Ed was closer than some of the other friends Alan had been thinking about. They were scattered even further, in all corners of the country—Texas, Minnesota, Washington state.

The sixty-one-year-old Kardoff hated to see Ed "Muzzy" Rudd and the others fall out of touch with each other. The presidential election had brought them together in an online community, and as the energy created by the crazy campaign dwindled, Alan hoped the group would somehow stick together. They felt like family to him.

In the spring of 2000 Syracuse University (SU) recruited one hundred people, from all over the country, for interviews about how they use the Internet for political purposes. The group included Kardoff and Rudd, who were among a smaller group of twenty-five, taken from the original group of one hundred, who joined an online discussion set up by the university. The school did not nurture the group in any way or partici-pate in it, yet it flourished without direction or a designated "e-leader." The group bonded. Members posted some 1,600 messages to each other through December 2000, and their coast-to-coast neighborhood buzzed with talk.

They and the other groups we have introduced in this book are instructive not for the election—albeit that's the glue that initially held them together—but for the type and the strength of the bond that developed and for what it might tell us about the Internet's potential political power.

The open question is whether the large-scale, formal social institutions—parties and the campaigns, the government, the nonprofits, the big media, and big business—can support the Internet's effective use in improving the civic environment. At times, we saw the parties and candidates use online tools effectively in 2000, and we can reasonably hope that they will build on their modest successes in future elections. Improved technique and technology will help bring in more money, help build longer e-mail lists, and attract more donors and volunteers. Campaigns will include their Internet strategists in their inner circles. And although the large media institutions were largely an online disappointment in 2000, there were nonetheless a few glimmers of hope among them too, especially early in the election cycle. We can debate the relative speed and the extent of these changes, but intuition tells us the Internet's influences will inevitably grow in these areas.

But much more needs to be done. How must the large institutions change their approach to using the Internet in order to better encourage the kinds of success stories we traced in our four chapters on community? How can we bridge the digital divide to get the Internet into more hands and homes? How fast will broadband and high-speed connections spread, and who will have access to them? How will television and online media converge?

These questions are much more pressing, and the answers less certain. We've seen that everyday Americans used the Internet as a means to some interesting ends politically. We close by being more prescriptive than predictive. In this chapter we will briefly offer some lessons that the large institutions could learn from the stories we've told. What might these institutions do to advance a better civic life through the Internet?

Success Stories

The stories of community we tell illustrate one of the tensions inherent in the very notion of community. On one hand, bonding in community is stimulated and reinforced by traits that are commonly shared and that therefore distinguish members of that community from others who do not share those traits. The ancient Greeks deeply understood this and were perhaps obsessed by it. But their vigilant preservation of the individual integrity of their city-states resulted in a collective political weakness on the Hellenic peninsula, which ultimately led to their conquest by the Macedonians. The Greeks did not hang together, so they hanged separately.

Broadening communities too far, however, can dilute them to the point where real bonding becomes difficult if not impossible. Geographic expansiveness is one of the primary obstacles in this regard. Indeed, James Madison banked on the diluting effects of geography when he argued for an expansive republic in *The Federalist Papers*, for he was more worried about the political harms that people acting in concert, through their government, could inflict. He may not have anticipated the politically unifying effects brought by the technological advances that would soon follow, as well as the political and social changes brought about by modern nations and modern political parties. It is both one of the great historical triumphs and tragedies of humankind that the modern nation-state has often been able to generate a strong set of bonds among its entire citizenry.

There is no unique solution to this problem; there will always be trade-offs. Communities based on points of view, identities, particular kinds of shared discussions, shared experiences, and so on are good things. They are good for political participation, social capital, and civic life. But they also carry with them—if not in each individual case, then certainly as a whole—inherent dangers of exclusion, intolerance, and injustice.

In the case of our research on the Internet, it is important to note that some of the most successful communities built by citizens were not the traditional online associations with which we are most familiar and that the Internet critics are most apt to single out. These new political communities were not entirely closed societies; they were not confined to extremely narrowly defined boundaries. The bonds they generated were more broadly based and therefore in some ways more deeply held, because they were grounded in the mutually experienced, shared humanity of the participants. This underpinning—more than a common electoral goal, a shared point of view, or a common ethnicity—is exactly what inspired Kardoff not only to trade e-mails about politics with Ed Rudd but also to want to stay in touch with him after the election was over. And in 80-20, a grassroots group built on ethnic identity, unanimity of opinion was not required. True, the 80-20 group did ultimately seek to unite everyone behind a single candidate, but conformity was not a requirement for membership or for acceptance. Indeed, its founders acknowledged in the very name they chose that everyone would not agree. Furthermore, 80-20 had an expanded agenda that included such issues as ethnic bias and racism. Even in Have Gun Will Vote, a group that at first looks to be geared toward a fairly specific political aim, the central idea was not whom to support but to get involved. And even here, real conversations across different beliefs occurred.

Both Kardoff and Rudd happened to support Gore, but their association was rooted in more than a particular political end. There was also a social fabric. Indeed, it was spontaneous conversation that strengthened the group, the very kind of thing that is frowned upon in many traditional e-neighborhoods, where apparently casual chatter is discouraged as "off topic" or simply ignored. It is this very phenomenon that has prompted Internet analysts to suggest that one drawback of the Internet is that it encourages people to narrowly seek out others who are like themselves in extremely particular ways. Their critique is that these people simply trade their similar opinions, biases, and interests in a virtual but static universe that, at its worst, reinforces all of their prior prejudices. As a result people online further wall themselves off from perspectives that they would otherwise run into accidentally while at work, while socializing, or while reading or watching the news. For example, a Bush supporter might encounter—and actually read—a contrary viewpoint about the Texan on the editorial page of a newspaper, a view that would be weeded out by custom news reports delivered via e-mail.

This hardly seems an epiphany. In the nonvirtual world, we choose our own exclusive neighborhoods, friends, and social circles, our own professional associations, the colleges our children attend, even the grocery stores we shop in, all based on what makes us most comfortable, or on our desire to move upward in the social hierarchy, or sometimes because we are suspicious, fearful, or hateful of others who seem to threaten us. And we have been doing this for centuries. We look for people like us, with opinions like our own. There is no reason to suspect that we would choose our virtual neighborhoods any differently. If anything, our online associations are just as likely as not to increase the odds of accidental exposure to different thoughts and people, since some of the typical physical clues are missing when we are online. We might talk online to people we would cross the street to avoid.

It may not have been obvious at the start to everyone, but it is in hindsight: The idea that the Internet would quickly democratize America was wishful thinking. But its potential should not be grossly underestimated either, just because unrealistic expectations were not fulfilled. The key to the future will be how the grassroots and the large institutions intersect. Suggestions that this will somehow happen out of altruistic forces may seem as naïve as our original high expectations. But institutions and individuals could nurture the hopeful signs and learn from them.

Four Lessons

Based on our experience listening in on the SU chat-room and our observations of the behavior of both the large institutions and the communities and individuals we have described throughout this book, we offer the following four recommendations.

Invest more

This is an obvious point—it does not need to be belabored, but it nonetheless needs to be made. The large institutions must be willing to invest more of their resources in their Internet efforts. They must do so with a long-term perspective and be willing to take short-term losses in virtual space. For all the hype generated by the anticipation of a wired election in 2000, the large institutions ultimately put relatively meager amounts of their vast resources into online efforts, and they were quick to pull the plugs on them when they didn't pay off quickly or at the first signs that the patina of their freshness was wearing off.

Youth-e-Vote is one of the more distressing examples of this problem, because it seemed to hold some real promise of making a positive difference for civic engagement among youth. A big disappointment of Youth-e-Vote, according to organizer Doug Bailey, was that the big corporate sponsors supplied in-kind contributions but not what the effort really needed: money. He's somewhat sympathetic, but puzzled. "Every day they hear [Internet] proposals of one kind or another, and maybe some of those projects are worthwhile, but how would they ever know, because most of them amount to nothing? In this instance, in terms of major foundation and major corporate sponsors, we have to prove ourselves to be a success this year to have that kind of support in the future. It's the corporate sponsor thing that stuns me. Why, if you're going to be in 15,000 schools and in front of anywhere from 15 million to 18 million students, wouldn't you think that a Coca Cola or a Nike or a Gap or somebody who wants to have an impression with those students would want to be there with us? The answer to that is 'no.'"

John McCain's campaign, in contrast, did make a relatively large investment in the Internet, and it did pay off. Being to some degree an outside candidate, at least vis-à-vis George W. Bush, he arguably had less to lose by pursuing votes and funds more heavily online, but nonetheless it worked for him. Future campaigns could take note of his success, particularly as a way to get an early head start in a campaign.

As we mentioned earlier in this chapter, we are reasonably confident that the resource problem will be addressed, if not solved. Relatively more resources are likely to flow online in the next election cycle. The more problematic and pressing issue is *how* that increased investment should be directed.

Treat citizens and citizenship as ends rather than means to an end

For obvious reasons, the electoral ends of the large political institutions' use of the Internet are readily apparent in their online activities. In almost every campaign e-mail sent, for example, someone wants citizens' money, their time and effort, and their vote. In a similar vein, the media institutions want advertising dollars, and to generate those dollars, they need citizens to stay locked on their site. They want Americans, therefore, to do certain things that they are controlling.

They want citizens to be active in a particular way, but from a broader civic perspective, they are engaged in a more passive enterprise—one institution communicating directly to many individuals, with those individuals only responding directly back to that institution. Under the guidance of parties and campaigns, political conversation in 2000 flowed from top to bottom, out to the e-mail lists but seldom back in. And the citizens who did write to the campaigns often got canned responses from software programs that scanned e-mails for key words, then replied with a best guess (and seldom useful) answer.

Our research indicates that the Internet is far more useful when it is employed to seek citizens' active participation and interest, in ways that extend well beyond the narrow ends that initially spawn most institutions' interest in the Internet. In an ironic twist, they would probably be much more successful at achieving these narrow ends if they employed a broader purpose in their Internet endeavors and stimulated activities that extended beyond their control. It is not enough just to provide more information, of different kinds, presented in different ways. What the Internet offers to large institutions willing to use it in a more democratically appropriate way is an avenue toward building community. A felt sense of community is one of the most effective stimulants of civic engagement.

Can we really expect parties, interest groups, politicians, media conglomerates, and even nonprofit organizations to see beyond the narrow goals they seek for themselves online and to work on their own and together to build communities that will enhance civic life? It would be naïve to suggest that these narrower purposes be abandoned. In 2000 the large institutions got their Internet feet wet, and their top-down, one-to-many model logged its successes. But they must see that there is more to political life online than the already abused favorite of viral marketers, the e-mail pass-along.

From the Election 2000 experience, the cyberdebate should get special congratulations and notice, but it also illustrates the problem. The cyberdebate employed the Internet as a means for all the candidates to participate in a daily exchange of ideas and arguments, without putting forward any special interest or seeking any special result except to make more candidates available to more people. Unfortunately, the cyberdebate didn't fully realize its potential, mainly because the candidates failed to employ it in a way that mattered. Failing to see much in it for them, they put little into it. Ralph Nader, in fact—just the kind of candidate who might seem to have the most to gain from such an arrangement—complained about online campaigning in a visit to the Freedom Channel, according to CEO Doug Bailey. Candidates who took part in the cyberdebate did little more than cut and paste issue statements onto a Web page. Their contributions were dense in policy and stylistically bland and looked like everything else on the Web: electoral politics as usual.

Another campaign feature with some potential was Al Gore's Web page, or more specifically the feature it contained that facilitated instant messaging between individuals from the same geographic areas visiting his site. The participants in this enterprise were preselected by their interest in, if not complete support for, Al Gore's presidential campaign, but once they were linked through the instant messenger, they were on their own to generate connections and activities of their own choosing. This is closer to what we mean by the facilitation of interconnectivity, of the many-to-many or bottom-up (or bottom-out) approach. Community members need to be able to talk to each other and to feel the need, the responsibility even, to respond to other members of the community.

The central aspect of our recommended change in approach that will be most difficult for the large institutions to implement is the partial relinquishing of centralized control. This runs against their very nature. The day-to-day management of political campaigns, for example, is in large part organized around avoiding the unscripted embarrassing incident, the gaff, the incorrect off-the-cuff comment. Turning their Internet supporters loose in cyberspace only heightens the danger. We do not know of a silver bullet to cause the institutions to change their orientation. But change it they must.

Rick Segal, Webmaster for Steve Forbes's campaign, notes that citizens may not seem interested in politics as it is practiced, but that does not mean they are uninterested in civic life. Partisanship cannot motivate those who are not partisan. And technology will not change that, even if it moves the partisan message faster, cheaper, and wider. A more thoughtful deployment of these new Internet tools is therefore called for, and ironically, this includes a surrender of some control.

"My general sense is that the technology is certainly capable of breaking a logjam," Segal says. "But I don't think the lack of citizen participation is a consequence of their lack of interest. My contention is that they remain very interested. They search in a variety of different ways for a voice: the explosion of talk radio, for instance, or bulletin board postings on the Internet. There's a lot of pent-up expression. I think it's still kind of locked up, however, in that the mercenary class that runs our politics is still very heavily wedded, and perhaps properly so at this point, to television. I think in most cases the Internet proved to be little more than a novelty and what I would call info-fashion in this particular campaign cycle. I think a lot of these candidates went to the Web, launched Internet programs, but mainly for the buzz it would give their campaign because of the way the Internet was high fashion, high pop culture, not so much as the practical medium for making things happen.

"My thought at the beginning was if you could give a candidate's site some of the utility and functionality of the best Internet community sites, not only bulletin boarding but the exchange between its members, that that was the best way to do that. But frankly, in the presidential election, we ended up not being able to do that, and the reason was you could not allow that kind of freedom of exchange on a presidential campaign site. As soon as you allowed uncontrolled, unmediated exchange, then you would see on CNN, 'Tonight we see Nazi hate ramblings by someone on the George W. Bush site.' And he is stained by association. So the handlers were really opposed to anything going on that site that had not been scrubbed clean."

Wes Gullett, who helped manage the McCain campaign, says the Internet can help build social capital, but the problem is that this goal has little business appeal in politics. He's a bit more optimistic about the future than Segal, however. "It's hard to sell that today, but in the future, everybody's going to look back on it and say, 'That was a no-brainer,' because what the Internet does is create opportunities for new communities to exist that are not restricted by geography or other physical limitations. The neat thing about the Internet is any single person who has an interest can find a community. Now the challenge is that in the first phase of the Internet, we saw this whole thing, 'Oh great, I'm into rock climbing, so I can go to this rock-climbing site and find out where the best climbs are.' The second phase of the Internet will be not only having those people come there but having them coalesce as a community together in an interactive way."

Gullett adds, a little bitterly, "The Internet is not the new paradigm in politics, absolutely not. It's a paradigm. It's not a new paradigm. And the reason why is because I think this new economy thing looked good to a lot of people, but it was squandered so quickly. And it's really a shame because these guys who got all this money pissed it away so quick that it set back all the innovations."

Put a computer in every pot

What can government do? Our third recommendation is that before anything else, government must address the digital divide. Here our recommendation is simple and doable but difficult to achieve politically. Government must take real actions to ensure that, to the greatest extent possible, every citizen has real access to the Internet. And what we mean by real access is not placing computers at a local community center; it is placing computers in every home. From our research, it is clear that there is no substitute for having a computer down the hall, where one can log on before bedtime, after school, or before breakfast.

A national commitment to this kind of access would be costly but is well within the capacity of this nation, even during an economic downturn. And there are plenty of precedents and metaphors that one might draw upon in making the case. Frequently, due to changes in technology and perceptions of national need, certain goods previously thought to be private are deemed to be essential to the functioning of democracy and the very living of one's life. These goods are then guaranteed by the state when they cannot be provided to everyone through private means. Prominent examples from the nation's past include education up to college (and in a more limited respect through it), old-age pensions, old-age health care, and in a more limited fashion, health care more generally.

There is another model that one might also invoke to make this case. Due to a similar recognition of the importance of having universal access to an important technology, combined with the recognition that it will likely not be provided through private means to everyone and everywhere in the nation, certain goods become seen as public and therefore subject to governance, and sometimes provision, by the state. Examples of these would include the transportation system (Eisenhower's 1956 Federal Highway Act initiated the interstate highway system and was at the time the single biggest government works project in the nation's history), telephone service, and electricity.

Of course we would have to do more than simply provide the computers and the dial-up and cable connections. We must also ensure that everyone knows how to use them effectively. This is even more difficult. There are already early efforts in this vein, however, that might be expanded upon or copied. Drawing on the university-based service-learning and community-service movements, which are now quickly gathering momentum across the nation, two programs, one at Drake University in Des Moines, Iowa, and the other here at Syracuse University, are currently working to bridge the digital divide in their own communities. Stuart Shulman, a political science professor at Drake, and William Coplin, a public affairs professor at Syracuse, lead the two efforts. Shulman has been successful in obtaining a major grant from the National Science Foundation to support and study his program. In both programs, undergraduate students are being trained to provide coaching, guidance, and instruction in computer skills to less privileged citizens who have been recruited from the community, in order to raise their "fluency in information technology," as Shulman puts it. Shulman's program includes the establishment of a fieldwork laboratory in Des Moines that will link the undergraduate students, the faculty, and the participating citizens. In addition, he will employ the scientific methods of pre- and post-testing and experimental and control groups in order to track the program's effectiveness. Both programs are still in their infancy but should generate some useful lessons over the next few years.

The best broad policy method to employ in order to guarantee universal Internet access—direct provision, subsidy, tax credit, regulation, and so on—is an important issue but not one that will concern us in this brief conclusion. Our point here is that it must be done. Until the digital divide is largely closed, any other positive developments in the use of the Internet to develop active political communities will be at best only partial successes and, at worst, reinforcements of current patterns of privilege between the haves and have-nots.

Reach out to youth

If, in America's long-term future, the Internet is going to make a positive contribution to civic engagement and social capital, it will do so primarily through the nation's youth. This is true for three obvious reasons. First, youth represent the nation's future. Second, youth are the most Internet-friendly age cohort in the nation. Third, youth are presently the least politically engaged and active age cohort.

The generation born after 1976, now numbering about 90 million, is the spearhead of what futurist and author Don Tapscott termed the Internet Generation, so called because they are the first generation to grow up with the Internet in home, school, and workplace. They use it for school projects, homework, entertainment, and instant messaging with friends. As a medium, it belongs to youth, and according to Tapscott, they have taken control of it. With Election 2000 the first in which the Internet Generation could vote in significant numbers, trend watchers naturally assumed that young voters would tap into democracy by logging on. Tapscott refers to the Internet Generation as knowledge seekers, the antithesis of that passive TV generation, the baby boomers. "At the heart of N-Gen culture is interactivity," he explains. "Children today increasingly are participants, not viewers. They are incited to discourse."[1]

Even Internet watchers and political theorists who had never read Tapscott's ideas about youth and the Internet sensed the same as the 2000 election approached, and many Web sites and online events were created—primarily by dedicated adults—to draw youth into the political process. Convinced they could reach the youth where they live—online—

Web sites were established to educate, motivate, and register young people. Some targeted young, first-time voters but others, such as
Youthevote.com, targeted pre-voting-age youth. Even the World Wrestling
Federation (WWF) and MTV got into the act by sponsoring and encouraging online registration efforts. It was an uphill battle. Although there
were notable successes, such as the online registration of over 1.5 million
new voters, young people generally displayed little interest in U.S. political life, and there are reasons for this.

Compared with older adults, young people are more transient, less established in a particular local community, more likely to be single, and
more preoccupied with individually oriented pursuits versus community
affairs. But there appears to be something different at work concerning
today's youth. They seem to be more dramatically afflicted by the social
capital ills plaguing American society more generally, in particular poor
voting turnout.

Not only do today's young adults vote at lower rates than do older
adults, they also vote at lower rates than those older adults did when they
themselves were young. Data from the U.S. Census Bureau show that only
32.3 percent of all eighteen-to-twenty-four-year-olds voted in the 2000
election, down from 32.4 percent in 1996.[2] In 1972, 50 percent of voters
in this age group voted, and as recently as 1992, 40 percent did.

Two telling data points help to illustrate the generational difference in
voting turnout. The first of these is contained in an intriguing national
survey of college freshmen administered every year since 1966 by UCLA.
The students are asked to identify from a list of values which ones are essential or very important to them personally. Over the past thirty-five
years, there has been a dramatic reversal in the frequency of identification
of two values in particular: developing a meaningful philosophy of life
and becoming financially very well off (see Figure 10.1). In 1966 the
freshmen chose a meaningful philosophy of life twice as frequently as financial well-being, but by the late 1970s they chose these two values
equally, and by the late 1980s they had almost completely reversed the frequency of their choice—a position they have maintained steadily to the
present.

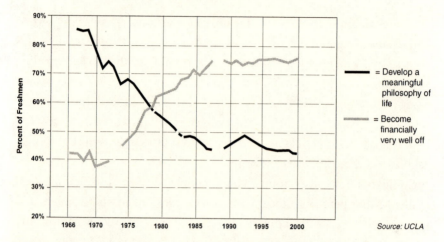

FIGURE 10.1   Trends in university freshman values.

The second data point indicates both the promise and problem of today's youth. It turns out that youth do volunteer in valuable social and civic efforts, and in fact they do so in higher numbers than other previous generations of youth. In 1998 three-quarters of college freshmen reported that they volunteered their services to some organized public effort in their last year of high school (note that only 21 percent of those had service-learning requirements in order to graduate).[3] But they do not experience these activities as *political.* Eighty-five percent of college students polled by Harvard in 1996 preferred volunteering to political involvement as a solution to community problems, and six in ten preferred volunteering to voting as a solution to national problems. Youths thus tend to see their volunteer activity as doing good (and no doubt also as building a good résumé), but more traditional political and electoral activity remains corrupted in their eyes. Nature, it seems, has played a cruel prank on American politics. The generation most likely to be online is the least likely to be engaged in what they regard as political activities, especially voting.

How to reach the youth? The polling firm Zogby International of Utica, New York, contacted 402 randomly selected persons between the ages of eighteen and twenty-four from October 13 to 18, 2000. Hamilton College students worked with Zogby to compose the survey, and Zogby executed it. The margin of error for the full sample was +/– 6 percentage points. The Zogby survey found:

1. Just 11 percent of students said they depend on the Internet for most of their political news. TV was 54 percent and newspapers 23 percent.
2. 65 percent said it would help "a lot" if it were possible to vote online. 20 percent said it would help "a little," and 15 percent said it would not help at all.
3. 53.5 percent said it would help "a lot" if more information were available online. Another 33 percent said it would help "a little."
4. 43.5 percent said it would help "a lot" if the candidates tried to reach them more through nontraditional means (e.g., the WWF, MTV).

In our interviews with college freshmen, one message came through again and again from this generation, and this we advise for future cybercandidates, political Web sites, and online get-out-the-vote efforts: Whether your message is on the Web, on television, or in print, speak *to* the youth, not at or down to them. Address issues that concern them and take them seriously (many youth complain that political candidates pander to Social Security recipients and ignore college loan seekers). Use the Internet as a communications device, not as a broadcast medium. Tapscott's Net Generation is far more conversant with the Internet than mesmerized by the television, and they expect the back channel to be open at all times. Do not focus on spinning a message, concentrate instead on establishing a dialogue, hold up your end of it, and establish trust, honesty, and reciprocity with the youth. It *is* possible online.

From the Bridge Club to the Civics Club

Drew McGarr, the insurance salesman from Chapter 1 who participated in the SU group, loves politics. Sure, he says, he goes online for policy. But he also enjoys community, just talking many-to-many to other group members. How it *feels* is just as important as what is said.

"Someone said it reminded you of being in a bar," McGarr says of one tight-knit community—the News Club—that he used to belong to on AOL. "People would drift in and out and conversation continued, and it would change and flow and come back just as it would in a conversation. . . . When people came in you'd greet them because they were old-timers."

The News Club and the SU group, he said, reminded him of the television program *Cheers,* the comedy set in a neighborhood bar in Boston. It's no surprise that one of the markers of the decline in social capital identified by Putnam is the drop-off in drinking at local bars with friends. "We had this lady out in Nebraska; she said her nearest neighbor was four miles away," McGarr said. "She said, 'I can't even see anybody else's house. Just wheat fields and stuff.' Mrs. Monster was her name—that's what her children called her. She was one of the anchors to the [chat] room, she was there all the time. And then we had this lady who was in Sonoma County in California. Salted Grass was her name. She was probably in her seventies; her husband was a retired doctor."

The group also included an insurance adjuster from New Jersey, a fireman's wife from the San Diego area, a couple of people from Texas, and a man from Clearwater, Florida, who ran a shop selling costumes to strippers. "He was one of the most knowledgeable people in the group," McGarr laughs. "He would send catalogs to some of the ladies in the room."

"We had this lady who had a panic disorder. The computer was just a savior for her. She was in western Massachusetts. The most radical guy was of Chinese descent who grew up in Brazil. Nobody agreed with him."

Alan Kardoff, the Florida resident, said the SU group reconnected him politically. And his online associations generally have improved the quality of his life. He goes online to shop and makes friends in the process. It's another "accidental" consequence that the traditional political operations on the Web are lacking and must take notice of.

Kardoff says the unmediated SU political group "opened the doors to political involvement that now I have burning in my soul. But I wouldn't have it but for the chance to interact with people. For here is a community that was right there. Here was a community I could get involved in and get responses to."

The institutions would do well to listen, watch, and learn.

EPILOGUE

INTERNET USERS WERE THE REAL INSPIRATION FOR THIS WORK, and they will be for future projects as well. Visit clickondemocracy.com to share ideas, advice, and support or to seek partners or inspiration to promote your own grassroots efforts like the ones described in this book. The authors plan to nurture, encourage, and facilitate more of these efforts, by encouraging a dialogue with you and among you.

Please get in touch. Consider it a nationwide brainstorming. Seize the opportunity to join—or to create—new civic-minded communities.

Robert Arnold, a fifty-nine-year-old freelance writer in San Francisco, told us how he sank $10,000 of his own money into the darkhorse2000.com site, devoted to 235 presidential candidates who were never written about and never noticed.

For the most part, Arnold says, "Here are these normal people like you or me, and they're willing to risk the ridicule of their friends and family or the world at large for tilting against windmills. I think it's pretty admirable."

Arnold has already bought up three dozen domain names, from usvoters.com to voterville.com. "There's a guy who wrote a very interesting piece about Nader's campaign and about the possibility of electing Nader," Arnold said back in summer 2000, as the serious election season was about to dawn. "His basic premise is, 'There's 100 million people out there who are eligible to vote, and don't. If those people who don't vote and are so disgusted and disenchanted with politics registered and voted, they could swing the election to someone like Nader.' And it would be really great to see those people interested."

We agree.

NOTES

Foreword

1. See Chapter 8 for the origin and meaning of the name "80-20."

Chapter 1

1. As part of our research, we set up a bulletin board on a commercial Web site and invited people whom we had interviewed regarding their political uses of the Internet to join the online political community. Once the community formed, we looked in on the discussions but did not actively participate.

2. Peter Kollock and Marc A. Smith, "Communities in Cyberspace," in *Communities in Cyberspace*, ed. Smith and Kollock (New York: Routledge, 1999), 13.

3. Paul Rogat Loeb, *Soul of a Citizen: Living with Conviction in a Cynical Time* (New York: St. Martin's, 2000), 193.

4. Robert D. Putnam, *Bowling Alone: The Collapse and Revival of American Community* (New York: Simon & Schuster, 1998), 46.

5. Ibid., 19.

6. Robert N. Bellah et al., *Habits of the Heart: Individualism and Commitment in American Life* (New York: Harper & Row, 1986).

7. William Greider, *Who Will Tell the People: The Betrayal of American Democracy* (New York: Simon & Schuster, 1992).

8. James Carville, *Stickin': The Case for Loyalty* (New York: Simon & Schuster, 2000).

9. Thomas E. Patterson, *Doing Well and Doing Good: How Soft News and Critical Journalism Are Shrinking the News Audience and Weakening Democracy—and*

What News Outlets Can Do About It (Cambridge, MA: Joan Shorenstein Center, Harvard University, 2000).

10. Bill Kovach and Tom Rosenstiel, *The Elements of Journalism: What Newspeople Should Know and the Public Should Expect* (New York: Crown, 2001), 17–19.

11. Patterson, *Doing Well.*

12. The Voting Rights Act (1965) did increase registration and voting among African-Americans, but this increase did not offset the decrease in registration and voting in other populations.

13. Donald A. Norman, *Things That Make Us Smart: Defending Human Attributes in the Age of the Machine* (Reading, MA: Perseus Books, 1993), 78.

14. Bonnie A. Nardi and Vicki L. O'Day, *Information Ecologies: Using Technology with Heart* (Cambridge, MA: MIT Press, 1999), 49.

15. Ferdinand Tönnies, *Community and Society (Gemeinschaft und Gesellschaft)*, trans. C. P. Loomis (New Brunswick, NJ: Transaction, 1988 [originally published 1887]).

16. Putnam, 176.

17. Ibid., 178.

18. Ibid., 177.

19. Ibid., 179.

20. Note that Putnam's consideration of the telephone's social effects is more complicated than rendered here; for more, see *Bowling Alone*, pp. 166–169.

21. Carville, *Stickin',* 18.

22. Howard Rheingold, *The Virtual Community: Homesteading on the Electronic Frontier* (Cambridge, MA: MIT Press, 2000).

23. Jan Fernback, "The Individual Within the Collective: Virtual Ideology and the Realization of Collective Principles," in *Virtual Culture: Identity and Communication in Cybersociety,* ed. Steven G. Jones (Thousand Oaks, CA: Sage Publications, 1997), 39.

24. Andrew Calcutt, *White Noise: An A–Z of the Contradictions in Cyberculture* (New York: St. Martin's Press, 1999), ix.

Chapter 2

1. Pew Research Center for the People and the Press, "Internet Election News Audience Seeks Convenience," *Pew Internet and American Life Project,* December 3, 2000. URL: http://www.pewinternet.org/reports/toc.asp?Report=27.

2. Karen A. B. Jagoda et al., *E-Voter 2000: Measuring the Effectiveness of the Internet in Election 2000* (Washington, D.C.: E-Voter Institute, 2001), 11.

3. Arthur Lupia, *Do Web Sites Change People? The Impact of Web White & Blue on Citizens in the 2000 Election Cycle* (report for the Markle Foundation, 2001), 9.

4. Figures from our study on the number of Web sites are based on daily searches and an audit of political Web sites from November 1999 through January 2001.

5. Neil Postman, *Technopoly: The Surrender of Culture to Technology* (New York: Vintage Books, 1993), 53.

6. Ben Green, in an interview with the authors, February 7, 2001, Syracuse, NY.

7. Interestingly, "Electoral College" became a top-listed search term for a brief period immediately after Election Day.

8. Green interview.

9. Susan Page, "Gore Proposal Could Narrow Digital Divide," *USA Today*, February 15, 2000, sec. A.

10. Green interview.

11. National Opinion Research Center, "Confidence in Institutions: The Executive Branch," *The General Social Survey* (2000). URL: http://www.icpsr.umich.edu/GSS/.

12. Michael Cornfield, "The Internet and Democratic Participation," *National Civic Review* 89(3) (2000), 235.

Chapter 3

1. Ernest Angelo Jr., phone interview by authors, June 26, 2001.

2. Cliff Angelo, phone interview by authors, June 19, 2001, and July 2, 2001.

3. Charles Bowen, "Campaign 2000: The Internet's Political Impact," *Editor & Publisher*, October 2, 1999, 29.

4. Ben White, "On Politics: Electrons as Electors? Probably Not Yet," *The Washington Post*, April 16, 2000, A10.

5. "Participation in Elections for President and U.S. Representatives, 1930 to 1998," U.S. Census Bureau (released online July 31, 2000). URL: http://www.census/gov/population/socdemo/voting/proj00/tab02.txt. The percentage of the voting-age population in 1930 that cast a vote for president was 52.5 percent. That percentage spiked in the 1960 election to its highest recorded level, 62.8 percent,

before dropping to 48.9 percent in the 1996 election. That was quite a dip from the 1992 election, in which 55.1 percent of the eligible population voted.

6. Leslie Wayne, "On Web, Voters Reinvent Grass-Roots Activism," *The New York Times,* May 21, 2000, 30. According to the *Times,* such independent and home-grown Web pages, created by individual voters, numbered about 6,700 at the story's publication date. "As of last week, 3,775 home-grown Web sites had the Bush name in them and 3,066 had Mr. Gore's name, compared with virtually none containing candidates' names in the last presidential campaign. Not all, of course, support one of the two candidates. Some praise, some mock, some parody and others simply repeat much of what the two candidates have said or post news articles about them from other sources."

7. Ben Green, speech at Syracuse University, February 6, 2000.

8. Green quoted in Andrew J. Glass, "Bush, Gore Battle with Divergent Online Strategies," *Atlanta Journal and Constitution,* September 5, 2000, A8.

9. Scott Hogenson, "Forbes Announces for President on Internet," Conservative News Service, March 16, 1999.

10. Ibid.

11. Dick Morris, interviewed by authors via e-mail, December 21, 2000.

12. The seventeen organizations and their corresponding Web sites on the Web White & Blue network were ABC News, America Online, CNN, Excite, Fox News, ivillage.com, MSN, MSNBC, MTV's Choose or Lose, Netnoir, NPR, *The New York Times,* Oxygen media, PBS, *USA Today, The Washington Post,* and Yahoo! Accessed online at http://www.webwhiteblue.org/about/#charter.

13. Courtney Macavinta, "Web White & Blue Launches," CNET (October 6, 1998). URL: http://www.news.cnet.com/news/0–1005–200–333922.html?tag= pmfr.

14. Jill Rosenfeld, "Web White and Blue," *Fast Company,* no. 35 (November 2000), 431; URL: http://pf.fastcompany.com/online/40/ifaqs.html.

15. "Voting and Registration in the Election of November 1996," U.S. Census Bureau (released August 4, 1997). URL: http://www.census.gov/population/ www/socdem/voting.html. Only 32.4 percent of eighteen-to-twenty-four-year-olds voted in 1996, even though 48.8 percent were registered. For twenty-five-to-twenty-nine-year-olds, 40.2 percent voted; 54.9 percent were registered.

16. Lee Rainie and Dan Packel, principal authors, "More Online, Doing More," Pew Internet and American Life Project, February 18, 2001, 2. This report is based on the findings of a daily tracking survey on Americans' use of the Internet. The results are based on data taken from two surveys conducted by Prince-

ton Survey Research Associates. One took place between May 2 and June 30, 2000. Some 4,606 adults eighteen and older were interviewed, of whom 2,277 were Internet users. The second took place between November 22 and December 21. Some 3,493 adults were interviewed; 2,038 of them were Internet users. The sample for this survey is a random digit sample of telephone numbers selected from telephone exchanges in the continental United States.

17. "Youth Have Replaced Old Media with Web, Study Shows," www.mediacentral.com, April 12, 2000. Available online at http://www.roundtablegroup.com/about/article.cfm?ID=14. The Round Table Group is a Chicago-based consortium of 3,000 university professors that consults on high-tech start-ups and provides high-level executive education. The telephone survey of 1,014 American households was conducted with the assistance of Opinion Research Corp. International of Princeton, N.J.

18. Claudia Buck, "Coming of Age on the Web," *California Journal,* September 1, 2000.

19. Bill Castner, interviewed by authors, October 23, 2000, Syracuse, NY.

20. Ben White, "The Web Provides a Closer Link Between Candidates and Voters, but There Are Potential Dangers, Too," *The Washington Post,* May 17, 2000, G18.

21. "Features of Jesse Ventura's Web Site," *Politics Online,* (January 9, 2002). URL: http://www.politicsonline.com/jv/features.html.

22. Bob von Sternberg, "Exit Polling Shows Ventura Fueled Surprising Turnout," *Minneapolis Star Tribune,* November 4, 1998, A1.

23. Phil Madsen, "Notes Regarding Jesse Ventura's Internet Use in His 1998 Campaign for Minnesota Governor." URL: www.jesseventura.org/internet/netnotes.htm.

24. Don Van Natta Jr., "The 2000 Campaign: The War Chest; GOP Plans Year of Raising Money and Reaching Out," *The New York Times,* January 17, 2000, A15.

25. Rebecca Raney, "Campaign Lessons from the Bradley Camp," ZDNet News, July 3, 2000. URL: http://www.zdnet.com/feeds/cgi/framer/hud0002500/www.zdnet.com/intweek/stories/news/0,4164,2597304,00.html.

26. "Campaign 2000: Party Politics on the World Wide Web," Media Metrix, Jupiter Media Metrix (October 2000; no longer available online). In nonpresidential year 1999, 55.7 percent of online users reported that they voted; 88 percent said they planned to vote in the 2000 elections. All data in this report are based on Media Metrix's sample of over 55,000 people under measurement in U.S. homes and businesses.

27. "The Dollar Divide: Demographic Segmentation and Web Usage Patterns by Household Income," Media Metrix (August 2000). URL: http://ca.medi-ametrix.com/xp/ca/press/releases/pr–082100.xm. The report's key findings were as follows: While the number of Internet users with annual household incomes under $25,000 has grown nearly 50 percent, outpacing the growth of total users, they still only represent 9.7 percent of the overall Internet population. Media Metrix's clickstream Internet behavorial data shows the digital divide gradually narrowing as lower-income households increase their ranks online by a significantly wider margin than the total population. The overall composition of the Web, however, still skews toward a higher-income base. If there is a marked digital divide today, it exists primarily in the distribution of household income level online. Early adopters of Internet technology tended to be those who could afford the requisite equipment, or who had access to the Internet in the workplace.

28. Richard Wolf, "Going Online Is Fine, but GOP Sees E-mail as the Key," *USA Today,* August 3, 2000, 7A.

29. Ben Green, interviewed by authors, February 7, 2000, and February 8, 2000, Syracuse, NY.

30. Glen R. Simpson and Bryan Gruley, "Far-Flung Volunteers Gave Forbes a Boost in Iowa via the Internet," *Wall Street Journal,* January 26, 2000, A1.

31. Joseph Burns, interviewed by authors, March 5, 2000, and November 15, 2000, Syracuse, NY.

32. Christina Hinchey, interviewed by authors, March 9, 2000, Syracuse, NY.

33. "The Profile of the Internet," eMarketer (report released October 19, 1999). URL: http://www.emarketer.com/about_us/press_room/press_releases/101999_profile.html.

34. Deb Price, "Candidates Hit E-Campaign Trail: They Tap the Powers of the Net to Reach Voters, Their Pockets," *The Detroit News,* November 26, 1999, A1.

35. Lynn Reed, interview with authors, August 2000, Washington, D.C.

36. Max Fose, interview with authors, July 7, 2000, Washington, D.C.

37. Tom Hockaday, interview with authors, June 23, 2000, Washington, D.C.

38. Michael Isikoff, "How He's Catching a Cash Wave," *Newsweek,* February 14, 2000, 35.

39. Tom Brazaitis, "Campaign Money Just a Mouse-Click Away," *The Plain Dealer,* February 7, 2000, A1.

40. Glenn Simpson, "The Internet Begins to Click as a Political Money Web," *Wall Street Journal,* October 19, 1999, A28.

41. J. Scott Orr, "Internet Becomes New Source of Untapped Campaign Cash," *New Orleans Times-Picayune,* April 5, 2000, 10A.

42. Susan B. Glasser, "Consultants Pursue the Promising Web of New Business," *The Washington Post,* May 3, 2000, A1.

43. Dan Morgan, "The TV Bazaar," *The Washington Post,* May 2, 2000, A1.

44. CMR/Mediawatch for the Top 75 Markets, cited in "Political Advertising on Broadcast Television," Television Bureau of Advertising (December 15, 2000). URL: http://www.tvb.org/tvfacts/tvbasics/basics30.html. The bureau estimates that political advertising in 2000 totaled $606 million.

45. "Online Political Ads Sway Voters," Cyberatlas, February 4, 1999. URL: http://cyberatlas.internet.com/big_picture/demographics/article/0,1323,5941_154611,00.html.

46. Glasser, "Consultants Pursue the Promising Web of New Business."

47. Joel Deane, "Online Presidential Ads a Certainty," ZDNet News, February 5, 1999. URL: http://www.zdnet.com/zdnn/stories/news/0,4586,2204211,00.html?chkpt=zdnnsmsa.

48. Ibid.

49. David Halprin, "Will the Web Cannibalize Traditional Media?" eMarketer, December 8, 2000. URL: http://www.emarketer.com/analysis/eadvertising/2001208_web_trad_media.html. EMarketer estimated 1996 U.S. online advertising spending at $175 million and was projecting a 2000 online spending amount of $7.1 billion. EMarketer prepares each market report using a four-step process of aggregating, filtering, organizing, and analyzing data from leading research sources worldwide. Using the Internet and accessing an electronic library of research reports, the eMarketer research team first aggregates publicly available e-business data from hundreds of global research firms, consultancy firms, and news organizations. This comparative source information is then filtered and organized into tables and graphs. Finally, eMarketer analyzes the facts and figures along with its own estimates and projections.

50. Rebecca Gorny, phone interview with authors, July 27, 2000.

51. "Political Ads Target Wired Voters," ZDNet News, December 7, 1999. URL: http://www.mediacentral.com/channels/advertising/944601234_99.html.

52. Pamela Parker, "Political Campaigns Discover Online Advertising," www.internet.com, February 4, 2000. URL: http://www.internetnews.com/IAR/articlephp/299331.

53. Fose, interview with authors, July 7, 2000, Washington, D.C.

54. Kevin Poulsen, "McCain Campaign Targets the Web," ZDNet News, December 17, 1999. URL: http://www.zdnet.com/zdnn/stories/news/0,4586,2411330,00.html.

55. Ben White, "Cyber-Squatter Gives Site to Gore Ticket," *The Washington Post*, August 9, 2000, A19.

56. William Welch, "Cheney's Voting Record Gives Gore Campaign Ammunition," *USA Today*, July 28, 2000, A10.

57. Gore interview quoted in Andrew J. Glass, "Gore Looks at Installing a White House Webcam," *Atlanta Journal and Constitution*, October 15, 2000, 6B.

58. Carin Dessauer, phone interview with authors, December 18, 2000.

59. Tim Noah, phone interview with authors, December 30, 2000.

60. Barbara Matusow, "Two Jakes," *Washingtonian*, May 2000, 47.

61. Catherine Candisky and Roger K. Lowe, "Networks Tuning Out Political Conventions: Cable News, Web Sites Pick Up Slack," *The Columbus Dispatch*, July 31, 2000, 1A.

62. "Online TV Gets Access to Conventions; Pseudo.com Will Conduct First Webcasts from Democratic, GOP Skyboxes," *Milwaukee Journal*, May 17, 2000, 12B.

63. Michael Rust and Timothy Maier, "GOP Convention Ready for Bush," *Insight on the News*, July 31, 2000, 10. In a 1998 study for Harvard University's Shorenstein Center for the Press, Politics and Public Policy, Zachary Karabell found that over-the-air networks broadcast about sixty hours of each party convention in 1952, and 80 percent of U.S. households, or about 65 million viewers, tuned in for ten to thirteen hours. By 1996 live network coverage averaged eight hours, and only 10 percent of households watched any.

64. Ben Macklin, "Broadband Content—Who's Your Target Audience?" eMarketer, January 12, 2001. URL: http://www.emarketer.com/analysis/broadband/20010112_broadcontent1.html.

65. Mary Leonard, "Conventions Face Battle for Audience," *Boston Globe*, June 26, 2000. Accessed online at http://www.boston.com/dailyglobe2/178/nat. . . nventions_face_battle_for_audienceP.shtml.

66. Candisky and Lowe, "Networks Tuning Out Political Conventions."

67. Ronna Abramson, "Revving Up the Conventions," *The Industry Standard*, July 24, 2000. URL: http://slate.msn.com/netelection/entries/00–07–24_86910.asp.

68. Michelle Rafter, "Web Sites Cannot Get Enough Convention Time," Reuters Limited, July 27, 2000. Accessed online at http://dailynews.yahoo.h/nm/20000727/pl/campaign_internet_dc_1.html.

69. Ronna Abramson, ibid.

70. Associated Press, "Internet at Political Conventions," *The New York Times,* July 10, 2000. URL: http://www.nytimes.com/aponline/p/AP-Dot-Com-Conventions.html.

71. Ellen Gamerman, "Breaking into the Mainstream," *The Baltimore Sun,* July 31, 2000, 2A.

72. Sam Allis, "Pseudo Mixes Chat with Gonzo and Wacko," *Boston Globe,* August 2, 2000, A19.

73. Howard Kurtz, "Political Coverage Clicks; Webcasts Target New Audiences," *The Washington Post,* August 1, 2000, C1.

74. Tammy Braman, phone interview with authors, July 31, 2000.

Chapter 4

1. Justin Friedland, phone interview with authors, January 31, 2001.

2. One category of sites monitored by the authors was news sites not affiliated with traditional media. These included drudgereport.com, politics.com, politics1.com, primarydiner.com, rollcall.com, salon.com, slate.com, vote.com, yahoo.com, and 2000election.com.

3. Aaron Pressman, "Grassroots.com Trims Staff by 25%," The Industry Standard, March 14, 2001 (accessed July 10, 2001; no longer available online).

4. Ross Kerber, "Voter.com Closed Its Doors after Discovering the Most Basic Lesson in Politics and Business: People Have to Buy What You're Selling," *Boston Globe,* February 19, 2001 (available on Lexis-Nexis).

5. Carrie Kirby, "The Party's Over," *San Francisco Chronicle,* November 6, 2000, D–1.

6. Online news organizations also saw cutbacks after the election, due more to the slumping industry than the lack of interest in political news. In June *Salon* fired thirteen staffers to slow its "burn rate" of cash. CBSNews.com fired most of its graphics staff midyear. By year's end foxnews.com shuttered its online division and moved its scaled-down Web site to the TV news division, nytimes.com cut 17 percent of its staff, and CNN Interactive laid off more than one hundred. And news organizations struggled with how to find a workable business model for Internet news—whether to keep the Internet component within an existing unit, as Fox did, or to grow it out on its own as a new-media entity.

7. "Post Election 2000 Survey on Internet Use for Civics and Politics," Democracy Online Project, December 4, 2000. URL: http://www.democracyonline.org/databank/dec2000survey.shtml (accessed June 27, 2001).

8. Ibid.

9. Ben Green, interviewed by the authors, February 7, 2001, Syracuse, NY.

10. Larry Purpuro, Republican National Committee deputy chief of staff, said the GOP collected 225,000 e-mail addresses as of the convention, 440,000 by the middle of September, and 935,000 by Election Day (L. Purpuro, phone interview with authors, April 9, 2001).

11. An impression is the number of times an ad banner is presumably seen by visitors ("Election Data by Advertiser," report provided by research analyst David Martin of AdRelevance, which was a Jupiter Media Metrix firm, April 8, 2000. Now it is owned by Nielsen //Net Ratings.). Total impressions calculated from July 2000 through November 2000 totaled 29,112,642.

12. Ibid.

13. The GOTV effort ran in Maine, New Hampshire, Pennsylvania, Michigan, Wisconsin, Minnesota, Missouri, Washington, New Mexico, and Florida (Green, interview).

14. Nick Anderson, "Internet Ads Click with Candidates," *Los Angeles Times,* January 13, 2000, A5.

15. Leslie Wayne, "Voter Profiles Selling Briskly as Privacy Issues Are Raised," *The New York Times,* September 9, 2000, A1.

16. J. Phillips, phone interview with authors, January 10, 2001.

17. M. Fose, interview with authors, July 7, 2000, Washington, D.C.

18. "18 Million Voters Visited Presidential Candidates' Web Sites during Primary Campaigns," Harris Interactive (February 2000). URL: http://www.harris-interactive.com/harris_poll/index.asp?PID=79 (accessed June 27, 2001).

19. Ibid.

20. Ibid.

21. "Campaign 2000: Party Politics on the World Wide Web," Media Metrix, October 18, 2000 (no longer available online).

22. The thirteen were Lamar Alexander, Gary Bauer, Bill Bradley, Pat Buchanan, George W. Bush, Elizabeth Dole, Steve Forbes, Al Gore, John Kasich, Alan Keyes, John McCain, Dan Quayle, and Bob Smith.

23. William L. Benoit and Pamela J. Benoit, "The Virtual Campaign: Presidential Primary Web Sites in Campaign 2000," *American Communication Journal* (June 2000). URL: http://acjournal.org/holdings/vol3/Iss3/rogue4/benoit.html (accessed June 26, 2001).

24. The Harris Poll included 10,768 adults online.

25. Seventy-nine percent of online adults surveyed by Harris Interactive said they used the candidate sites to find views on specific issues, while 41 percent

looked for biographies. Respondents were allowed to select more than one response. Cliff Angelo, phone interview with authors, July 2, 2001.

26. Wesley Dale Wilson, "A Different Kind of E-publican: An Analysis and Critique of the 2000 Presidential ECampaign of George W. Bush" (May 2001). URL: http://www.wesleywilson.com/pr/ (accessed June 26, 2001). Wilson, a campaign staffer, reports that in October 2000, the site attracted only 48,824 page views.

27. This estimate covers design, content, promotion, computer infrastructure, and staffing (Purpuro, interview).

28. The first incident came the day after its launch in October 1999, when an interloper put up a graphic of a hammer and sickle along with Marxist propaganda. The second happened during the height of the presidential debates in October 2000 (Wilson, "A Different Kind of E-publican," 12).

29. C. Angelo, interview.

30. Greg Sedberry, Web strategy manager for georgewbush.com, reported that the campaign sent out over 2 million e-mails a week. (Stephen Coleman, ed., "Elections in the Age of the Internet," Hansard Society (n.d.). URL: http://www.hansardsociety.org.uk/ElectionsInTheAgeofInternet.pdf [accessed June 26, 2001].

31. In a foreshadowing of sorts, this first e-mail focused on the importance of one vote, noting: "1960. JFK wins the election because he receives 1 more vote per precinct in Illinois (8,858 votes), 3 more votes per precinct in Missouri (9,880 votes), 3 more votes per precinct in New Jersey (22,091 votes). Without those 40,829 votes, the election goes to Nixon. Your vote does matter." (Quoted in Wilson, "A Different Kind of E-publican.")

32. Kathryn Coombs, interviewed by authors, July 7, 2000, Alexandria, VA.

33. Green, interview.

34. Purpuro, interview.

35. Green, interview.

36. Ibid.

37. K. Coombs, interview with authors, July 7, 2000, Washington, D.C.

38. D. Chakin, interview with authors.

39. "Post-Election 2000 Survey on Internet Use for Civics and Politics," Democracy Online Project, December 4, 2001. URL: http://democracyonline.org/databank/dec2000survey.shtml (accessed June 26, 2001).

40. The Pew study reports: "On a typical day in late 2000, 17 percent of Internet users were getting political news . . . a tripling of the number getting political news at mid-year." It also states that in November and December about 50 mil-

lion people, some 48 percent of all U.S. Internet users, read news about the campaign (Lee Rainie and Dan Packel, "More Online, Doing More," Pew Internet and American Life Project [February 18, 2001] URL: http://www.pewinternet.org/reports/toc.asp?Report=30 [accessed February 19, 2001]).

41. MediaPost reported the political pages at ABCNews.com jumped 366 percent on Election Day over the previous day and Yahoo!'s political news area increased 357 percent for a similar period ("Traffic to Candidates' Sites Soar," MediaPost Communications [November 12, 2000]. URL: http://www.mediapost.com.)

42. Pew reports that during the week after the election, "between 11 percent and 15 percent of all Americans followed the story online on any given day." ("Internet Election News Audience Seeks Convenience, Familiar Names," Pew Research Center for the People and the Press [December 3, 2000]. URL: http://www.people-press.org/reports/ [accessed November 30, 2000].)

43. Whereas 74 percent of Americans told pollsters for The Pew Research Center for the People and the Press in 1994 that they had watched some kind of news on TV the day before, the tally dropped to just 55 percent in 2000. One in every two of us reported watching an evening news broadcast in 2000, compared to 71 percent in 1987, according to Pew ("Internet Sapping Broadcast News Audience," Pew Research Center for the People and the Press [June 11, 2000]. URL: http://people-press.org/reports. [accessed November 30, 2000]). Cable news remained flat from 1998. Then, and in 2000, 40 percent reported watching news on cable the previous day. The Internet is gaining over newspapers too. Pew's numbers show that 63 percent read a newspaper regularly, though only 46 percent responded "yes" when asked if they'd picked one up the day before ("Internet Election News Audience Seeks Convenience").

44. Media Metrix reports that more than 12 million unique visitors traversed CNN.com and MSNBC.com in November 2000, mirroring trends earlier in the year.

45. "Internet Election News Audience Seeks Convenience."

46. Being on top of the news 24/7 comes at some cost for reporters. It challenges them in time management and priorities. One of the authors who spent time with reporters on the campaign trail, found that members of the traditional media who had to also file for Internet editions didn't pay the Internet as much attention as their main edition or broadcast. One journalist who was covering the Democratic convention for a paper in the Northeast told her, "The concern is that if you have to write for a Web edition you won't have time to

make that extra phone call or two that would have made your story in the paper better."

47. Reporters coming from print seemingly had more difficulty than online converts from broadcast. A study done by one of the authors showed that the sites affiliated with broadcasters were routinely faster in reporting news than those affiliated with newspapers. For example on Super Tuesday, CNN.com and CBSNews.com, among others, announced the winners at 7:00 P.M. (EDT) for the states where polls had closed. Meanwhile over at washingtonpost.com the headline read, "Four candidates await their fates." While MSNBC.com and ABCNews.com gave Web surfers exit poll results from multiple states, nytimes.com was running a story nearly three hours old, noting simply that voters were going to the polls that day.

48. "EPolitics: A Study of the 2000 Presidential Campaign on the Internet," Committee of Concerned Journalists, April 9, 2000. URL: http://www.journalism.org/ccj/resources/epolitics.html.

49. Two comments from interviews with the authors summarize these points. Refet Kaplan, managing editor of foxnews.com, said: "I've learned that a lot of people on the Web are very, very interested in politics. We are constantly challenged to satiate the appetite for more and more political news and information." Craig Staats of MSNBC.com said Internet news has finally arrived as a valid medium, adding, "People are used to going on the Web to see what's happened."

50. One of the authors followed political news on ten Web sites affiliated with traditional media: ABCNews.com, CBSNews.com, CNN.com, foxnews.com, MSNBC.com, npr.org, nytimes.com, pbs.org/newshour, usatoday.com, and washingtonpost.com.

51. Ben de la Cruz, producer, "Ballots to Bits: Conventions Then and Now," *The Washington Post*, July 28, 2000. URL: http://www.washingtonpost.com/wp-srv/mmedia/politics/072800–3v.htm.

52. *The Drudge Report*. URL: http://www.drudgereport.com (accessed June 29, 2000).

53. "EPolitics: A Study of the 2000 Presidential Campaign on the Internet." The study, released in April 2000, by the Committee of Concerned Journalists, examined the political front pages and lead stories of twelve of the most popular Web sites during six days in the heat of primary seasons. The study covered five portals: Netscape, AOL News (the portal, not the subscription site), Yahoo!, MSN.com, go.com; three news sites: MSNBC.com, pathfinder.com, and CNN.com; and two online magazines: salon.com and nationalreview.com; along with two online sites related to newspapers: nytimes.com and washingtonpost.com.

54. "Despite Uncertain Outcome Campaign 2000 Highly Rated," Pew Research Center for the People and the Press (November 16, 2000). URL: http://www.people-press.org/post00mor.htm (accessed November 30, 2000).

55. In a focus group of first-time voters at Syracuse University, several persons expressed disappointment that many news sites didn't include comparisons among all the candidates. Andrew Shin noted that usatoday.com compared only Bush and Gore positions. He wanted to see what Nader and Buchanan believed. "When you go to the Web, you're not expecting less, you're expecting more. It's not like TV or radio, where they have only an attention span of a few seconds," said Shin, a nineteen-year-old from Potomac, Maryland.

56. "Choosing A President: Assessing Online Election Coverage," Poynter Institute (November 8, 2000). URL: http://www.poynter.org/election2000/writing/lessons1.htm (accessed May 11, 2001).

57. Noah isn't alone. Other news editors interviewed for this book said they received a lot of viewer feedback, ranging from the wording of a headline to story content to sourcing. At foxnews.com managing editor Refet Kaplan said they got responses as quickly as the stories went up.

Chapter 5

1. Bill Lambrecht, "Web Activity Grew, but the Internet Election Fizzled," *St. Louis Post-Dispatch*, December 3, 2000, sec. A.

2. Martha T. Moore, "Messages Urging Gore to Concede Flood E-Mail," *USA Today,* November 22, 2000, sec. A.

3. Ibid.

4. Ibid.

5. Tom Kirchofer, "Election 2000: Grassroots Group Sends E-Mail Flood to Editors," *Boston Herald*, November 17, 2000, Sec. News.

6. Robert D. Putnam, *Bowling Alone: The Collapse and Revival of American Community* (New York: Simon & Schuster, 2000), 45.

7. Lisa Napoli, "Empowering Voters via the Net," MSNBC (August 14, 2000). URL: http://www.msnbc.com/news/445947.asp (accessed August 14, 2000).

8. Rita Kirk Whillock, "Age of Reason," *Understanding the Web: Social, Political and Economic Dimensions of the Internet,* ed. Alan B Albarran and David Goff (Iowa State University Press, 2000), 172.

9. Howard Rheingold, "A Slice of Life in my virtual community," (1988) URL: http://mirrors.ccs.neu.edu/EFF_Net_Guide/eeg_263.html (accessed July 20, 2001).

10. Andrew Calcutt, *White Noise: An A–Z of the Contradictions in Cyberculture* (New York: St. Martin's Press, 1999), 2.

11. Zack Exley, telephone interview with authors, June 19, 2000, Syracuse, NY.

12. David Legard, "Yin, Yang, and the Internet," IDG, January 16, 2001. URL: http://www.idg.net/go.cgi?id=399017 (accessed January 16, 2001).

13. Mitchell Kapor, "Mitchell Kapor on Dharma, Democracy, and the Information Superhighway," *Tricycle: The Buddhist Review* (summer 1994), 49–56.

14. Alan Wolfe, *One Nation, After All: What Middle-Class Americans Really Think About* (New York: Viking Press, 1998), 217.

15. Edward Markey, "Keynote Speech: Networked Communities and the Laws of Cyberspace" (Washington, D.C., February 1993), in *The Rights and Responsibilities of Participants in Networked Communities*, ed. Dorothy E. Demming and Herbert S. Lin (Washington, DC.: National Academy Press, 1994), 146.

16. Ibid.

17. William Greider found many examples of this in *Who Will Tell the People*.

18. We wish to set aside the debate over whether there can be bad communities; that is, whether a dysfunctional community ceases to be a community.

19. Ferdinand Tönnies, *Gemeinschaft und Gesellschaft (Community and Society)*, trans. Charles P. Loomis (New York: Harper & Row, 1953).

20. Richard P. Hiskes, "Emergent Citizens: Keeping Faith with Democratic Politics," *Kettering Review* (winter 2001), 19.

21. Robert N. Bellah et al., *Habits of the Heart: Individualism and Commitment in American Life* (New York: Harper & Row, 1986), 135.

22. Jan Fernback, "The Individual Within the Collective: Virtual Ideology and the Realization of Collective Principles," in *Virtual Culture: Identity and Communication in Cyberspace*, ed. Steven G. Jones (Thousand Oaks, CA: Sage Publications, 1997), 39.

23. Steven G. Jones, *Virtual Culture: Identity and Communication in Cybersociety* (Thousand Oaks, CA: Sage, 1997), 30.

24. Mitchell Kapor, "Dharma in Cyberspace."

25. These are the four main causes cited by Putnam as contributing to the decline of social capital (*Bowling Alone*, 284).

Chapter 7

1. For the relevant figures, see M. Margaret Conway, *Political Participation in the United States*, 3rd ed. (Washington, D.C.: Congressional Quarterly Books,

2000). Conway defines the kind of efficacy we are referring to here as "the belief that public officials are responsive to the interests of individuals like oneself and that governmental and political institutions help make them responsive."

2. Elisabeth Noelle-Neumann, *The Spiral of Silence: Public Opinion—Our Social Skin* (Chicago: University of Chicago Press, 1986). Similar spirals can exist even among those whom we normally think of as having power and strong egos. For a description of the workings of the spiral of silence within a state legislature, see Grant Reeher, *Narratives of Justice: Legislators' Beliefs about Distributive Justice* (Ann Arbor: University of Michigan Press, 1996).

Chapter 8

1. "Who Voted: A Portrait of American Politics, 1976–2000," *The New York Times*, November 12, 2000. Percentages of the two-party vote are necessary here in order to see one party's relative level of support across the elections, given the varying strengths of the third-party candidates Ross Perot, Patrick Buchanan, and Ralph Nader.

Chapter 10

1. Don Tapscott, *Growing Up Digital: The Rise of the Net Generation* (New York: McGraw-Hill, 1998), 78.

2. Richard Morin, "A Record Low, and No One's Cheering," *Washington Post National Weekly Edition*, January 14–20, 2002, 34.

3. All survey results in this paragraph found on Service Vote 2000 Web site. URL: http://servicevote.org/votedata.htm (accessed January 18, 2001).

INDEX